# PIETRO LONGHI

PHAIDON

# PIETRO LONGHI

## PAINTINGS AND DRAWINGS

### COMPLETE EDITION

BY

TERISIO PIGNATTI

PHAIDON

TRANSLATED FROM THE ITALIAN
BY PAMELA WALEY

SBN 7148 1376 1

COLOUR PHOTOGRAPHS BY CLAUDIO EMMER
BLOCKS ENGRAVED BY CLICHÉ ELETTRA MILAN
AND NUOVA EDITORIALE VENICE
PRINTED BY FANTONI ARTEGRAFICA VENICE

PRINTED AND BOUND IN ITALY

# CONTENTS

# INTRODUCTION

# INTRODUCTION

## CRITICAL HISTORY

In many ways the history of the critical appreciation of Pietro Longhi is the story of a series of mistaken ideas of the thematic and social motives which informed his art. During the active life of the artist, the Venice of casinos and of amiable but vapid patrician society had chosen him as its favourite painter, making him a kind of smiling chronicler of its own vacillating fortunes. In the nineteenth century, neo-classicism and then romanticism accorded him little respect, except for his scenes of masked figures and a nuance of gallantry easily reconcilable with the sentimental-tourist image of the adorable 'dying city', the goal of peregrinations in search of evocative atmosphere. For the beginning of our own century, Longhi was still rather indistinct, halfway between a *petit-maître* and the charming illustrator of a decaying civilization. The critical revaluation of the artist is the work only of the most recent generation of scholars, in the light of a more careful and sensitive interpretation of his qualities as a painter, which at last have been recognised and specified.

A fundamental element in the formation of a critical judgement of Longhi, and one that was acknowledged by his contemporaries, is undoubtedly his relationship with the playwright Carlo Goldoni, who mentions him explicitly several times. In a sonnet of 1750 he praises his skill as a portraitist — his 'brush which seeks the truth' — and in the preface to *Il Frappatore*, in 1755, he claims for Longhi an outstanding ability to express 'the characters and passions of men' (1). Gaspare Gozzi, with, it must be said, a certain encomiastic lack of discrimination when he compares him with Tiepolo, gives a surprising account of him, and calls him a 'painter of reality', in contrast to those who paint 'figures dressed in ancient fashion' (1762).

To the patrician Pietro Gradenigo, a valuable diarist of his times, Longhi's art was more generic than penetrating; the painter of reality is for him a recorder of 'speaking caricatures'. Guarienti's *Abecedario pittorico* of 1753 noted the 'whimsical and capricious skill' of Longhi's conversation pieces, which comprised groups of easily identifiable portraits, a merit which ensured high prices for them. His success as portraitist of a social class and painter of its customs was thereby assured, but his potential as an advanced thinker, a revolutionary, an artist ready to the call of aesthetic enlightenment, faded. The seal was set upon this development by the official biography of the painter by his son Alessandro in 1762. Following Guarienti, he emphasizes the genre aspect and the social nature of the portraits, insisting on their originality in the context of the Venetian art market. Alessandro Longhi is even more explicit than his predecessors on the subject of his father's success: Pietro Longhi 'gave great pleasure so that his paintings are desired not only by all the patrician families but by whomsoever esteems singular works of art; and thus they are sent even to the courts of Europe'. Clearly this was success in a restricted social circle, which inevitably imposed restrictions upon Longhi in the milieu of a conforming aristocracy, utterly alien to revolutionary notions and quite prepared to renounce any claim to liberty.

There is little information to be derived from these early testimonies that sheds light on the training and stylistic inclinations of Longhi. Guarienti tells us something of his youthful period of study with Crespi at Bologna, an experience that was decisive after the early years with Balestra, which were judged by Alessandro to have been ineffective since he showed no ability to distinguish himself in history painting. No doubt partly from national pride, it was the French critics who took a new line, characterising Longhi's taste for social subjects as imitation of the Parisian tradition. For Mariette, Longhi 'became another Watteau'; for Edmond de Goncourt, his drawings, which he saw at the Museo Correr, seemed to have been inspired by the technique of Watteau and Lancret (1894). These are indeed important suggestions which have been taken into account by more recent criticism. But the French writers, pursuing this analogy with the charming eighteenth-century *petits-maîtres*, reduce Longhi more and more to the role of a chronicler, a *peintre de moeurs*, and untiring illustrator of a Venice seen through the languid veil of romanticism (Monnier, 1908). Berenson awards to Longhi the palm of prince of illustrators of this Venice, gazing intent upon its own reflection 'as if there were nothing else in the world that wanted doing'; but no attempt is made to examine the efficacy of his palette (1911).

Meanwhile Italian scholars were looking again at the painter in a first valid attempt at analysis and characterisation. In 1909, Ravà produced a real monograph, reproducing a hundred or so paintings and about fifty drawings by Longhi. Ravà's critical approach reflected the classifications of genre painter and society painter which had previously been attached to Longhi, but at the same time he succeeded in tracing a clearer outline of his personality, open to inspiration by the illustrious English and French painters whose conversation pieces had preceded his own, but still good-humouredly Venetian, a little provincial, perhaps, but above all intent upon the effective application of colour. Again in the second edition of his work, in 1923, which contained more illustrations and was more accurate in distinguishing Longhi's own work from that of his followers, Ravà emphasises the novelty of his work in Venice, and demonstrates its stylistic validity.

This positive phase in the history of the criticism of Longhi's art was followed, contrary to what might have been expected, by numerous studies expressing doubts and reservations and often questioning the poetic quality of the artist. For Damerini, many of Longhi's smaller paintings are occasional works, a kind of social diary, and the spirit of realism does not suffice to save them; in fact the analogy with Goldoni is unjustified (1928). Fiocco (1929) questioned his 'brain' if not his 'exquisite technique'; Arslan (1943) even questioned the expressive power of his painting, 'a clumsy translation of the wonderful drawings'.

The strong reaction of Roberto Longhi (1946) was therefore particularly timely. He reasserts

I - SHEPHERD GIRL WITH A FLOWER (detail of plate 10). *Bassano, Museo Civico.*

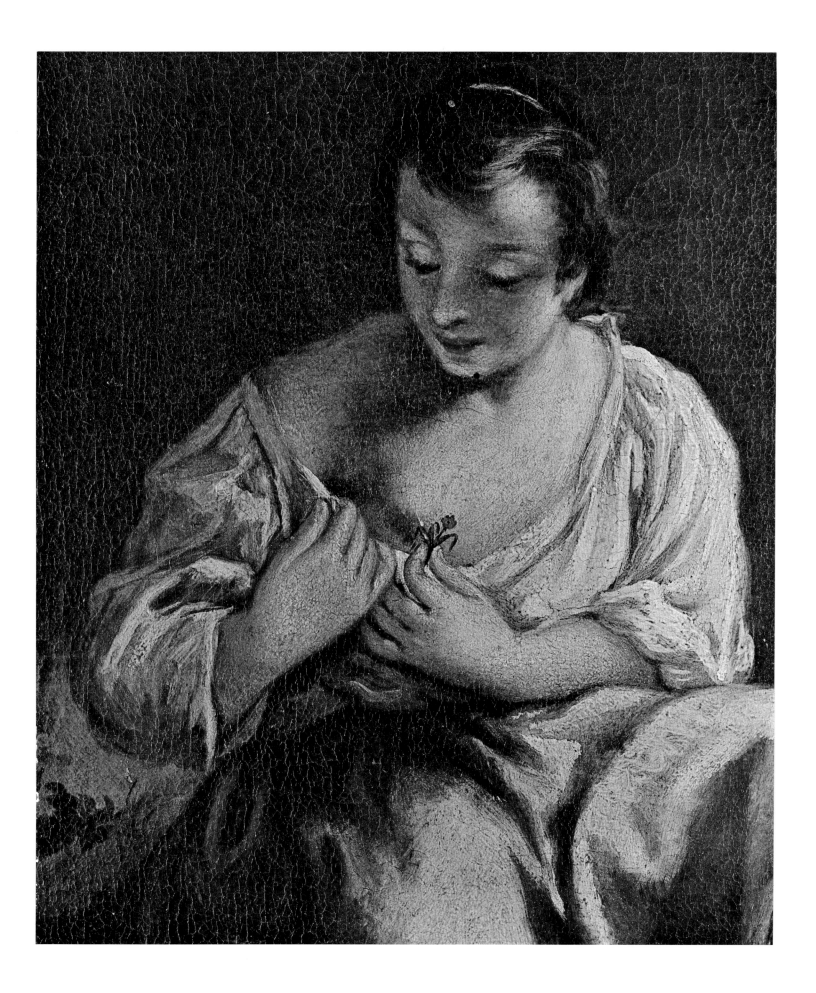

the topicality of Longhi in his interpretation of 'truth' and shows how he descends, as a painter of bourgeois and low life, from the schools of Brescia and Bergamo, associating him with the European movement of Watteau and Chardin. From this decisive revaluation there has sprung a series of recent contributions which have gone a long way towards defining the individuality of Pietro Longhi. In 1946 Pallucchini rediscovered an important chapter in the youth of the artist when he identified as his the series of *Shepherd Boys* and *Shepherd Girls* now at Bassano and Rovigo, which are fundamental for the understanding of the initial stages of his work under Crespi prior to 1740. Another very important discovery was made by Valcanover, who attributed to Longhi the series of frescoes in the chapel of the Holy House of Loreto in San Pantalon, Venice, which until then had been completely unknown (1956). These afford a more precise knowledge of the stylistic values of the artist, who in these history paintings datable to 1754 — that is, to the height of his career as painter of conversation pieces — shows himself clearly allied to some of the more delicate aspects of contemporary painting, from Rosalba to Amigoni. The analysis of Longhi's creative process has led recent criticism to a careful study of his drawings. About a third of those known to us (about 162) have proved to be related to his paintings (Valcanover and Moschini, 1956) and they provide a criterion by which the painter's sensitivity to 'truth' may be judged. By means of the drawings other critics have shown the affinity of certain of Longhi's fundamental stylistic tendencies to the French manner, from Watteau to Chardin (Moschini, 1956; Pallucchini, 1960; Pignatti, 1965). Finally, Antal (1962) has made new contributions to the question of the influence of eighteenth-century English painting, particularly through the medium of prints.

Thus the volume of documentary evidence and the critical investigation which has made use of it now provide the basis required for a reasonably mature and complete reappraisal of Longhi's art. The difficulties and uncertainties of attribution have been overcome by this valuation, and Longhi can be seen in a European context, as befits the historical environment in which he worked, a Venice which, with Paris, was undoubtedly one of the chief centres of eighteenth-century figurative art.

The present corpus of Longhi's work brings together for the first time 225 paintings and 162 drawings from his hand. Many of these, as can be seen from the catalogue entries, have hitherto been unpublished. The known works have almost all been examined by the present writer, and a bibliography is given for each, in which the relevant information can be found. A complete bibliography is to be found at the end of the catalogue, and on pp. 51-56 a collection of documents relating to the artist, all of which have been examined. In the compilation of the entries of the catalogue an attempt has been made to arrive at a plausible chronology, by grouping the works by reference to the many dated or datable paintings and often using as evidence prints made from Longhi's paintings by professional engravers. These prints, together with other material evidence, are illustrated in proximity to the catalogue entry. In the same way, next to the paintings are reproduced all preliminary drawings and sketches related to them, with the purpose of providing as complete a documentation as possible of the creative process involved in Longhi's art, based as it is upon the observation of truth. All other known drawings of the artist are reproduced separately together with a short catalogue, thus offering the first complete graphic corpus of his work.

4

# BIOGRAPHY

All that we know about the life of Pietro Longhi comes from a few contemporary documents and references and some self-portraits. Unfortunately, only a very indistinct idea can be formed of Longhi's personality. Little can be deduced from the autograph letters preserved at Bassano (see below, p. 51 *Documents*): a placid man, who can resign himself to mediocre engravings of his works and who seems almost too preoccupied with the wine and sausages which the printer was to send him from Bassano. We have therefore to rely on the few and rather impersonal references to him by his contemporaries Carlo Goldoni and Gaspare Gozzi, and the pompous phraseology of the biographer whose polished rhetoric accompanies the portrait of the artist etched by his son Alessandro in 1761.

Goldoni wrote a sonnet to:

| | |
|---|---|
| *Longhi, tu che la mia musa sorella* | Longhi, you call my comic muse |
| *chiami del tuo pennel che cerca il Vero...* | the sister to your brush which seeks the truth... (2). |

Is this merely eulogy or does it indicate a friendship which extended beyond this incidental reference, and a genuine affinity of spirit? Certainly, from our viewpoint in history the second possibility seems more probable, and this would imply a deliberate and intelligent choice on the part of Longhi in favour of the justly famous reformer of Venetian comedy, the acute observer of customs and human character, as perhaps the painter too wished to be.

The information supplied by authentic biographers is also rather vague: Orlandi and Guarienti mention his 'whimsical and capricious skill' and the high prices already being paid, in 1753, for his paintings, which were also being engraved, a proof of their popularity (3). Little is added by the brief page in Alessandro Longhi's *Vite dei pittori*, which provides some details of the painter's training as an artist but echoes Guarienti in describing his 'whimsical and brilliant spirit' (4). His claim that 'his paintings are desired not only by all the patrician families... they are sent even to the courts of Europe' is further proof of popularity.

No more is learnt from the brief references to him in the *Diario* of Gradenigo, usually well informed, who refers to Longhi's reputation for 'speaking caricatures' (5). The most lively impression of him is given by Gaspare Gozzi, who compares him with Tiepolo and praises his curiosity, which leads him to neglect 'figures dressed in ancient fashion and characters of fancy' in favour of representing in his canvases 'what he sees with his own eyes', studying situations with 'certain sentiments which evoke a genial good humour' (6).

Pietro Longhi's eyes are indeed his great strength and ensure the poetic vitality of his work, able to penetrate and describe objectively the everyday variety of his world: sentiment and action, psychology, with here and there a dash of Venetian irony.

Let us take a closer look at him as he is portrayed in Cattini's first print, at the age of about forty: a long, smiling face, delicate, noble features beneath thick eyebrows, and a very long nose. This is even more a prominent feature in the portrait etched by Alessandro in 1761, but here the face is more good-natured; and in the third portrait, a print decorated with the insignia of the painter's craft, dated 1766, a faintly ironic smile gives life to his lips (Figures 1-3).

6

It certainly cannot be said that the artist had any pretensions about his own appearance nor that he was particularly drawn to self-portraiture, since he features in only four of his many paintings. The first shows his back as he sits in his *Studio* painting a young lady and her escort (Plate 47; repeated in Plates 48 and 49); the second, in the gathering of gentlemen at *Coffee Time* (Plate 187), where he is seen standing slightly at an angle, making a sketch with pencil and paper; in the *Conversation among Gentlemen* at Stanford (Plate 193); and finally as an oldish man in a rather decaying drawing-room, among figures presented almost as caricatures (Plate 281).

This is all we know of the personality and physical appearance of Pietro Longhi, born in Venice in 1702, son of a goldsmith named Falca; we know moreover that he married Caterina Maria Rizzi in 1732, and he became father of Alessandro — who was also to win fame as a portraitist — in 1733; and he was a founder member of the Venetian Academy of Painters in 1756, instructor to the life class until 1780, and the director of an academy founded by the Pisani family in 1763; and he died from a chest complaint on 6 May 1785, in the house by the Pontesello in the quarter of San Rocco where he had lived since 1740 (7). After his early training at Bologna he had probably never left Venice, where he lived — as Alessandro's biography tells us — applauded and loved by all the nobility of Venice.

## SOCIAL MILIEU

There are many references in the eighteenth-century sources to the goodwill of the patrician families towards Longhi, and there is no doubt that they constituted the sphere of his greatest activity. He was painting for the Sagredo family in 1734, lived in the house of the Emo family in 1740, was suggested by Goldoni to paint some portraits for the Grimani family in 1740, and in 1751 painted Doge Pietro Grimani twice; in the same year he painted *The Rhinoceros* for Giovanni Grimani, for whom he also painted *Magrath the Giant* in 1757. In about 1752 he painted the Sagredo family, in about 1758 the Rezzonico family; in 1762 he made an inventory of the paintings in the possession of the Sagredo family, in 1763-6 he was director of the Pisani school, in 1764 he painted Ludovico Manin, in 1772 the Querini family, in 1779 Adriana Giustinian Barbarigo and the Michiel family (8).

This association with an aristocratic clientele is indeed strange for one who was, after all, perhaps the most independent painter of his time and almost the only one to undertake social subjects, or at least who looked at nature with open eyes. The truth is that Longhi took his patrons wherever he could find them. Perhaps too, halfway through the century, it was too early to receive commissions from middle-class collectors on a small scale, the cultured priests, foreign travellers and merchants who were later to give work to Francesco Guardi (9). Historical research reveals in fact that a true bourgeoisie was lacking in a city that was still inhabited largely by patricians, who dominated the typical activites of the merchant and professional classes, and by the poorer classes. About the palaces of the nobles revolved a whole world of servants and dependents: in 1760, for example, the number of household servants registered was 12,819 (10). How often these are to be seen in Longhi's pictures, wearing the master's cast-off cutaway coat and three-cornered

IV - THE PAINTER IN HIS STUDIO (detail of plate 47). *Venice, Ca' Rezzonico.*

hat, busy buying doughnuts or salad, dancing the furlana or serving chocolate, holding up a mirror or arranging the crinoline of a swooning mistress!

The society portrayed, in its several aspects, in the paintings of Longhi reflects the only milieu in which he moved: the nobility of Venice, somewhat impoverished, by no means brilliant (with few exceptions) either as to social life or as to culture, fervently conservative and excessively repectful of public authority, careful not to provoke the vigilant curiosity of official censure (11). It has been said of Longhi that he was a realist and sought to portray truth. But how much prudence he needed, not to stir too vigorously the problems which were developing beneath the surface, from the restriction of freedom of thought and expression to the infinite wretchedness of the lower classes, driven both in the city and in the countryside to the direst expedients in order to survive! It is a fact that of the 25,000 and more paupers registered in the Republic not one makes an appearance in the paintings of this 'faithful chronicler of his time' (12). Nor do we see any attempt to extol the public and private charity which nevertheless was freely and beneficently exercised. That these were 'revolutionary matters' was doubtless the opinion of Longhi, who preferred to delight his patrons with his 'speaking caricatures' and to provoke sentiments of 'genial good humour' (13).

It is therefore not surprising that Longhi rarely takes us outside the patrician palace or its immediate surroundings. Apart from the few country inns and the genre scenes of peasants eating polenta, the poorer classes (so familiar to his contemporaries Ceruti, Crespi, Gamberini, Hogarth, Chardin, who are so often irrelevantly compared with him) hardly appear at all in Longhi's Venetian scenes. On the other hand, they frequently inhabit Goldoni's comedies, where sometimes sentiments quite other than respectful are expressed with regard to the established order and the nobility.

In short, it is evident that the claim 'interpreter of eighteenth-century Venetian life', taken in an absolute sense, as it often has been, is an exaggeration for many reasons. On the social plane, it is only true that Longhi chronicled a limited sector, restricting himself to the moral status of the painter of a class, exposed to inevitable compromise with the conservatism of his customers.

## LONGHI'S VERNACULAR SUBJECTS

Far from assuming any character of social protest, Longhi's idiom thus reflected the good-natured, paternalistic and somewhat provincial attitude which typified the placid patrician element of Venetian society: when, for instance, the young ladies of the household are benevolently intent upon giving refreshment to the faithful old servant (Plate 70), or when the gentleman bestows a smile upon the wretched beaters in the *Shooting in the Valley* (Plate 233). Often too the scenes are circumspect and reactionary, as when he includes the worthy clerical tutor in his portraits of noble families, and constrains into poses of smiling devoutness the plump, sugary peasant girls of his *Sacraments* or his many *Sermons*.

What then are the real feelings of Longhi the artist, where does his humanity truly manifest itself? Perhaps it can be identified most clearly in the good-natured but ironic observation of the

V - A FEMALE MARTYR (detail of plate 73). *Venice, Church of S. Pantalon.*

kind of sentiments conveyed in the candid and unequivocal manner of vernacular poetry, tinged with gentle Venetian malice, in pungent and fluid language. It is relevant to recall, even more than Goldoni (who is sharper-tongued and with greater powers of psychological penetration) a whole series of verses, typical of eighteenth-century Venetian dialect literature:

| | |
|---|---|
| ... *Vardè là in quel campielo* | Look over there, in the square, |
| *Cara Siora Prudenza benedeta* | Dear Signora Prudenza, |
| *Chi xè quela siorazza spetenada* | Who is that untidy little madam, |
| *Che fa tutti quei sesti, e che camina* | Making all those gestures, walking |
| *Con quel ninarse e quel bocon de mina?* | With that mincing step, that pouting mouth? |

This is more than reminiscent of one of the many strolls in the piazzetta, with masked and cloaked figures busy about their scandal-mongering, which Longhi shows us; here it is from *La Momoleta*, attributed to Barbaro or Gritti. And how much of the vernacular spirit of Pastò is echoed in Longhi's *Girls spinning*, or preparing the *Polenta*:

| | |
|---|---|
| ... *Ben venuti, ben venuti,* | ...Come in, good people, |
| *Via da brave, le se senta* | Welcome, take a seat |
| *Le se comoda qua tute,* | Make yourselves comfortable. |
| *Che xè ora de polenta,* | It's time for some polenta, |
| *Disnaremo qua in cusina,* | We'll eat it here in the kitchen, |
| *Zà la vede che zogièlo,* | Here it is, bubbling away; |
| *Co mi g'o la polentina,* | When I eat my polenta |
| *Questo è sempre el mio tinelo.* | This is always my dining-room. |

Caricature, irony: these abound in his pictures, whether peasant or patrician, but never real satire. Unlike Gaspare Gozzi, and even more unlike Hogarth, it is impossible to believe that Longhi was ever inclined to pillory the well-loved Venetian nobility, nor yet the middle class. If sometimes he lets himself go a little, he uses a gentle touch, a good-natured smile rather than a bitter grimace. Almost with a feeling of daring he depicts some clerics playing cards (Plate 37) or who carry out their duties munching biscuits and sipping coffee (Plate 279), or an indiscreet gentleman surprising a lady at her toilet (Plate 85), an apothecary or a mountebank cajoling customers (Plates 112, 160), a few abbés or friars with a roving eye (Plates 100, 103), a peppery milord or a learned lady, two noblemen who lethargically test their niece's knowledge of geography (Plates 83, 201, 126).

There is neither gall nor fire in Longhi's mild characterisation, but merely a little pleasant caricaturing, in the same way as Gritti in his *Marchese Merliton*:

| | |
|---|---|
| ... *El Marchese gravemente* | The Marquis gravely |
| *Sente tuto come gnente,* | Hears everything as though it were nothing, |
| *Tuto esamina, corege,* | Examines, corrects everything, |
| *E stranùa sentenze e lege.* | And yawns out sentence and law (14). |

12

# BEGINNINGS: FRENCH INFLUENCE AND CONVERSATION PIECES

How is it that Longhi, within this framework of characters, with the means and possibilities that have been indicated, yet managed to secure for himself a unique and original place in the history of eighteenth-century Italian painting and comparison with Watteau and Chardin? First and foremost, the individuality of his 'realistic' angle of vision must be recognised, which places him, with the portraitists and the view-painters, in the category of artists who to a greater or lesser degree, and in a variety of different ways, are drawn to new interests beyond the customary subjects of rococo painting. Fundamentally, Longhi's voluntary restriction of his subject matter to the depiction of social customs does not unduly limit his figurative imagination nor his poetic language. The choice itself shows that he belongs to a movement of innovation in European culture, and testifies to his critical intelligence.

It was probably not merely his evident inability to distinguish himself as a history painter which made Longhi throw to the winds the training he had received from Balestra and the Bolognese decorative painters, turning his back on altar-pieces and frescoes in order to dedicate himself to 'conversation pieces, games, ridotti, masquerades, parlours' painted 'in a new and individual style' as Orlandi and Guarienti put it (15). But let us first examine in detail the beginnings of his career.

First, according to Alessandro Longhi, he was for several years a pupil of Antonio Balestra; then he went to study at Bologna under Giuseppe Maria Crespi, with whom he remained 'for several years'. One may assume that the painter, who was born in 1702, was with Balestra until about 1719, the year in which he left Venice, and that he spent the following decade in Bologna, returning to his native city in about 1730, since there are documents recording his transactions with the parish of San Pellegrino in Venice during that year. Moreover he married in Venice in 1732. The lost 'historical' paintings may date from around this time, in S. Pasquale Baylon and Sta Maria delle Grazie, Venice, and in S. Biagio, Verona. The recent discovery, in the Scuola di S. Giovanni Evangelista, of the *Adoration of the Magi* formerly in Sta Maria Materdomini confirms the influence of Balestra in his work (16). The frescoes in the Sagredo palace, signed on their completion in 1734, appear to mark the end of Longhi's false start: after this he suddenly changes direction.

There appears no room for doubt that Longhi's crisis occurred in the late 1730s. After the large academic figures of *San Pellegrino* (1730), the saints, commanders, torturers, endeavouring to rectify the baroque superabundance of their number by the foreshortening of the composition, comes the downpour of giants and storm-clouds of the Ca' Sagredo staircase, seen from below in the Bolognese manner (17), but painted with such thick colour and such straining after plastic and chromatic effect that one wonders whether he had ever raised his eyes towards the luminous ceilings of Piazzetta or Pellegrini, Ricci or Tiepolo, in Venice.

There is no signed painting which gives any idea of his activity during the years 1734 to 1741, but the next signed and dated work is a masterpiece, the *Concert* (Plate 37) in the Accademia, Venice. Various hypotheses have been put forward to explain Longhi's break with his previous manner. One suggests the influence of Italian paintings of low life, maintaining that in his training with Crespi at Bologna he had most enjoyed the little scenes of everyday life such as the *Seven Sacraments* and the *Peasant girl searching for a flea* (Fig. 12), while others have suggested the influence,

14

VII - THE FRIARS' SERMON (detail of plate 114). *Bergamo, Private collection.*

in the same line, of Ceruti and Ghislandi (Fig. 14). More recent critics have looked further afield, postulating an acquaintance with Dutch and Flemish works (Cornelis Troost) or with English ones (Hogarth, Highmore, Hayman); and it has also been suggested that he had seen French drawings and paintings, reproduced in prints, the work of Watteau and his successors. The latest suggestion is the influence of the French artist Joseph Flipart, who was in Venice from 1737 to 1750 and engraved several of Longhi's works (18).

While this wide acquaintance with the figurative arts is claimed for Pietro Longhi, it is almost always hastily added that his rendering of these models is in fact very limited, even provincial. Some fundamental points, however, can be established with certainty. First of all, it is relevant to investigate the relationship, in this early phase, of the idiom of Longhi to that of contemporary Venetian painting. His colours, glazed with gradual transitions of colour, the brushwork in small dabs, the harmonious use of the palette, are in fact typically Venetian, even when the themes he treats have no local reference. To digress briefly on the subject of theme: it does indeed seem obvious that the conversation pieces of Longhi are versions as it were in Venetian dialect of English ones which became fashionable between 1720 and 1730, from Mercier to Dandridge, Highmore, Hayman and Devis. Hogarth is in a class apart with his 'serial paintings' where he shows himself a savage critic of his times. How Longhi knew of this type of painting is not clear, but it is not difficult to imagine that prints of them may have come to his notice (19).

Now we turn to consideration of the French illustrators, led by Watteau. Here also the relevant dates are the 1730s and 1740s, and it is very probable that Longhi knew engravings such as those made by Cars from Watteau's *Fêtes Vénitiennes* (1732), and even the complete collection of engravings of his work printed during those years by Jullienne (Fig. 6). It is known that the *Figures de différents caractères* appeared between 1726 and 1728, and the complete set, entitled *L'Oeuvre gravé de Watteau*, was ready in 1735. It seems unlikely that Flipart, who was active in Parisian studios and also the engraver of some of Chardin's paintings, arrived in Venice in 1737 without bringing with him this *Summa* of French 'rocaille'. It would hardly be surprising if, while he worked at engraving Longhi's paintings for Wagner's press, he introduced his Venetian colleague to his 'complete Watteau'. Moreover, the great works of French literature, printed in the early decades of the century with engravings of the Parisian *petits-maîtres*, must not be left out of account in connection with someone like Longhi, who was seeking to free himself from the conventional rhetoric of Baroque art (Fig. 4). The *Comédies* of Molière, illustrated by Boucher and engraved by Cars (1734), are a case in point: they were certainly well known in Venice (20) (Fig. 5).

Between the pages of the *Oeuvre gravé* which Longhi may have studied in his search for a new graphic idiom there may well have been some original drawings by Watteau, Lancret, Pater, Bernard Lépicié and other Parisian artists. The long, firm line, the heightening with white chalk on dark paper, show him more closely in the line of Watteau and his followers than in that of his Venetian contemporaries (Figs. 8 and 9). And it would not be surprising if Longhi's artistic inclination to softness and delicacy responded also to some sketch or other of Chardin's which might be found in this hypothetical collection that we are attributing to Flipart. *The Sedan chair* (Fig. 10) in Stockholm is a drawing which is so close in character to Longhi as to make one doubt the historically justified attribution to Chardin (21). Turning towards the graphic style of Chardin, Longhi

16

was marking a decisive choice not only as far as the Venetian tradition was concerned, but also within the French one.

It is evident from a study of the most characteristic examples, in the Museo Correr and the Berlin Kupferstichkabinett, that the style of Longhi's drawings differs from that favoured by other Venetian artists of his time. His technique is individual, with black chalk or soft pencil heightened with white chalk on light brown or grey blue papers which afforded a contrast. The strokes of white chalk which animate the linear structure produce modest effects of light; and often a gradation of tone very similar to that obtainable with pastels and achieved by rubbing with the tip of the finger suggests rounded shapes. The style gives importance to the figures, which are realistic and suggestive and almost always evoke the intimate peace in which the drawing was made (22).

It has already been suggested that in his very personal choice of style and medium Longhi was not without some slight, if isolated, encouragement in Venice. This may well have come to him above all from an artist who has herself something in common with the French artists, the Venetian pastellist Rosalba Carriera. She knew the work of the Paris school from her triumphant visit to Paris in 1720-21, when she became friendly with Watteau himself, with whom she exchanged paintings and drawings. No one knows how Rosalba drew, but from what can be learnt from the line of her paintings and from a few drawings which have been attributed to her, it is not difficult to assume that her manner was somewhat similar to that of Longhi (23). Both Rosalba and Longhi were of the same mind in their search for 'the truth', and both looked at their subjects 'with their own eyes'. And above all in the sphere of painting this affinity was to influence Longhi, perhaps helping to liberate himself from an element of heaviness and darkness in the use of colour which were the effect of Crespi, in favour of a lightening of touch and colour and even a more careful application of colour. Between the Bassano and Rovigo *Shepherds*, which are obviously youthful Bolognese works, and the *Concert* of 1741, he cannot have failed to see and study Rosalba's work, and it had its due effect in the change in Longhi's idiom (Figs. 17, 18).

The name of another Venetian must be mentioned beside that of Rosalba in the discussion of Longhi's tendencies in the years around 1740, that of Jacopo Amigoni. Apart from the similarities of some of his family groups and portraits, such as the *Two Ladies* in the Museo Correr (formerly thought to be by Flipart), Amigoni's Arcadian canvases show the subtle, short strokes of the brush, the careful use of shaded colour and soft pastel-like tones, somewhat frail and precious, which appear in *The Concert* for the first time, and in other works of that period, from the *Dancing Lesson* (Plate 41) to *The Tailor* (Plate 38) and The *Toilet* (Plate 42) and the sparkling *Introduction* (Plate 44), the composition of which, however, reveals influences from France (Fig. 13).

It cannot be said that in the years between 1741 and 1756 Longhi's line of development was a straightforward development of these beginnings. The two initial tendencies continue to coexist — on the one hand that of Crespi, particularly in the brushwork and the typically Bolognese use of light, and on the other what might be called the Rosalba influence, aiming at more delicate tonal effects, the juxtaposition of colours applied with very fine, thread-like strokes, with little spots and sudden patches of luminosity, with a range of light and transparent colours (24). Thus we have on the one hand the scenes of peasant life, outstanding among which are those at Ferrara, Zoppola and Venice (Plates 15-36), and on the other are the canvases which are French in cha-

IX - THE APOTHECARY (detail of plate 112). *Venice, Gallerie dell' Accademia.*

racter — the *Gentleman's Awakening* (Plate 57), *Blind Man's Buff* (Plate 62) at Windsor, the *Faint* and the *Game of the Cooking-pot* at Washington, (Plates 67-8) and others in the Accademia, which are all reminiscent of the transparent palette of Rosalba and Amigoni. In 1745 come the frescoes of San Pantalon, in the Loreto chapel, which confirm further Longhi's liking for the light and luminous painting of Rosalba and Amigoni. What other style is closer to the assembly of youthful saints and smiling Madonnas intent upon holding the children who are gently slipping from their arms, the little angels like curly-headed peasants?

Valcanover has remarked how the pale tones of Rosalba's palette are matched by the soft gradation of colour in these frescoes, which are mostly in sky-blue, pale green and gold lines on grey, pink, silver, white and cloudy yellow grounds (25). It is certain, because of the stage which the painter had reached by 1745, that this is not merely a question of casual influence but the result of a deliberately weighed choice.

Thus, at the end of his fourth decade, Pietro Longhi freed himself from the manner of the history painter, acquired from Balestra and from the twilight effects of Crespi's palette, which were certainly too limiting for one whose inclination was above all to paint 'scenes which evoke a genial good humour' and sought to establish himself in an artistic world in which the dominant voice was that of Venetian rococo, with the dazzling cascades of light to be found in the virtuoso late works of Ricci, Pellegrini and Gian Antonio Guardi.

The uniqueness of Longhi's figurative manner is the result of this synthesis; with the achievement of complete independence with regard to theme, rivalling the most highly esteemed European models, he can approach, even if with prudent conservatism, an authentic aspect of the ethos of his time, in making himself a penetrating chronicler of contemporary society; and he is able to select from the most highly developed styles of Venetian painting the forms which could best give artistic substance to his fragile but genial people. He finds a 'new and individual style' to portray a world 'seen with his own eyes'.

## SERIAL WORKS

It is a curious but characteristic fact about Longhi as a person that, having resolved his crisis in these cultural conditions, throughout his long active life, which comprised fifty-five years of productivity, he apparently did not ever want to change his means and manner of expression. There was inevitably some development, from the more thoughtful manner of the 1750s to the more ingenuous forms of his old age, and he was affected also by the middle-class spirit of Alessandro's portraits.

But in general terms one must acknowledge that Pietro Longhi shows a singular consistency as to style, so that he was able to return to subjects in replicas and variants only slightly different from their originals, even after decades. The choices that he made at thirty-five, 'seeing that it would be difficult to distinguish himself as a painter of History', were decisive ones, and they were fortunate ones, because they provided him with an original iconographic repertory and opened to him a wide range of human interests, and at the same time brought his painting closer to that of some of the most delicate colourists of the eighteenth century.

20

X - THE MOOR'S LETTER (detail of plate 119). *Venice, Ca' Rezzonico*

A study of the 'evolution' of Longhi's style after 1745 can hardly be more than that of an elementary chronological development, and for many details of a purely philological order the catalogue entries have seemed the most suitable place. It is perhaps more useful to study the thematic grouping of Longhi's paintings, the result of design rather than chance, in order to understand his method of work, which is always based on detailed graphic documentation in his drawings.

The production of 'serial works' — that is, of several works in a series illustrating a single theme — is typical of the eighteenth century. They are encountered particularly in those fields which were most familiar to Longhi in his early years. He knew the *Life of a Singer* and the *Sacraments* of Crespi; at one time or another, directly or indirectly, he knew, perhaps through prints, Hogarth's series: *The Harlot's Progress*, *The Rake's Progress*, *Marriage à la Mode*, or *The Four Times of the Day*, and there is a trace of Longhi's spirit in Highmore's series for *Pamela* (Fig. 16). Now that in the present volume all Longhi's paintings are brought together for the first time it is not difficult to feel that many of his works fall into similar series, and there is no need to force the chronology in order to form hypothetical groups which can stand beside the acknowledged series of the *Sacraments* and *Shooting in the Valley*. Between his fourth and fifth decades Longhi shows, in his own fashion and without the sharp irony of Hogarth, after the *Shepherds* (Plates 7-13), *Peasant Life* — girls spinning, preparing polenta, washerwomen, the sturdy suitor, rustic dances, drunkards (Plates 15-35). Between 1740 and 1750 comes the *Life of a Lady* — her toilet, the choice of a dress, music and dancing lessons, visiting the library, her presentation in society (Plates 38-54). Another series illustrates *Family Life*, from rising in the morning, games of Blindman's Buff and the Cooking-pot, to the more or less genuine swoon after the interrupted game of cards (Plates 57-68). Again, still during the 1740s, another series can be perceived, that of a *Gentleman's Amusements*, including gay receptions, strolls in the piazza, surprise visits to the boudoir (Plates 84, 85, 132, 200 etc.). And finally there is of course a series devoted to the *domestic servants*, from buying doughnuts and salad from street vendors, to cooks and maidservants dancing the furlana in the courtyard when the master and mistress are out or asleep (Plates 86-94).

At this stage, series illustrating a thesis or argument, especially one with moral or satirical intention, are hardly to be expected. These, if any are to be admitted, belong to the following decade, 1750-60, when the influence of Rousseau and the polemical renovation of Venetian comedy by Goldoni, and some of Gaspare Gozzi's pamphlets, might encourage a more marked social content. But it is hard for Longhi to achieve more than a benevolent irony, still conservative in his attitude, in the various 'temptation' pictures, in the embroidery workrooms, the young friars with roving eyes, the milords ready with their 'protection', the old abbés or the military seducers (Plates 100-6). There is perhaps an implied criticism of the superabundance of quacks, tooth-drawers, gypsies and soothsayers who infest the arcades of the Doge's Palace — a common background to many paintings of the 1750s. At the same time the *Education of a Noble Young Lady* is lightly ridiculed in the lessons of geography, music and singing, reading aloud, visiting elderly aunts, grandmothers and greatgrandmothers, which ends the artist's most productive period, around 1770 (Plates 54, 126, 127, 201, 208, 283, 285).

It is surely exaggerated to believe what has been asserted without evidence, that for this superficial irony Longhi actually clashed with authority, and the assertion misrepresents the peace-

XI - THE GEOGRAPHY LESSON (detail of plate 126). *Venice, Pinacoteca Querini Stampalia.*

loving and conservative nature of the artist. This side of his personality is represented in the series of the *Sacraments*, devoutly religious, which is based on the Crespi series but sweetenend with soft tones, smiling and tranquil.

Undoubtedly Longhi's concentration on serial painting from the end of the 1730s sharpened and fostered his talent for observation of reality and led him towards portrait painting pure and simple. He understood portraiture as the recording of events as much as the portrayal of individuals. The famous *Rhinoceros* commissioned in 1751 by Giovanni Grimani de' Servi clearly includes portraits of members of the family of his noble client. Close in date are the various *Family Groups* (Plates 117, 119, 120, 123, 128, 132) and *The Moor's Letter*, and all these paintings have a certain rarefied atmosphere which confers importance on the rather childish attitudes of the sitters, whose expressions and gestures certainly do not suggest any preoccupation with problems of moment. But the subtlety of the preparatory drawings for so many of these, from the guitar player (Plate 127) to the gentleman of the *Patrician Family* in Ca' Rezzonico (Plate 121), from the embroideresses (Plate 134) of *The Embroidery Workroom* to the maid (Plate 125) in *The Geography Lesson*, serve to underline his concern for realism; and the colour graduates more than ever by means of small strokes, like a miniature. The exquisite sensitivity to detail is exemplified in the famous inscription on one of the drawings in the Museo Correr (26) which describes a parrot: 'The front of the face dark, the patch running to beneath the neck yellow, red round the eyes and above them, the body greeenish, some feathers reddish above, yellow below, the eye reddish and the pupil black.'

Between 1750 and 1755 he painted a number of portraits in the strict sense of the word, from those of Doge Grimani (Plates 139, 141) to the equestrian portrait of William Graeme and the group of young noblemen (Plates 142, 143), which fully justify the reputation that Longhi had and that Gradenigo records in his reliable diaries for those same years (27).

## 'SPEAKING CARICATURES'

With the series of *Quacks*, beginning with the example of 1757 in Ca' Rezzonico there is a distinct modification of the palette of light colours which had been typical of the first conversation pieces (*c.* 1741 to 1755). This suggests a point of departure for a second phase in Longhi's activity, in which the tonality becomes darker and tends towards brown tints, while even his drawing becomes more rapid and approximate, losing a certain degree of plasticity.

We can only conjecture what may have been the cause of this variation in style, although the difference is in fact slight and more of a technical than a stylistic order. We may seek it in the disappearance of the first immediate inspiration of Rosalba and Amigoni, and its supersession by the arrival of a stronger influence of Rembrandtesque modes through the medium of portraitists such as Nazzari and pastellists such as Nogari — a manner which later was to become straightforward imitation as in the case of Novelli. This development in Longhi is probably more apparent than substantial and there are in fact many reworkings, even after 1760, of subjects in light tones, executed with the subtle *sfumatura* effects of ten years previously: such are *The Hairdresser* (Plate 206),

24

*The Toilet* (Plate 210) in Ca' Rezzonico' and conversation pieces formerly in the Perera collection.

In this period, which might be defined as one of transition if the expression did not seem a restricting one — which it is not —, Pietro Longhi often returns to the production of serial works. Thus we have the series of *Quacks, Fortune-Tellers, Perfume-Sellers, Showmen*, the crowd of swindlers, tricksters, meddlers, which throng the arcades of the Doge's Palace to the delight of foreigners and of the masked patricians (Plates 160-6, 242-5).

The masked figures are one of the typical themes of the years between the mid 1750s and the mid 1760s. They are to be found in the many *Ridotti* (Plates 168-73), in the scenes in the Piazza and the Piazzetta, beneath the arcades, even in the domestic *Visits* (Plate 203). There is no need to stress how congenial the theme was to the smiling and intimate muse of the artist: even more than in the little pictures of customs and environments he seems to find the rather eerie presence of figures wearing the domino, or 'bauta', a subject which inspired him to intensely pictorial expression — he plays with the cloudy white of lace and the suggestive black of the shawls (28).

At the end of the 1750s there is a limited return to portraiture, a type of work to which he turned at increasingly long intervals throughout his life. In 1757 he painted *Magrath the Giant* (Plate 141) and at about the same time the portraits of *Clement XIII* (Plate 175), a *Lady* (Plate 178), and a *Gentleman* (Plate 177). Many of these portraits are an extension of the conversation piece or family group, and they include the outstanding series of canvases which formerly belonged to the Perera collection. A characteristic common to this group is the use of rather blurred, sweet colours, with yellows, green-greys and luminous blues predominating. Longhi seems to have moved away from the enclosed atmosphere of the preceding decade, and here the light is more open and diffused. The spatial composition also shows some improvement, with more successful organisation in depth. To the years around 1760 probably belong some family groups of larger proportions in horizontal format, like those in the Albrizzi, Salom and Verona collections (Plates 216, 218, 220). In an attempt to achieve a more convincing setting in a wider space Longhi shows a curious tendency to incline the ground plane forwards, raising considerably the vanishing point. It is a technical shift which reveals a certain awkwardness, but it does not detract from the sharp verisimilitude of the scenes.

## MASQUERADES AND CONVERSATION PIECES OF HIS MATURITY

The declining phase of Longhi's career is usually taken to begin with the works dated 1761, such as the *Monks, Canons and Friars* (Plate 221), or 1762, such as *The Lion Show* (Plate 252) — paintings with rather fragmentary outlines, faded-looking colours, misty in quality. But this is perhaps a partial judgment: it is to this period that the series of *Shooting in the Valley* belongs (Plates 233-42), a real masterpiece in the lively observation of manners, which evokes a genuine atmosphere, damp with lagoon mist and humidity, and with many penetrating and unforgettable portraits, And between 1764 and 1772 there is an increasing number of paintings of people in their natural surroundings, all touchingly real and never without the trace of humour which always characterised Longhi's conversation pieces. There is no doubt that in his later years his activity as a portraitist was of increasing importance. It is partly a reflection of his status but it also reflects the

26

situation of the art market. With Rosalba and Nazzari dead, Nogari, Uberti and Pasquetti old, the office of portraitist of the Venetian nobility passed to the Longhi family, with Alessandro also by now a successful artist.

It is true that the Longhi portraits continue to be by way of a compromise, between the 'speaking caricature' of which Pietro was the master and the greater demands made, both in psychological penetration and in the dimensions of the canvas, in which he did not always feel at home. There is a feeling of mild reluctance in the renderings of *Francesco Guardi*, *The Doge's Steward*, the *Polish Gentleman* and the *Gentleman* at Treviso (Plates 227, 231, 232, 260), and the Querini portraits seem on the stage for a moment, out of the embalmed silence of one of the little conversation pieces. When Pietro Longhi attempts full-length figures, such as the *Procuratore Manin* at Udine (Plate 230) he poses a problem for the critics, who have to explain certain incongruities by a supposed collaboration of his son.

There are also a number of paintings of public events, examples of which Longhi had painted earlier, such as the curious sights commissioned by Giovanni Grimani, which are one of the typical features of his work in this decade. After the strange group of the *Monks, Canons and Friars of Venice* (Plate 221) of 1761 come the *Lion Show* of 1762, *Borgogna's Show*, the *Quack* of after 1763 and the *Elephant* of 1774 (Plates 252-5). It is true that Longhi is no longer capable of attaining the level of quality of so many previous paintings which were similarly inspired by popular events, but it must be acknowledged that he retains intact the freshness of his interest, expressed in innumerable details, which are as always guarantors of direct and lively observation (29).

## FOLLOWERS OF LONGHI

While it seems problematic whether Alessandro ever in fact collaborated in Pietro's work — it is more likely to have been the other way round, that Pietro had a share in works attributed to his son, as in *The Pisani Family* — there is no doubt that in the last decades of his life a number of works were produced alongside his own by imitators. Rather than these being workshop productions (unlikely because the intervention of assistants would be detrimental to Longhi's individual manner) it is possible to identify some individual imitators and followers — artists who adopt certain of Longhi's forms and subjects without having direct contact with him (30). Mention will be made of some of these, and further details appear in the catalogue entries. First is Charles Joseph Flipart, who is still something of a mystery in Venetian art, but who seems identifiable as the artist of the *Concert* and the *Hairdresser* in the Topic collection (Plates 437 and 439), because they correspond to signed prints. These are not very different from the two small portraits of singers at Hartford and Milan which have been referred to as his (Plates 441, 443) nor from the *Painter* (Plate 422) recently attributed to him. Flipart, born in 1721, worked first in Paris in the studio of Cars, the engraver of Watteau, Chardin, Boucher and Lancret. He arrived in Venice in 1737 and by 1740 was engraving for the printseller Wagner; in 1750 he left Venice for Madrid. During his twelve years in Venice he made many engravings from works by Longhi with an expert technique of etching achieving, particularly successful effects of shading and lights. His work as a painter during his Venetian period is naturally affected by this technique: examples

XIV - THE QUACK (detail of plate 160). *Venice, Ca' Rezzonico.*

of his work are now being rediscovered. However, even in close proximity to Longhi, Flipart's manner remains unmistakably French, and the plastic clarity of his colours, refined and luminous, belongs to the realm of Watteau and his followers.

Closer to Longhi, and certainly a Venetian, is the painter known as the Master of the Ridotto, from one of his canvases in Ca' Rezzonico. His style is characterised by elongated thin figures and uncertain perspective, but also by some effective use of colour reminiscent of the brilliant palette and stabbing touch of Diziani and Fontebasso; while iconographically his drawing belongs to the tradition of the view painters, Carlevaris and Marieschi. He is without doubt the most prolific of Longhi's followers, and the paintings of masked subjects in Amsterdam, Rome and some private collections should be attributed to him.

Very similar to the Master of the Ridotto is a painter who is known at present as the Master of the Reflections for his idiomatic technique, an iridescent effect of lively brushwork. The work of this artist is very pleasing and has some affinity with that of Flipart; his *Declaration* (Plate 469) is painted from a print of Flipart's, and a companion piece to *The Game of Cards* (Plate 467). Others of his canvases are *The Jewish Wedding* (Plate 468), *The Spinet* (Plate 466) and the *Awakenings* (Plates 473, 478). Further from the authentic Longhi quality are paintings such as *The Geography Lesson* in Ca' d'Oro (Plate 446), *Goldoni in his Study* (Plate 447), *The Family Gathering* (Plate 445) in Ca' Rezzonico, which are all close in style to another *Family Gathering* in the Museo Civico, Udine, signed by Lorenzo Gramiccia, a mediocre artist who copies Longhi's style at a distance, in blurred and brownish tones.

Goldoni describes in *Il Burchiello* in 1756 a certain Andrea Pastò as 'a good painter especially of small figures in the manner of the famous Longhi' (31), but so far efforts to identify the man and his work have been unsuccessful. The Veronese artist Giuseppe de Gobbis, however, may be identified as the author of a group of paintings similar in style to those of Longhi, in Ca' Rezzonico, Philadelphia and Segromigno (Plates 449-453), on the basis of Pallucchini's study of paintings formerly in Palazzo Stucky; his style is characterised by a smooth application of colour, with rather plump-faced and doll-like figures. Possibly the famous *Ridotti* of the Grand Dukes of Bavaria are by him, and also the similar canvases formerly in the Sundin collection (Plates 454-7).

## THE BOURGEOIS MANNER

It has often been asserted that Longhi's last paintings, from 1770 onwards, descend to the level of modest ex-votos, but this is an injustice. It cannot be denied that *The Elephant* of 1774 (Plate 255) and other paintings of fairground curiosities (some of which are not of certain attribution) are pictorially impoverished when compared, for example, with *The Rhinoceros* (Plate 116) of twenty years earlier. The subtle gradations of lively and charming colour are replaced by a subdued and almost uniform tonality, and the narrative interest is confined to a few touches of local colour which do nothing to 'evoke a genial good humour'. But these are also the years in which *The Advocates* (Plate 271), *Coffee Time* (Plate 274) and *The Morning Cup of Chocolate* (Plate 279) were painted, all of which are real masterpieces; they portray now people who are middleclass, rather than patricians, almost to symbolise the fallen fortunes of the Most Serene Republic of St Mark.

30

XV - THE QUACK (detail of plate 160). *Venice, Ca' Rezzonico.*

The starting point for this period is perhaps the *Portrait of Benedetto Ganassoni* (Plate 261) of 1774. Longhi tends increasingly to portraiture centred on the sitter, his personality rather than his social milieu. The painter of manners yields to the painter of individuals, and in this he follows the ethos of the time, in an increasing interest in the private aspects of middle-class life.

It is significant that at this time the similarity of the work of Pietro Longhi to that of his son, now the most celebrated portrait-painter in Venice, becomes more obvious and indeed is so marked that in some cases, such as that of Bishop Ganassoni, there exist two portraits, a smaller one by the father (Plate 261) and a larger version by his son (Feltre, Seminary) (33). Pallucchini has suggested that it is wrong to consider that of these Pietro's painting is a *modelletto* for Alessandro, an opinion shared by the present writer (34). It is indeed probable that Pietro, then aged over seventy, was gradually adopting the 'middle-class portrait' manner of his son, to the point of copying one of his paintings, either from memory or commissioned by a collector (Fig. 20). The famous picture in the Lady Lever Gallery, the *Poet reciting his Verses* (Plate 278) may be another example of this: the existence of a drawing traditionally ascribed to Alessandro caused the painting also to be attributed to him rather than to his father (35). It appears to us that this is another case of Pietro working in Alessandro's manner, with the more subtle, precise and slightly ironic touch which is typical of him.

In these portraits of the last period there is often a tendency to insist on the details of a face and to go over profiles, or the folds of a garment, several times with the brush, in such a way that the pleasant effects of colour which Longhi achieved in his best period are lost. The infinite variety of tints, graduated and juxtaposed with a predominance of misty, soft pastel-like colours is now replaced by a rather crude chiaroscuro and a more trite, monotonous line. The paint is applied thinly so that in many of the paintings of the 1770s the grain of the canvas and the greyish ground can easily be seen. This does not however reflect any physical decline of the artist, as some scholars have implied, nor does it deserve the qualification of an 'ex-voto' standard. The *Family Groups* (Plates 280-1), *The Advocates* (Plate 271), the *Literary Gentlemen* (Plate 290) and the *Barbarigo Giustinian* portraits (Plates 286-7), which were painted up to 1779, have their own atmosphere, rarefied and detached, as if the artist had deliberately renounced the charms of a palette that was now old-fashioned — in an age of neo-classicism — to concentrate on the psychological aspects, which interested him more.

Certainly, the pose of the Michiel family of *c.* 1780 (Plate 293) is of a distressingly middle-class anonymity compared with the patrician family groups of the 1750s. But there is no real comparison possible between the rhythmic vitality of groups such as the Sagredo and the Rezzonico (Plates 120, 175) and the frail melancholy of Giustina Renier Michiel.

In this sense, even when academically speaking the technique of the old painter is most hesitant, his line wavering and returning repeatedly over the outline to construct features with his customary deep honesty in the face of reality — in *The Dancer Binetti, The Tutor, The Quintet, The Usurers,* in the series of portraits in the Orsi collection and the portraits of husband and wife (Plates 288-99) — in all these the very personal style of Pietro Longhi is by no means either lost or withheld, but it rather acquires a more profound, more delicate humanity.

# NOTES

1. For this and the following quotations relating to critical opinions upon Longhi, see the *Anthology of Longhi Criticism* and the Bibliography, which are both arranged chronologically.

2. C. GOLDONI, *Componimenti poetici per le felicissime nozze di Sue Eccelenze il Signor Giovanni Grimani...*, Venice, 1750.

3. A. ORLANDI - P. GUARIENTI, *Abecedario Pittorico*, Venice, 1753, p. 427.

4. A. LONGHI, *Compendio delle vite dei pittori veneziani*, Venice, 1762.

5. L. LIVAN, *Notizie d'arte tratte dai notatori e dagli Annali del N.H. Pietro Gradenigo*, Venice, 1942, p. 62.

6. G. GOZZI, *L'Osservatore Veneto*, Venice, 14 February 1761, p. 28.

7. From the *Catastici* of the State Archive, Venice, year 1740, it appears that Longhi lived in the house registered as no. 343, the property of the Nobleman Lunardo Emo. The rent was 44 ducats a year (Ravà, 1909, p. 155). The house was near the 'pontesello S. Rocco', and is described as such in the registration of Longhi's death (v. Document 2). The 'pontesello S. Rocco' is today the Ponte della Scuola, which leads to the Calle della Scuola, in which the houses numbered 3800, 3801, 3802 probably correspond to the site of the former no. 343, which has been destroyed.

8. For the portrait of the Grimani see the *Componimenti poetici* cited in note 2. For the Sagredo inventory, see M. BRUNETTI, *Un eccezionale collegio peritale; Piazzetta, Tiepolo, Longhi* in 'Arte Veneta', 1951, p. 158.

9. See F. HASKELL, *Francesco Guardi as vedutista and his patrons* in 'Journal of the Warburg and Courtauld Institutes', 1960, XXIII, p. 256.

10. D. BELTRAMI, *Storia della popolazione di Venezia*, Padua, 1954, pp. 212-3.

11. For the historical background to Venetian society see M. BERENGO, *La società veneta alla fine del Settecento*, Florence, 1956, pp. 43-87.

12. See M. BERENGO, *Op. cit.*, 1956, p. 74.

13. There is no evidence that Longhi had dealings with the Venetian censorship, in spite of the assertion of P. PAOLETTI, *Continuazione della storia della Repubblica di Venezia*, Venice, 1832, p. 122. See also F. HASKELL, *Patrons and Painters*, London, 1963, p. 323.

14. For the verses see M. DAZZI, *Il fiore della lirica veneziana*, Venice, 1956, II, pp. 273, 374.

15. A. ORLANDI - P. GUARIENTI, *Op. cit.*, 1753, p. 427.

16. R. PALLUCCHINI, *La pittura veneziana del Settecento*, Venice-Rome, 1960, pp. 178-9. After remarking that Balestra left Venice in 1719 and that Longhi could therefore have studied under him only for a short time, when he was still very young, Pallucchini suggests that the artist then devoted himself to the production of the works of historical and religious nature which are mentioned in the documentary sources and of which some have been rediscovered. Among these are the S. Pellegrino altar-piece, of 1730, the *Adoration of the Magi* recently identified in the Scuola di San Giovanni Evangelista (E. MARTINI, *La pittura veneziana del Settecento*, Venice, 1964, p. 106, no. 239), and the frescoes in Ca' Sagredo of 1734. According to this theory, only after the execution of the last, unfortunate, work, which made him determine to change his direction, did Longhi go to Bologna. It is of course not impossible that the move to Bologna took place several years earlier, especially if it is accepted that there are Bolognese elements — however slight and misapplied — in the 1734 frescoes. Apart from the difficulty of solving this problem of chronological detail, Pallucchini is certainly right when he suggests that the Bolognese training was more likely to direct Longhi towards the production of scenes of 'popular' life (the *Shepherds* of Bassano and Rovigo) than to reaffirm his rather barren

pursuit of decorative painting along the lines of his training with Balestra. The fact that this tendency to paint low-life scenes such as the *Shepherds* exists alongside the French inspiration visible in his early works (*The Concert*, dated 1741) shows that Longhi's conversion was the result of a somewhat complicated process into which many different factors enter.

17. Pallucchini (*Op. cit.*, 1960, p. 178) draws attention to the influence of Dorigny, active in the Veneto as a decorative painter and in Venice itself, in Ca' Zenobio.

18. A. RAVÀ, *Pietro Longhi*, Bergamo, 1909 (2nd ed. 1923, pp. 6-8); G. FIOCCO, *La Pittura Veneziana del Seicento e del Settecento*, Bologna, 1929, p. 66; R. PALLUCCHINI, *Capolavori dei Musei Veneti*, Venice, 1946, p. 160; R. LONGHI, *Viatico per cinque secoli di pittura veneziana*, Florence, 1946, p. 36; V. MOSCHINI, *Pietro Longhi*, Milan, 1956; R. PALLUCCHINI, *Op. cit.*, 1960, p. 190. The prevalent opinion among critics is that the origins of Longhi's 'popolar' scenes are to be sought in eighteenth-century art. Older views which suggested that seventeenth-century painters provided his inspiration do not, on investigation, seem fruitful. It is in fact unlikely that Longhi had seen paintings of the type of Pasqualino Rossi's *The Lacemakers* (now in the Louvre), nor that the *bambocciante* school of Pietro Bellotti and others had any significance in relation to his art. Longhi's genre painting is essentially Bolognese, and is not affected, even indirectly, by Caravaggesque realism.

19. F. ANTAL, *Hogarth and his place in European art*, London, 1962, pp. 203-4. In the chapter on 'Hogarth's impact on European Art', Antal describes how Hogarth prints had a certain vogue in Italy, especially among intellectuals. Beccaria, for instance, mentions '*The Rake in Bedlam*' in his essay on 'Public Happiness'. As far as Longhi in particular is concerned, Antal thinks it probable that the influence of these prints was transmitted primarily by the first few of Hogarth's serial works (he cites *Marriage à la mode*), which must obviously have seemed more French in the eyes of the painter.

20. For French eighteenth-century prints see L. RÉAU, *La gravure d'illustration*, Paris and Brussels, 1928; E. DACIER, *La gravure de genre et de moeurs*, Paris and Brussels, 1925; Id., *La gravure française*, Paris, 1944. Anna Pallucchini kindly informs us that a series of prints after Watteau had been sent from Paris to Rosalba Carriera.

21. The drawing is on light brown paper, in black and white chalk, 284×405 mm. (reproduced in Fig. 10).

22. L. RIZZI, *Carlevarijs*, Venice, 1967, p. 67, draws attention to the relationship between the drawings of Carlevaris and Longhi's taste for anecdote. This is an acute observation, and there seems no doubt that some of Carlevaris' notebooks — such as those in the Museo Correr and in the Victoria and Albert Museum — may have been seen by Longhi, and to some effect. As to figure-drawing, his tendency to use an unbroken line and a touched-in profile is unlike any other contemporary example, but it has a direct antecedent — besides in the French artists — in the manner of the Friulian Carlevaris.

Another comparison relative to Longhi's linear technique that is worthy of note is with the drawings of Gian Paolo Panini. This Roman painter also used to fill small books with drawings from life, often in black pencil or in red chalk. Some of his ladies with a fan or gentlemen intent upon their music-making in the British Museum (vol. 1858), have undeniably an aura of Longhi about the (Fig. 11). Again, his peasants and smiling country wenches in the Berlin Kupferstichkabinett (nos. 17536-40), in soft pencil, have a characteristic outline with strong shading, producing a pictorial effect similar to that of Longhi (reproduced in F. ARISI, *Gian Paolo Panini*, Piacenza, 1961, *passim*). The great novelty and poetic power of Pietro Longhi's drawings is however in their direct relationship with reality, the carefully noted details of colour, distance, effects of light; there is hardly a sheet which is not brought to life by this particular expressive power, the riche endowment of his figurative technique.

23. We refer to drawings such as the *Portrait of a Lady* in The Hermitage (reproduced in L. SALMINA, *Disegni Veneti del Museo di Leningrado*, Venice, 1964, p. 42), which have elsewhere been compared — with many reservations — with two other similar drawings in the Museo Correr (inv. 387 and 1369) (T. PIGNATTI, *I disegni veneti di Leningrado alla Fondazione Cini*, in 'Arte Veneta', 1964, p. 225).

24. The clarity of tone of Longhi's colour around 1750 has suggested to Pallucchini the possibility of contact with Liotard. Algarotti acquired his *Chocolatière* (later in Dresden) in Venice in 1745 (*Op. cit.*, 1960, p. 181).

25. F. VALCANOVER, *Affreschi sconosciuti di Pietro Longhi*, in 'Paragone', 1956, no. 73, p. 24.

26. Museo Correr, drawings, inv. 535.

27. L. LIVAN, *Op. cit.*, 1942, p. 62.

28. As Pallucchini has pointed out, perhaps the coincidence is not a fortuitous one, bearing in mind the particular revival of the gay life, which led the masked nobleman from one ridotto to another in an exhausting round of gossiping and flirtatious encounters. The various sumptuary laws enacted by the Republic during this period against luxury and gaming give indirect evidence of this situation. In 1768 the most famous gaming-house, the Ridotto of Ca' Giustinian, was refurbished and redecorated, and the stage of preparation is recorded in the painting by Francesco Guardi in Ca' Rezzonico, as the casino itself is in many paintings by Longhi and his followers, from those in the Salom collection to that at Baden Salem. The festive and gallant life of the period is symbolised by personalities such as Caterina Dolfin Tron. See G. DAMERINI, *Settecento Veneziano*, Milan, 1939; M. PETROCCHI, *Il tramonto della Repubblica di Venezia*, Venice, 1950, pp. 43-57.

29. The up-to-dateness of Longhi's interests hardly needs further emphasis; he follows very closely the developments in the culture of the social milieu which he frequented. These are the years of interest in the natural sciences, and as an indication of this, the famous work of Buffon was re-published in Venice by Bossaglia in 1781.

30. For a first critical approach to the question of Longhi's followers see R. PALLUCCHINI, *Op. cit.*, 1960, pp. 179-192.

31. C. DONZELLI, *I pittori veneti del Settecento*, Florence, 1957, p. 176.

32. R. PALLUCCHINI, *Op. cit.*, 1960, p. 191, fig. 492.

33. See F. VALCANOVER, *Un nuovo ritratto di Alessandro Longhi*, in 'Archivio Storico di Belluno, Feltre e Cadore', May-June, 1854, no. 135; T. PIGNATTI, *Il Museo Correr di Venezia, Dipinti del XVII e XVIII secolo*, Venice, 1960, p. 184.

34. R. PALLUCCHINI, *La pittura veneziana del Settecento (dispense)*, Bologna, 1951-52, II, p. 73.

35. F. WATSON, *An unfamiliar conversation piece by Alessandro Longhi*, in 'Bollettino dei Musei Civici Veneziani', 1964, IV, p. 20. Watson in fact acknowledges in his article that if it were not for the existence of the drawing attributed to Alessandro, the painting in the Lady Lever Gallery could be taken for a typical work by Pietro Longhi. Indeed, it does seem doubtful whether the drawing is necessarily by Alessandro, of whom nothing is known as a draughtsman, and it may be by his father, whose manner in such works as the drawing with the *Rustic Scene* in the Pierpont Morgan Library it approaches. (See T. PIGNATTI, *I disegni veneziani del Settecento*, Rome, 1965, no. 107, p. 207).

*Many years of research in the compilation of the* corpus *of Longhi's works have put me so deeply into the debt of friends and colleagues that it would not be possible to thank them all individually. My special gratitude to Antonio Morassi and to Francesco Valcanover, who put at my disposal their collections of photographs and their advice, cannot be passed over in silence. Michael Levey has been of great assistance in tracing the paintings which have featured in collections and sales in England, as has Jean Cailleux for France. Dealers, collectors and the Directors of Museum have kindly collaborated in providing factual details of paintings and drawings as can been seen from the Catalogue.*

*I am particularly grateful to Rodolfo Pallucchini for having accepted the present volume for the series of books on art published by Editore Alfieri, and for the warm and friendly interest he has shown at every stage of this work.*

T.P.

Fig. 1. A. LONGHI: *Portrait of Pietro Longhi* (from the *Compendio...*, 1761).

Fig. 2. G. CATTINI: *Portrait of Pietro Longhi* (1740-50).

Fig. 3. *Portrait of Pietro Longhi as an Academician* (1766).

Fig. 4. Engraving by LARMESSIN after N. LANCRET: *Le Rémois* (from the *Contes* of La Fontaine, Paris, 1738).

Fig. 5. Engraving by L. CARS after F. BOUCHER: *The Visit to the Library* (from Molière, *Les Femmes Savantes*, Paris, 1734).

Fig. 6. Engraving by L. CARS after F. WATTEAU: *Fêtes Vénitiennes*, 1732.

Fig. 7. Engraving by J. AUDRAN after F. WATTEAU: from *Figures de différentes caractères*, Paris, 1726-28.

Fig. 8. J.B. PATER: *Lady with a Fan*. Paris, Private collection.

Fig. 9. F. WATTEAU: *Three Studies for an Actor*. Paris, Louvre (no. 33365).

Fig. 10. J.B. CHARDIN: *The Sedan chair*. Stockholm, National Museum (no. 42-1898).

Fig. 11. G.P. PANINI: *Lady with a Fan*. London,
British Museum.

Fig. 12. G.M. CRESPI: *The Flea*. Florence, Uffizi.

Fig .13. J. AMIGONI(?): *The two Ladies*. Venice, Museo Correr.

42

Fig. 14. J. CERUTI: *Young Girl with a Fan*. Bergamo, Accademia Carrara.

Fig. 15. W. HOGARTH: *The Strode Family*. London, Tate Gallery.

44

Fig. 16. J. HIGHMORE: *Portrait of Samuel Richardson* (detail). London, National Portrait Gallery.

45

Fig. 17. ROSALBA CARRIERA: *Self-portrait* (c. 1730). Venice, Ca' Rezzonico.

Fig. 18. P. LONGHI: *Portrait of Francesco Guardi* (detail) (1764). Venice, Ca' Rezzonico.

Fig. 19. B. NAZZARI: *Portrait of Samuel Egerton* (1732).
Venice, Ca' Rezzonico.

Fig. 20. A. LONGHI: *Portrait of an Admiral*. Milan, Orsi
Collection.

48

# CHRONOLOGICAL TABLE

1702 Pietro Longhi is born in Venice, according to the biography in the *Compendio* published by his son, Alessandro. The registration of death, in the Archive of the church of San Pantalon, Venice, and in the State Archive show his age as 85 years, which would date his birth to 1700. His family name was Falca, later replaced by the nickname Longhi (see Documents 2-3).

1732 8 July. In a payment made to the stucco-worker Francesco Camozzi, Pietro Longhi is mentioned as the painter of the altar-piece in the parish church of San Pellegrino (*Libro dei sindaci della Scuola del Sacramento*, Galizzi 1942). 27 September. He marries Caterina Maria Rizzi, in San Pantalon, Venice (see Document 1).

1733 12 June. His son Alessandro is born, in the parish of San Zulian, and is baptised on 10 July (Register of Baptisms, Archive of the Basilica of San Marco. See Document 4).
Zanetti mentions the *Adoration of the Magi* by Longhi in Sta. Maria Materdomini, now in the Scuola di San Giovanni Evangelista (Zanetti, 1733; Martini, 1964).

1734 Date on the fresco of the principal staircase, Ca' Sagredo, Venice.

1737 Entered the guild of the painters of Venice, where his name appears until 1773 (Pignatti, 1965).

1740 He lives in the parish of San Pantalon, in the house of Leonardo Emo, where he remains until his death (Catastico Emo, State Archive, Venice). Ca' Emo was probably on the site now occupied by nos. 3800-3802 (Ravà, 1923).

1741 Date on *The Concert*, Gallerie dell'Accademia, Venice.

1744 Date on *The Gentleman's Awakening*, Royal collection, Windsor.

1745 Consecration of the Chapel of Our Lady of Loreto, San Pantalon, 'completely finished' and hence probably with Longhi's frescoes (*Brevi notizie...*, 1756).

1746 Date on *A Lady receives Visitors*, Metropolitan Museum of Art, New York.

1748 7 December. Bassano, Museo Civico: Letter of the painter to Remondini about the engraving of a painting of *Ladies at the Coffee-House at Mira*. The print is by Faldoni (see Document 5).

1749 13 May. Bassano, Museo Civico: Letter to Remondini about the engraving of *Milord's Visitor*, Metropolitan Museum of Art, New York (see Document 6).

1750 Eulogistic sonnet to Longhi, written by Carlo Goldoni on the occasion of the marriage of Giovanni Grimani and Caterina Contarini (Goldoni, 1750).

1751 10 April. Bassano, Museo Civico: Letter to Remondini about the consignment of a quantity of wine to Longhi (see Document 7).
23 April. Bassano, Museo Civico: Letter to Remondini about the reproduction of various paintings, with *Dominoes at the Coffee-House* and other subjects which have not been identified (see Document 8).
8 May. Bassano, Museo Civico: Letter to Remondini, about a print for Wagner (see Document 9).

Date on *The Rhinoceros*, Ca' Rezzonico, Venice.

Bartolozzi engraves *The Tooth-Drawer* and *The Singing Lesson*, by Longhi (Calabi, 1928).

1752  5 December. Bassano, Museo Civico: Letter to Remondini in which the painter asks for four prints, and complains about the bad quality of their execution (see Document 10).

1753  12 January. Bassano Museo Civico: Letter to Remondini which mentions twelve prints, two of which are for Cecilia Morosini 'who possesses the original of *The Coffee-House* (see Document 11).

The first biographical note on Longhi appears in the new edition of Orlandi and Guarienti's *Abecedario pittorico* (Orlandi-Guarienti, 1753).

Date on *The Fortune-Teller*, National Gallery, London.

1755  The tenth volume of Goldoni's comedies published by Paperini; the dedication refers to prints of the *Seven Sacraments*, which Pitteri hoped to finish 'in a short time' (Goldoni, 1755).

1756  Date on *The Fortune-Teller*, National Gallery, London.

1757  Date on *The Quack*, Ca' Rezzonico, Venice.

Date on *Magrath the Giant*, Ca' Rezzonico, Venice.

1759  Date on *The Tooth-Drawer* formerly in the Ravà collection, Venice.

1760  13 August. Gaspare Gozzi, in the *Gazzetta Veneta*, no. 55, compares Pietro Longhi with Tiepolo (Gozzi, 1760). 3 September. Gradenigo, in his diary, mentions Longhi as 'the painter for natural situations and speaking caricatures' (Livan, 1942).

Pietro Longhi is among the subscribers to Piazzetta's *Studi di Pittura*, published by Albrizzi (Fogolari, 1913).

1761  14 February. In *L'Osservatore Veneto*, Gaspare Gozzi praises Longhi, who 'portrays what he sees with his own eyes' (Gozzi, 1761).

Date on the *Monks, Canons and Friars of Venice* in the Pinacoteca Querini Stampalia, Venice.

Alessandro Longhi writes the biography of Pietro, which appears in the following year in the *Compendio* (A. Longhi, 1762).

1762  The Venetian Academy requests a canvas from Longhi. He probably paints *Pythagoras* (Fogolari, 1913).

After Piazzetta and Tiepolo, Pietro Longhi compiles an inventory with a valuation of the Sagredo inheritance at Venice, which is preserved only in part in the Museo Correr, Venice (Brunetti, 1951).

Date on *The Lion Show*, Pinacoteca Querini Stampalia, Venice.

1763  He is the director in the school of drawing and engraving in the Pisani palace until 1766 (Gallo, 1945).

1764  30 April. Gradenigo mentions in his Diaries the *Portrait of Ludovico Manin* (Livan, 1942).

Date on the *Portrait of the Procuratore Ludovico Manin*, Museo Civico, Udine.

Date on the *Portrait of Francesco Guardi*, Ca' Rezzonico, Venice.

1772  Date on the Querini portraits in the Musée National, Algiers, the Cailleux collection, Paris, and formerly in the Padoan collection, Venice.

1774  Date on the *Portrait of Benedetto Ganassoni*, Ca' Rezzonico, Venice, and *The Elephant*, Salom collection, Segromigno Monte.

1775  Date on the *Peasants playing Cards*, Paulucci collection, Ferrara.

1777  May. A *Confession* by Pietro Longhi is exhibited during the Feast of Ascension, in San Marco (Fogolari, 1913).

1779  5 April. Pietro Longhi is present at the session of the Academy in the course of which Canova is elected (Fogolari, 1913).

Date on the *Girl spinning*, Fornoni Bisacco collection, Venice; in the inscription by an unknown hand on the *Portrait of Adriana Giustinian Barbarigo*; and probably on *The Alchemists* in the Cagnola collection, Gazzada.

1781  Date on the *Portrait of a Painter*, Ca' Rezzonico, Venice.

1785  8 May. Registration of the death of Longhi in the archive of San Pantalon, at the age of '85 years'. The same in the Register of Deaths in the State Archive, Venice (see Document 2-3).

# DOCUMENTS

1 - Venice, Archive of the church of S. Pantalon

27 September 1732

Sig.ra Catt.na Maria, daughter of Do. Alvise Rizzi, of this parish, living by the Ca' Foscari bridge, and Sig. Pietro, son of the late Do. Alessandro Falca, painter of the Parish of S. Giuliano: were married in the presence of the Rev. Don Bernardo Bolla, Priest of the Parish of S. Margherita: Antonio Pasinetti, clerk of this Parish and Sig. Do. Gasparo Ganardina Corner, of Rome, of the Parish of S. Cassan, witnessed to their single status; and they received benediction at Mass in the church of S. Nicolò della Carità from the above-mentioned Parish priest.

2 - Venice, Archive of the church of S. Pantalon

8 May 1785

Sig. Pietro Falca known as Longhi, son of the late Alessandro, 85 years of age, died today at ten o' clock, after ten days of sickness, as the result of a chest complaint, and he can be buried this evening at 23 hours.
Certified by Doctor Pharmacist Agostino D. Stae.
At Pontesello, S. Rocco.
The Burial will be with Chapter.

3 - Venice, State Archive
Provveditori of Health, 972
(Register of Deaths 180)

8 May 1785

Pietro, son of Allesandro Falca known as Longhi, 85 years, from chest complaint, ten days, died at 10 o' clock, will be buried at 23 hours.
Doctor Stae.
Chapter. S. Pantalon.

4 - Venice, Archive of the Basilica of San Marco
Register of Baptisms in Parish of S. Giuliano

'10 July 1733. Baptised by the Rev. D. Giacomo Carletti, Sacristan, by licence from me, Zampirano, Parish priest, a son of sig. Pietro Falca known as Longhi, painter, son of the late Alessandro, and of Sa. Catt. a, daughter of the late Alvise Rizzi, husband and wife, born 12 June of this year. He gave him the names Alessandro Antonio, Godfather, Sig. Domenico Corner of Rome, known as Gasparo, living in S. Cassan. Godmother Pasqua Morosini Albini, of S. Provolo.

5 - BASSANO, Museo Civico, Remondini letters

XIII-25-3543

Venice, 7 December 1748

Illustrious sir and honoured master

I have received the favour of an esteemed letter from you just as I have a reason for writing to you, to say that the first drawing is finished, and I have managed to persuade the young man to disregard motives of interest and care only for study and to be content with a single zecchino given him by Sig. Abrizzi. I have hardly let a morning pass without going out to put the fear of God into the young man and give him my advice, and I should like with all my heart to print his drawing of the painting because I am anxious that he should succeed. He has worked diligently but it lacks grandeur, especially in the heads, as they are in the picture, but here Sig. Faldoni since he is an excellent engraver will be able to make adjustments and to give a good appearance to the heads and plenty of light to the central figure. This first matter is not very important, and I am more concerned that the second should be amusing and give pleasure; and it is up to these gentlemen to further our intentions and let the boy draw the paintings which for the most part are in the possession of noble families. I advise you again to carry the business forward with verve and enthusiasm as Wagner does with his prints. Meanwhile I will tell you what my subject was in this picture: two ladies at the Coffee-House at Mira courted by two strangers, one in a wig and the other a Pantaloon in a straw hat and a dressing-gown. Then it is up to the Poet. Wagner made a lot of money from the verses of Dr. Pinalli of Padua. I hear that your illustrious lordship wishes to know from me whether Sig. Wagner is continuing. To tell you the truth, it would be very much in his interest to continue, and he was longing to do so in view of the great success which his four prints have had, but I can tell you that as far as progress is concerned I am a witness that the gentleman has been a month and more waiting to have a painting and then he received the reply that he wouldn't let his paintings out of his room for three months as he had been told they would be, and the engraver did not want the trouble of going there to draw them, so he is content at the moment to let things go. I tell you that if the matter succeeds as you hope it will be a good piece of business for you since Wagner is held up. I am looking forward to hearing how Sr. Faldoni likes the drawing, and so encourage him to engrave it as best he can and then as many copies as possible cna be made of it, and meanwhile I sign myself, to your esteemed commands

Your illustrious lordship's most obedient and devoted servant

PIETRO LONGHI

6 - BASSANO, Museo Civico, Remondini letters

XIII-25-3544

Venice, 13 May 1749

Illustrious sir and honoured master

Thanks be to God I hope that I have recovered for the second time and that the illness will not come again, and I wish good health to your lordship. I have seen the proof, and so that it may be correct I have indicated all the points with pencil, especially the background which must be darker so that the figures stand out more and so that all the working that was badly done and spoiled the composition cannot be seen. The boatman should be more distinct and his face darkened and his legs more clearly outlined: I have marked in more hair towards the front of his head and altered the boot nearest the gentleman so that it is more foreshortened, his back from the neck upwards should be darker. In the gentleman's head the right eye squints because it is not done correctly, I have lengthened his shoulder towards the boatman and made his leg and slipper a little firmer and straightened the little table by the curve on the side of the shadow. The hair of the servant close to the face less hard. The chair below the seat more sharply defined, and the outline of the whole clearer. In the head of the girl the eyes should not be elongated but round, to give a better idea. The old woman shorter so that she is not in the light, and the floor by the girl darker. I have marked all these things with a pencil and I hope he will study it well, and it must be done this way, and done this way all will be well and I shall be pleased, and let us hope that it will turn out well, and I greet you.

52

Dear and revered Sig. Giovanni Battista, if I could do more I would do it for you at any cost. I beg you to send the metal tube so that I can send you the drawing of the masquerade that I have had before sending the picture to Dresden to have it engraved, and I will ensure that he will be content with just three filippi, and it is a drawing of value. Apart from this, give your orders so that the boy is satisfied. I await your news, and entirely at your command I am

Your illustrious lordship's devoted and obedient servant
PIETRO LONGHI

7 - BASSANO, Museo Civico, Remondini letters
XIII-25-3545

Venice, 10 April 1751

Illustrious sir and honoured master

I reply to a revered note from you dated the 7th inst. I at once presented the letter to his excellency but he replied that nothing has been seen at Ca' Grimani of any wine to be delivered to Longhi as arranged. The letter I wrote some time ago to your lordship mentioned his excellency Giovanni Grimani de' Servi and the said gentleman is ready to help me if you will. If you have sent it to any other of the Grimani houses by mistake, let me know by letter so that I can make sure of getting it. Awaiting news of your commands I sign myself your lordship's servant

PIETRO LONGHI

8 - BASSANO, Museo Civico, Remondini letters
XIII-25-3546

Venice, 23 April 1751

Illustrious sir and honoured master

I reply to your most kind letter and I must say that I am now almost as enlightened as before I was in darkness. Meanwhile in order to please my kind master Sig. Giovanni Battista Remondini I sought out my friend Marcello Robazza, who at once showed me the latest proof of the Leghorn engraver, whom I do not know, and to my mind this does not matter. The good eye of Marcello is enough and really I am satisfied with the proof both as to drawing and as to the harmony and lightness of the line, which is unlike the thick line of Faldoni, and if I may say so I think that this is enough to assure your lordship of the skill of this engraver. I know moreover that the person and the plate are at Bassano, and I am not happy that the plate should be published without the corrections to the faces, hair and masks, and also the head of the Coffee-House keeper, and other details and it is precisely these which make the work perfect, and these niceties are of importance both for your interest and my reputation, and should not be neglected by unconscientious engravers.

The young man you ask me about is that Florentine of Wagner's who tells me that he started a drawing from one of my paintings which he has had and has at present, and he says that it was on behalf of the Remondini, so you may act upon this piece of information. Speaking of Sig. Giovanni Picoli, I rate him a good engraver, but I wish he were near and not a long way away, if I make myself clear, but if one or other of these gentlemen engravers will not make a positive undertaking with me to let me see the first proofs and alter them according to their ability and my intention, I shall never feel like letting them make drawings, but if this can be arranged Longhi will with all his heart forward the interests of Sig. Giovanni Battista Remondini, who professes esteem and love for him and at whose revered commands I am and shall be.

And I beseech you to employ Marcello Robazza, who really understands how to engrave copper, as a general rule, and I then will give just the final touches that will make it pleasing to everyone, and without passing through any other hands, and this I think the wisest and most able. Servant to your lordship

PIETRO LONGHI

54

XVII - THE RIDE (detail of plate 144). *Venice, Ca' Rezzonico.*

9 - Bassano, Museo Civico, Remondini letters
XIII-25-3547

Venice, 8 May 1751

Illustrious sir and honoured master

I am indebted to you for a letter of 24 April. In reply I can tell you that I have discussed the matter with Wagner and I am sure that when the plate is sent back it will be attended to by the above-mentioned. In the matter of the Florentine, we cannot hope that he will be able to draw or engrave for your lordship because he has too much to do for his principal client, and for me, I will do what I can to serve Sig. Giovanni Battista Remondini according to his instructions and respond to them with method. I have only one bottle of wine left and the little barrel is finished, so I am waiting from day to day the favour of your kindness. I remain entirely yours. Your lordship's servant

PIETRO LONGHI


10 - Bassano, Museo Civico, Remondini letters
XIII-25-3548

Venice, 5 December 1752

Illustrious sir and honoured master

This humble letter of mine comes to the illustrious Sig. Giovanni Battista Remondini with a reverence, as is my duty, and at the same time to request you to order your agent to give me four prints two of each kind, to give to the owners of the originals according to the usual practice, although we have been unfortunate with these two engravers. One has to bear with this, but it would be as well to let the public know that the original works are by Longhi although they are badly drawn and engraved, if they are printed with my name the business will have far more success, in fact I have recently had to swear that the originals were by me. So I am now awaiting these copies to be sent with my name on them, and to your esteemed commands I am your illustrious lordship's servant

PIETRO LONGHI


11 - Bassano, Museo Civico, Remondini letters
XIII-25-3548

12 January 1752 M.V. (1753)

Illustrious sir and honoured master

With joy and delight I must rejoice with your lordship and your worthy consort on the birth of your son, the news of which has been received here with universal pleasure, an evident sign that our amiable Sig. Giovanni Battista Remondini is loved by all, and I hereby declare myself the first to welcome every occasion to serve and please you as I shall do in the expectation of a good engraver so that the series may be completed with as good a fame as possible. I am enjoying the sausages you were good enough to send me for which I must thank you and I have also received the twelve prints of which I shall deliver two to her excellency Signora Cecilia Ema Morosini, who possesses the original of the Coffee-House and the other at Ca' Zen, I will not tire you with any more at the moment, signing myself at your revered commands, servant of your illustrious lordship

PIETRO LONGHI


56

XVIII - SHOOTING IN THE LAGOON (detail of plate 180). *Venice, Pinacoteca Querini Stampalia.*

# AN ANTHOLOGY OF LONGHI CRITICISM

O Longhi, you who call my comic muse
the sister to your brush which seeks the truth,
here let your hand, conjoined with my idea,
now treat a lofty theme in novel form.

You can portray the maiden, noble, fair,
charming of face and stately in her mien,
you can depict Giovanni's arching brow
shooting the dart of love at his beloved.

I will extol his glories and his name,
his faithfulness, surpassing common boast,
and thus between us we divide the task.

You with live colour, I with poetry,
I paint the graces, you the golden locks,
— and all the while, they will enjoy their love.

CARLO GOLDONI, *Componimenti poetici per le felicissime nozze di Sue Eccellenze Giovanni Grimani e la Signora Catterina Contarini*, Venice, 1750.

Pietro Longhi, the Venetian painter, studied painting in the school of Antonio Balestra and in that of Giuseppe Crespi, called the Spaniard, in Bologna. But with his whimsical and capricious skill he forged for himself a new and individual style of painting conversation pieces, games, ridotti, masquerades, parlours, all on a small scale and with such veracity and colour that at a glance it was easy to recognise the places and people portrayed. With this great talent he rose to high fame, and his works fetch high prices; many of them are engraved by more than one artist and prints made from them.
A. ORLANDI - P. GUARIENTI, *Abecedario pittorico*, Venice, 1753, p. 427.

Fortunate will be also our mutual friend the celebrated Pietro Longhi, a distinguished painter, an outstanding imitator of nature, who having discovered an original manner of conveying on to canvas the characters and passions of men prodigiously increased the glory of the art of painting, which has always flourished in our country. Fortunate

58

will he be, as I say, since you have undertaken to engrave the notable work of the Seven Sacraments in seven pictures, wonderfully depicted by him and so true to life that they certainly deserve to be made available to the public, to his honour and to our glory.

*Le Commedie del Dottor Carlo Goldoni*, Florence (Paperini), vol. X, MDCCLV, p. 301.

The painter for natural situations and for speaking caricatures is Signor Pietro Longhi, of the quarter of San Pantalon, near San Rocco.

L. Livan, *Notizie d'Arte tratte dai Notatori e dagli Annuali del N.H. Pietro Gradenigo*, Venice, 1942, p. 62 (September 3 1760).

Pietro Longhi, Venetian, was born in 1702, the son of a silver-founder who, seeing him model, fostered his inclination and encouraged him to draw. He then had the good fortune to be aided by Antonio Balestra of Verona, the famous painter, who after several years sent him to Bologna with a recommendation to Giuseppe Crespi, called the Spaniard, also a famous painter; and after several years of study he returned to Venice; but seeing that it would be difficult to distinguish himself as a painter of History, he altered his aim, and being of a whimsical and brilliant spirit he set about painting small pictures of everyday matters such as conversations and entertainments; with scenes of love and jealousy which, since they were faithful portrayals of reality, made a great impression. He then painted also pictures of masked figures which were so realistically depicted in their natural attitudes that they were recognisable even behind the mask. And as this was a way not trodden nor sought by any before him, it gave great pleasure so that his paintings are desired not only by all the patrician families but by whomsoever esteems singular works of art; and thus they are sent even to the courts of Europe; and because the same merit is apparent also when they are printed, they are engraved on copper by the most famous engravers. He lives at home in Venice, applauded and loved by all the Venetian nobility.

A. Longhi, *Compendio delle vite de' Pittori Veneziani...*, Venice, 1762 (1761).

I see, above all, that the inventions of Signor Pietro Longhi are admired because he omits from the play of his imagination figures dressed in ancient fashion and characters of fancy, and portrays in his canvases what he sees with his own eyes, and contrives to introduce into his scenes certain sentiments which evoke a genial good humour. And I see that his success derives principally from a felicitous rendering of customs, which are shown in the situations of all his subjects.

G. Gozzi, *L'Osservatore Veneto*, 14 February 1761, p. 28.

Another Venetian was Pietro Longhi who learnt first from Balestra and then from Crespi to give pleasure in his pictures with those whimsical paintings of masquerades, conversations and landscapes which are to be seen in noble houses.

L. Lanzi, *Storia pittorica dell'Italia*, Bassano, 1795-96, pp. 218-9.

Longhi (Pietro) or Lunghi, born in Venice in 1702, began by learning from his father, who was a founder in silver, how to model, and this opened the door for him to painting and drawing, which he studied under Balestra and then at Bologna under Giuseppe Crespi, called the Spaniard, and it was doubtless in the school of the latter that he acquired a liking for conversation pieces, for festivities and masquerades and, in short, for all that happens in civil life. He was aware of his limitations and realised that he would not have the same success in painting historical works in the grand style. So he confined himself to the first kind, and gave much pleasure: he became another Watteau, and his work was greatly in demand. Several of his paintings have been engraved in Venice, where he lived. See in Guarienti and Longhi's Lives of Venetian Painters. He was the father of Alessandro Longhi, the author of a Compendium of Lives of Venetian painters who have lived and are living in our own times.

P.J. Mariette, *Abecedario...*, Paris, 1854-56, p. 221.

XX - THE CARD-PLAYERS (detail of plate 190). *London, Hallsborough Gallery.*

What a charming painter of manners is this Longhi! He gives a visual and spiritual account of his scenes, a décor and an environment not in an ideal rural or decorative setting but in the intimate interiors of Venetian private life. In his larger, decorative canvases he is a painter with some affinity to Goya. There are two notebooks of sketches kept in the Director's office which reveal that the painter had completely assimilated the pencil technique of Lancret, with firmly outlined legs in imitation of his master Watteau, with strokes of a pointed black pencil as is usual in the drawings of French artists... Longhi draws from life even chamber-pots.
E. and J. DE GONCOURT, *L'Italie d'hier. Notes de voyages* 1855-56, Paris, 1894, pp. 39-41.

And as Rosalba stands for the heroine on the threshold of love, Pietro Longhi, the genial little Lancret of Venice, who delights in the lively spectacle of the streets, who catches in the act a thousand and one little comedies, who muses, strolls, loiters always on the lookout, who ferrets in the back of shops, who insinuates himself into the closed circle of the casinos, who slips into the mysterious interiors of houses, Pietro Longhi stands for the social habits of the fantastic city. He is a charming painter of manners. He is a jovial, chubby painter of manners.
P. MONNIER, *Venise au XVIIIe siècle*, Paris, 1908, p. 177.

The love for pictures was by no means dead in Venice, and Longhi painted for the picture-loving Venetians their own lives in all their ordinary domestic and fashionable phases. In the hairdressing scenes we hear the gossip of the periwigged barber; in the dressmaking scenes, the chatter of the maid; in the dancing-school, the pleasant music of the violin. There is no tragic note anywhere. Everybody dresses, dances, makes bows, takes coffee, as if there were nothing else in the world that wanted doing. A tone of high courtesy, of great refinement, coupled with an all-pervading cheerfulness, distinguishes Longhi's pictures from the works of Hogarth, at once so brutal and so full of presage of change.
B. BERENSON, *The Venetian Painters of the Renaissance*, New York-London, 1911, pp. 73-74.

He is the faithful, slightly indiscreet reproducer of his world; his precise and colourful brush brings everything to light — the smiles, glances, affected poses, flattering simpers, precious mannerisms, bows and curtseys. He reveals a provocative mole or an impatient little foot beneath the gown; he catches a swift look through an eye-glass, a confidence whispered behind a fan; he follows the muttered but rapid spread of a little scandal, greeted by suppressed laughter, he conveys the graceful and measured cadence of a minuet or the mellifluous gesture of the singer of a madrigal; he teaches us how to wear a domino, how to hold oneself in a crinoline, how to offer a bonbon, how to introduce or take one's leave; how a perfect lackey should offer a tray of sweetmeats; all with wonderful delicacy, facility and effectiveness.
Thus Pietro Longhi finds his art, thus he can fully utilise his natural gifts, achieving such a degree of artistic perfection that he has won the name of 'the Goldoni of painting'.
A. RAVÀ, *Pietro Longhi*, Bergamo, 1909, p. 24.

To make a dispassionate judgment of the work of Pietro Longhi it must be said that his chief merit lies in having introduced genre painting to Venice, applying the teachings of his master Giuseppe Crespi to eighteenth-century Venetian society; that without aspiring to the moral purpose of Hogarth, without possessing the delicate grace or the sentimentality or the psychological acuteness of the contemporary French painters, he reproduced it faithfully and with amiable realism and inimitable local colour in hundreds of delightful little scenes realised from life.
A. RAVÀ, *Pietro Longhi*, Florence, 1923, pp. 22-23.

It should not be forgotten that many of the small canvases that he painted as genre scenes are really little family groups to celebrate an anniversary or a private event of some solemnity. The matter of his art is substantially the society gossip column... But the genre becomes stereotyped beneath his brush, gradually those very characteristics thanks to which the encomiastic literature of enthusiasts for eighteenth-century life incline to compare him to Goldoni for

XXI - PORTRAIT OF FRANCESCO GUARDI (detail of plate 227). *Venice, Ca' Rezzonico.*

his gifts of observations and, rather less, to Parini for the rather dubious evidence of his satire, become conventionalised and mannered.

G. Damerini, *I pittori veneziani del Settecento*, Bologna, 1928, p. 86.

And so all the lies are known to us, painted by Pietro Longhi with an exquisite technique, but no brain.

G. Fiocco, *La pittura veneziana del Seicento e Settecento*, Verona, 1929, p. 66.

And it seems likely that the artist was a slow worker, because in his paintings all the swiftness of vision of his wonderful drawings, not unlike those of Lancret of Watteau, completely vanishes.

E. Arslan, *Di Alessandro e Pietro Longhi*, in 'Emporium', August 1943, p. 56.

Pietro Longhi faces modern customs with a detachment, a superiority, which are far from being understood. Even Goldoni's praise of his 'brush which seeks the truth' has perhaps done him harm when quoted by those who probably understood neither Longhi nor Goldoni. As for his cultural formation, his derivation not only from the Bolognese Crespi but, above all, from the paintings of the low and middle classes of the schools of Brescia and Bergamo, which were, at the end of the seventeenth and beginning of the eighteenth centuries, with Ghislandi and Ceruti, the most sincere and serious paintings in the whole of the Venetian republic, must be further investigated and given greater consideration. But Longhi is to be thought of in European terms, and to be measured against Watteau and Chardin.

R. Longhi, *Viatico per cinque secoli di pittura veneziana*, Florence, 1946, p. 36.

The precious existence of the pictures depends entirely upon the colour, whose imperceptibly soft gradations and transitions can only be compared with the pastels of Rosalba Carriera, and cannot be imagined from black and white reproductions. It is a melody of magically pale tones, so fragile that it seems a breath might dissolve them; tender blues and pinks, luminous orange: of hushed and throbbing harmonies which achieve a wonderful delicacy.

F. Valcanover, *Affreschi sconosciuti di Pietro Longhi*, in 'Paragone Arte', 1956, no. 73, pp. 23-24.

How his art proceeds from the study of truth is particularly evident from his brilliant and fertile activity as a draughtsman. He recorded on paper figures and details, sometimes adding notes, and while in this way he assembled notebooks of great value for his paintings, it was already an art in itself. A whole world lives in these drawings, from the domestic interiors with their curtains and ancestral portraits, to the smart ladies in wide crinolines, the gentlemen in their cutaway coats, the equivocal dominoes, and so on down to the servants and the poor. The artist looked around him, in the brilliant Venice of polite society, in the enclosed and somnolent Venice of old houses, alert to the most fleeting aspects of fashion, the detail of a coiffure, a ribbon, a flower.

V. Moschini, *Pietro Longhi*, Milan, 1956, pp. 42-3.

A drawing is the first glance, the lens which focuses a particular detail, which sees and penetrates and knows all (it was said that if you wanted to know what a lady was doing at any hour of the day, you could ask Longhi: he would know). And from the drawing begins, line by line, verse by verse, this loquacious composition, civil and never impertinent, malicious without gall, almost imperceptibly caricatural, amiable, indulgent, affectionate: a poem of everyday life, more intimate and more domestic than that of his French contemporaries, from Lancret to Chardin; freer and more poetic in detail than that of a Flemish or Dutch painter, whose liking for noisy Kermesses or the rowdy gatherings of peasants or townpeople he does not share; because these people, the people of Longhi, are never common, but always distinguished by being Venetians, graceful and controlled even if they are gondoliers or beaters for a shooting expedition; however realistic the representation, his naturalism never touches vulgarity; and even the effeminacy and the arrogance and a particular incipient sensuality of these people are always rendered in a polite form with a pleasing air.

G. De Logu, *Pittura veneziana dal XIV al XVIII secolo*, Bergamo, 1958, pp. 191-2.

64

XXII - PORTRAIT OF BENEDETTO GANASSONI (detail of plate 261). *Venice, Ca' Rezzonico.*

He is a kind of Molière of painting or rather, as has often been observed, the pictorial equivalent of Goldoni, more incisive and ironic. In general, the documentary value of this illustrated diary has been greatly appreciated while its other pictorial qualities, showing an exceptional sensitivity to interiors, for subdued and well-calculated colour, have been neglected... An art which cannot be mistaken for that of a Hogarth or a Chardin.
A. CHASTEL, *L'Arte italiana*, Florence, 1958, II, p. 250.

The suggestions of unorganization in the scene, both as a composition and as a subject, are typical of Longhi and raise the question of whether he was naive or just falsely naive. He is a painter whose current fate is to receive the most extravagant and obtuse praise which can be given, even by Italian critics, to an artist. Where every clumsiness is supposed a touch of genius, and where Longhi is coupled with Watteau (to be fair, this dreadful analogy was started by Mariette) and paragoned with Renoir or Manet, it is not likely that he will be appreciated justly or reasonably. Because he is unique it has been presumed that he is invaluable. But it seems as if his clumsy handling of paint, his inability ever to establish the planes of a picture, and his incapacity to draw properly, were honest defects that he could not overcome even after many years of practice.
M. LEVEY, *Painting in XVIII-Century Venice*, London, 1959, p. 112.

He does not improvise, he does not create from memory. His fantasy does not consist in the flow of invention but in the way in which he re-elaborates pictorially, in the unity of an organic system of composition, the notes and impressions which he plucks from reality in a delicate, painterly fashion, plastic, but intent upon conveying effects of luminosity and colour. Through the practice of drawing, keeping in mind the examples of French artists — Watteau, Lancret, Portail, Mercier —, Longhi gradually refined his rather awkward, heavy line, inherited from the schools of Crespi and Gamberini, imposing on his figures a new elegance and a somewhat fragile flavour, and hence a subtly ironic character. But when, on the lines of these drawings, where the thematic situation of each figure is fixed, Longhi moves on to the painting, he composes the scene in terms of colour; exquisite colour, balanced in its transitions and in the subtle choice of harmonies.
R. PALLUCCHINI, *La pittura veneziana del Settecento*, Venice-Rome, 1960, p. 180.

But the comparison with French artists, in the case of Pietro Longhi, can be taken no further because it would be absurd to try to place him, on the plane of quality, on a level with universal geniuses like Watteau or Chardin. Pietro Longhi is of a more modest nobility, his vein is more domestic and his ambitions less evident. For forty years he continues to paint those rather dusty interiors, with old armchairs and curtains which deaden light and noise, and within them their inhabitants, devoid of ardent feelings, intent upon their comfort, attached to a peaceful life, remote from problematic ideals. Everyone can see that his characters share the cordial, rather parochial humanity of Goldoni's Pantalones and Rosauras: they are almost provincial — however unlikely that may seem in the cultured and cosmopolitan Venice of the mid-eighteenth century — because of this remoteness from the great aesthetic and spiritual problems that were then coming to a head in Paris. On the other hand, this unadventuring mind of Pietro Longhi was in the long run beneficial to his art, because from it derives an almost naive pictorial manner which allows the purity and sweetness of his colour to express itself freely and to characterise an unmistakable style.
T. PIGNATTI, *Pittura in Europa: il Settecento*, Milan, 1961, pp. 157-8.

It was certainly a sign of the new spirit in Venice — where in 1760 Gaspare Gozzi edited *L'Osservatore* in imitation of *The Spectator* — that Pietro Longhi (1702-85), the 'Italian Hogarth', who was only six years younger than Tiepolo, soon renounced painting baroque-mythological frescoes for genre pictures of contemporary life in an entirely new documentary vein. This changeover perhaps dates from as early as *c.* 1734, but most of these pictures were apparently painted during the last years of Hogarth's life and after his death. Longhi is said to have taken up this genre either as a result of studying under Crespi in Bologna or under the influence of Hogarth's engravings. However that may be — and it seems to me that individual figures in *Marriage à la Mode* could well have interested him — his pictures show more variety and greater penetration than Dutch seventeenth-century genre painting. He rendered the leisure

XXIII - THE MORNING CUP OF CHOCOLATE (detail of plate 279). *Venice, Ca' Rezzonico.*

pursuits and manners of the Venetian merchant aristocracy, which had certain urban, middle-class features and also occasionally of humbler people. This he did more systematically than had ever been done before in a faithful, journalistic manner with a strong feeling for atmosphere. Thus Longhi, but for whom we should know far less than we do about the life of the Venetian aristocracy, has a certain affinity with Hogarth. But Hogarth's art is not mere genre painting but critical and argumentative; and the faint, almost imperceptible humour in some of Longhi's pictures — far from the irony it is nowadays fashionable to detect in it — is no substitute for the spirit.

F. ANTAL, *Hogarth and his place in European Art*, London, 1962, pp. 203-3.

It is tempting to assume that Lodoli may have admired Alessandro's father, Pietro. For we know that Pietro Longhi was highly thought of in other advanced circles of Venetian society. Significantly, it was in 1750 that Goldoni first hailed him as a man 'who is looking for the truth'. This was the very period when Goldoni was making his deliberate and decisive break with the old masked comedies and was trying to reform the theatre by a return to nature. So it may well have been the painter who inspired the poet — Longhi had already been painting genre scenes for many years — rather than, as it is usually assumed, the other way round. Seven years later Goldoni returned to the subject and again praised Longhi for his 'manner of representing on canvas the characters and passions of men'. Goldoni's sympathies were 'advanced', at least by implication, and he was accused by his opponents of being a 'corrupter no less of poetry than of decent behaviour (buon costume). Could Longhi's pictures — those little 'conversations, meetings, playful scenes of love and jealousy' — have been interpreted in the same sense? The very idea seems absurd, despite the fact that early in the nineteenth century a Venetian historian claimed (with no supporting evidence) that he 'went so far in depicting the truth that he was several times punished by the laws'. None the less it is significant that the most enthusiastic praise of his work should have come from men who were anxious to look more steadily at the actual circumstances of Venetian life than was usual at the time.

F. HASKELL, *Patrons and Painters*, London, 1963, pp. 322-3.

Indeed, it is remarkable how, in the atmosphere that prevails in Longhi's little scenes, an atmosphere that in general one might say fosters the process of the intellectual decay of a certain class, the individuals nevertheless succeed in retaining a face, a detail, a frail, minute psyche, that is their own. Hence the strange but fascinating way in which Longhi's scenes act as a medium; they are halfway between the life of truth, to which the good Pietro attached so much importance, and that of puppets, a conception to which he was inevitably led by a not entirely obvious and in fact quite courageous view of the social conditions of his time.

It cannot be denied that into this role of a medium there enters a small measure, a finger, of complaisance, as much to enliven the portraits as to smile at them; the more so because this finger, however small, is the same which rubs the material of the painting, crumbling it like golden pap or gilded birdseed; it confers an illusion of elegance and simultaneously removes the disillusion of shadows, it powders it and 'makes it up'; but the heart is uncommitted and distant. A powder for a lagoon kaleidoscope, wherein there is a continual change of noses and large noses, lips and thick lips, cheeks and soft cheeks, legs and short legs, paws and little paws, curtains long and short, tables big and small, chairs and armchairs, coming and going; a powder which leaves everywhere a green and pink dust, like a fading dawn, and at the same time the suspicion that the festivities will not go on for ever, nor will the frivolity, nor the chatter and the gossip. So much for the little scenes, which will never cease to be praised. But what happens when Pietro takes one of his people out of the rooms of the patrician houses, so precariously poised, so damp with the salt air, and brings him to the centre of the stage? The least that can be said is that when there is no relationship with other persons, when the chatter and the gossip are missing, everything becomes motionless, dry, flat; and that this famous finger no longer intervenes to create that role of moral medium, so acidulated and stimulating, nor even to stir into expression the rosy powder, the delicious perfumed poultry-food of his material.

(L. MALLÈ) - G. TESTORI, *Giacomo Ceruti e la ritrattistica del suo tempo*, Turin, 1967, pp. 31-2.

68

XXIV - THE MICHIEL FAMILY (detail of plate 293). *Venice, Pinacoteca Querini Stampalia.*

# CATALOGUE

*The Catalogue is divided into three sections: accepted, attributed and lost works. In the accepted works are included all paintings and drawings which on documentary or stylistic evidence appear to be by the hand of Pietro Longhi. The attributed works include all paintings and drawings which have been associated with Longhi's name in critical writings but which, in the opinion of the present writer, cannot be fully accepted as his, and those of uncertain attribution which he has not been able to examine personally. Some works by followers of Longhi, many of them unpublished, have been included in an attempt to form as clear an impression as possibile of the artist's achievement. Among the lost works are included those which are mentioned in earlier writings but of which no trace can be found, and those whose existence can be asserted through contemporary prints made from them.*

*Together with the paintings recognised to be by Longhi are reproduced all the preparatory drawings which are related to them, and in the catalogue entries are mentioned reproductions of all drawings and prints made from the paintings. In addition, all other drawings by Longhi hand which have not as yet been shown to relate to the paintings are reproduced in a special section.*

*An essential bibliography in each entry of the catalogue indicates the first mention of the work and significant studies of it.*

*The entries are arranged topographically, for ease of reference; the artistic evolution of Longhi is evident from the arrangement of the illustrations, which is chronological.*

# PAINTINGS BY PIETRO LONGHI

**ALGIERS, Musée National**

PORTRAIT OF MATILDE QUERINI DA PONTE *Plate 256*

Oil on canvas, 84×73 cm.

*Collections:* Rawdon Brown, London; Cailleux, Paris.

Inscribed on the back 'Matilde Querini née da Ponte. Portrait painted by Pietro Longhi about MDCCLXII'. One of a series of three paintings of which one is in Paris (Pl. 257) and the other was formerly in Venice (Pl. 258).

*Literature:* Ravà, 1923, 114; Valcanover, 1956, 362; Moschini, 1956, 40.

**BASSANO, Museo Civico**

SHEPHERD BOY SEATED *Plate 7*

Oil on canvas, 61×48 cm.

One of a series which includes three similar paintings in the same museum and the *Shepherd Boy* in Rovigo (Pl. 13). As Pallucchini indicates, these are certainly among the earliest works of the painter, executed when he was still under the influence of Crespi, and can be dated to *c.* 1740 for the similarities between the *Shepherd Girl with a Flower* (Pl. 10) and Piazzetta's *Fortune-Teller*. The colour is applied with broad, full brush strokes and conveys characteristic light effects, while the rather opaque tonality, producing a general effect of greenish-brown, formerly suggested an attribution to Crespi himself. A preparatory drawing for the *Seated Shepherd Boy* is in the Museo Correr, no. 515 (Pl. 8), showing the strong shading typical of Longhi's early work (Valcanover, 1956, 24).

*Literature:* Pallucchini, 1946, 160.

**BASSANO, Museo Civico**

SHEPHERD BOY STANDING *Plate 11*

Oil on canvas, 61×48 cm.

*Literature:* Moschini, 1956, 44.

**BASSANO, Museo Civico**

SHEPHERD GIRL WITH A COCK *Plate 12*

Oil on canvas, 61×48 cm.

*Literature:* Pallucchini, 1946, 179.

**BASSANO, Museo Civico**

SHEPHERD GIRL WITH A FLOWER *Plates I and 10*

Oil on canvas, 61×48 cm.

Preliminary studies in the Museo Correr, no. 511 (Valcanover, 1956, 24), and in the Koenig-Fachsenfeld collection, Aalens (Pl. 9, 417a).

*Literature:* Pallucchini, 1946, 160; Deusch, 1967, 93.

**BERGAMO, Accademia Carrara**

THE RIDOTTO *Plate 172*

Oil on canvas, 61×49 cm.

*Collection:* Lochis, Bergamo.

Comparable with the paintings of the same subject in the Pinacoteca Querini Stampalia, Venice (Pl. 170, 171), datable to *c.* 1757.

*Literature:* Ravà, 1909, 98; Valcanover, 1956, 25.

**BERGAMO, Accademia Carrara**

THE VISIT TO GRANDMAMA *Plate 285*

Oil on canvas, 61×49 cm.

*Collection:* Lochis, Bergamo.

This painting can be dated to *c.* 1780, and it shows the psychological interest typical of Longhi's work towards the end of his life.

*Literature:* Ravà, 1923, 26; Moschini, 1956, 40.

**BERGAMO, Baronessa Maddalena Guffanti-Scotti Collection**

CONFESSION *Plate 270*

Oil on canvas, 59×46 cm.

Related to the *Sacraments* series in the Pinacoteca Querini Stampalia, this canvas is however probably of a very different period and should probably be dated to the 1770s, to judge by its affinities with *The Alchemists* at Gazzada (Pl. 269) which is perhaps of 1779. Fogolari (1913, 391) mentions a *Confession* by Longhi shown at the Venetian Academy Exhibition during the Feast of the Ascension in 1777.

*Literature:* Bassi-Rathgeb, 1952, 26.

**BERGAMO, Private collection**

THE FRIAR'S SERMON *Plates VII and 114*

Oil on canvas, 97×73 cm.

In this unpublished work Longhi takes great care to achieve a realistic representation of a spacious church, its congregation, altars, and an atmosphere of religious devotion. The painting includes several themes which he was to repeat in the following period, in the *Sacraments* and the *Sermons* now in Milan and Brescia. The painting can probably be dated to the early 1750 s for the similarity of its composition to that of *The Tooth-Drawer* (Pl. 107) and *The Betrothal* (Pl. 113), both in Milan. As in those paintings, the colour is dense and thickly applied, and there are many analogies in the figures and the furnishings. A study for the stool is in the Museo Correr (no. 534) (Pl. 115).

## BERGAMO, Private collection

THE INTERRUPTED GAME OF CARDS          *Plate 272*

Panel, 48×60 cm.

This painting, mentioned by Ravà and then lost sight of for some years until the present author found it in Bergamo, appears to be related to *The Advocates* at Padua (Pl. 271), of *c.* 1779, by virtue of the relaxed composition and marked characterization. The colour has delicate effects of *sfumatura* in the muted range characteristic of his maturity. A drawing for the man is in the Museo Correr, no. 559 (Valcanover, 1956, 25) (Pl. 273).

*Literature*: Ravà, 1923, 23.

## BERGAMO, Private collection

PORTAIT OF DOGE PIETRO GRIMANI          *Plates VIII and 141*

Oil on canvas, 48×32 cm.

This unpublished *modelletto* is a full-length portrait of the Doge Grimani, who is also depicted in the Museo Correr canvas (Pl. 139). The intense colouring with very lively highlights suggests a dating to *c.* 1752, the year of Cattini's print of the Doge.

## BERGAMO, Private collection

PORTRAIT OF A GENTLEMAN          *Plate 177*

Oil on canvas, 44×36 cm.

This unpublished work appears to be related to the *Portrait of a Lady*, formerly in New York (Pl. 178). The subtle gleam of the silvery grey of the coat against the transparent green of the wall gives a delicate chromatic perspective to the work. Perhaps of the late 1750s.

## BIELLA, Private collection

THE DRUNKARD          *Plate 35*

Oil on canvas, 53×71 cm.

*Collection*: Brass, Venice.

Signed 'Longhi Pie...'. There is considerable uncertainty about the dating of this work, but the present writer is inclined to attribute it to the early period of Longhi's activity, together with the first three scenes of the Paulucci collection (Pl. 20, 21, 22). Pallucchini suggests *c.* 1740, pointing out the Flemish influence. A preliminary drawing for the drinker and the jug is in the Museo Correr, no. 502.

*Literature*: Morandotti, 1941, 50; Arslan, 1943, 52; Pallucchini, 1960, 179.

## BOLOGNA, Giorgio Morandi Collection

A YOUNG GIRL EMBROIDERING          *Plate 297*

Oil on canvas, 39.6×29.5 cm.

Unpublished. Probably of the painter's last period, related to the paintings in the Orsi Collection, Milan (Pl. 295, 296, 298).

## BOSTON (Mass.), Museum of Fine Arts.

A GIRL SPINNING          *Plate 251*

Oil on canvas, 62×51 cm.

*Collections*: Wanamaker, Philadelphia; Weitzner and Holmes.

From Longhi's own hand, but deriving from various earlier paintings, especially *The Washerwomen*, Venice (Pl. 16). Probably of the 1760s. A study for the girl spinning is in the Museo Correr, no. 571 (Pl. 249).

*Literature*: Brosch, 1929, 357.

## BRESCIA, Mother-house of the Suore Ancelle della Carità

A MIRACLE OF ST LAWRENCE          *Plate 158*

Oil on canvas, 60×49 cm.

An outstanding work, apparently unpublished, which probably belongs to the period of the *Sacraments*, Venice (Pl. 148-154), although the chiaroscuro of the colouring is more marked, the atmosphere more dramatic and dark, in the manner of *Shooting in the Valley* (Pl. 233-242).

## CAMBRIDGE (Mass.), Fogg Art Museum

THE MILLINER          *Plate 250*

Oil on canvas, 59×48 cm.

This painting (inv. 1943.118) is part of the Grenville L. Winthrop donation; it is the prototype of various versions of the subject, of which the best is in the A. Crespi Collection, Milan (Pl. 102).

## CHICAGO (Ill.), Art Institute (Flora Erskine Miles Fund)

THE LADY'S TOILET          *Plate 137*

Oil on canvas, 56.9×49.3 cm.

Related to *The Embroidery Workroom*, London (Pl. 135), rather than to the works of the beginning of Longhi's career, this painting can probably be dated to the end of the 1750s. A drawing for the lady is in the Museo Correr, no. 449 (Pl. 136).

*Literature*: Moschini, 1956, 16.

## CHICAGO (Ill.), Art Institute (Worcester Collection)

PEASANTS DANCING          *Plate 90*

Oil on canvas, 61.7×49.7 cm.

*Collection*: Papadopoli, Venice.

Related to the series of scenes of lower-class life painted in the 1750s centred on the *Woman selling Doughnuts*, Venice (Pl. 88). The painting is reproduced in an engraving, in reverse, by Alessandro Longhi (Fig. 21).

*Literature*: Ravà, 1909, 149; *Catalogue of the Worcester Collection*, 1937, no. 25.

*Fig. 21.* PEASANTS DANCING. Engraving in reverse by Alessandro Longhi *(cf. pl. 90).*

## DUBLIN, National Gallery of Ireland

THE PAINTER IN HIS STUDIO                     *Plate 48*

Oil on canvas, 61×50 cm.

*Collection:* Langton Douglas.

A version in vertical format and with some variations of the well-known painting in the Ca' Rezzonico (Pl. 47) and that formerly in the Stirling of Keir Collection (Pl. 49). Another version used to be in the Kaufman Collection, Paris.

*Literature:* National Gallery of Ireland, *Concise Catalogue*, 1963, 79.

## FERRARA, Marchese Stefano Paulucci Collection

PEASANTS DANCING                     *Plate 20*

Oil on canvas, 61×49.5 cm.

*Collection:* Gatti Casazza, Venice.

With the two following paintings, it should probably be dated to Longhi's youthful period, and certainly not as late as 1775, as Valcanover has suggested.

*Literature:* Ravà, 1923, 110; Valcanover, 1958, 686.

## FERRARA, Marchese Stefano Paulucci Collection

PEASANT GIRL AND MAN DRINKING                     *Plate 22*

Oil on canvas, 61×49.5 cm.

*Collection:* Gatti Casazza, Venice.

An early work of Longhi's.

*Literature:* Ravà, 1923, 108; Valcanover, 1958, 686.

## FERRARA, Marchese Stefano Paulucci Collection

PEASANT GIRL AND MUSICIAN                     *Plate 21*

Oil on canvas, 61×49.5 cm.

*Collection:* Gatti Casazza, Venice.

An early work of Longhi's.

*Literature:* Ravà, 1923, 107; Valcanover, 1958, 686.

## FERRARA, Marchese Stefano Paulucci Collection

PEASANTS PLAYING CARDS                     *Plate 264*

Oil on canvas, 61×50 cm.

*Collection:* Gatti Casazza, Venice.

The signature 'Pietro Longhi, 1775', recently discovered on the back by Valcanover, provides valuable evidence for the dating of some scenes of peasant life which otherwise would be classified among the artist's earliest works (Arslan). It is clearly a new treatment on a large scale of themes of his youth, but distinguished from them stylistically by the dark, rather smoky colouring and firm linear technique.

*Literature:* Ravà, 1909, 109; Arslan, 1943, 52; Moschini, 1956, 64; Valcanover, 1956, 27; Pallucchini, 1960, 185.

## Formerly FLORENCE, Riccio Collection

THE INDISCREET GENTLEMAN                     *Plate 85*

Oil on canvas, 60×50 cm.

*Collection:* Papadopoli, Venice.

One of the chief works of the 1740s, belonging to the series of 'piquant' subjects of which several are in the Metropolitan Museum of Art, New York. There are no firm grounds for accepting Moschini's suggestion that the drawings in the Museo Correr, no. 511 recto and verso, which Valcanover relates to the *Shepherd Girl* at Bassano (Pl. 10), have any connection with this work.

*Literature:* Moschini, 1956, 18; Valcanover, 1956, 24; Pallucchini, 1960, 181.

## FLORENCE, Private collection

COFFEE TIME                     *Plate 274*

Oil on canvas, 61×46 cm.

Related to *The Advocates*, Padua (Pl. 271), of the 1770s.

*Literature:* Longhi, 1946, 161.

## FLORENCE, Uffizi Gallery

CONFESSION                     *Plate 156*

Oil on canvas, 61×50 cm.

An obvious derivation from the prototype in Venice (Pl. 154), and of the 1750s. A drawing for the lady's hands is in the Museo Correr, no. 565 (Moschini, 1956, fig. 120) (Pl. 155).

*Literature:* Salvini, 1952, 91; Moschini, 1956, 28.

**FLORENCE, Museo Stibbert**

BOYS RIDING                                        *Plate 143*

Oil on canvas, 70×56 cm.

Exhibited at the Museo Stibbert as a work by Longhi, this painting went unnoticed for a long time and was only recently reproduced by Martini. It is related to *The Ride* (Pl. 144) in Ca' Rezzonico, but differs in the palette, which is rather impoverished,
with the monochrome tonality of the last period.

*Literature:* Martini, 1964, 263, no. 244.

**GAZZADA, Villa Cagnola**

THE ALCHEMISTS                                     *Plate 269*

Canvas, 59×48 cm.

Published by Ciardi, who notes the bad state of preservation after a disastrous attempt at restoration in the early twentieth century. Even the signature and date, inscribed on the basin (lower
right) are partly illegible. The final figures, read by Ciardi as
'...79', allow a dating close to that of the paintings in the Bisacco
collection, Venice (Pl. 265-268).

*Literature:* Ciardi, 1965, 73.

**GENOA, Luigi Trucchi Collection**

PORTRAIT OF THE DOGE'S STEWARD                     *Plate 231*

Oil on canvas, 98×73 cm.

A recent addition to the series of Longhi portraits, this painting
is close to the *Portrait of Guardi* (Plate 227) dated 1764. On the
scroll can be read *Gastaldo Ducale* but the name of the sitter is
not legible. Its stylistic proximity to the early work of Alessandro
should be noted.

*Literature:* Longhi, 1946, 69.

**GENOA, Luigi Trucchi collection**

THE SCHOOLBOY'S PUNISHMENT                         *Plate 224*

Oil on canvas, 61×49 cm.

An unusual subject, of applied didacticism. Of the late 1750s or
early 1760s, with affinities to the *Sacraments* in Venice (Pl. 148-154).
A drawing for the schoolmaster is in the Museo Correr, no. 538
(Moschini, 1954, fig. 131) (Pl. 223).

*Literature:* Moschini, 1956, fig. 131.

**HARTFORD (Conn.), Wadsworth Atheneum Museum of Art**

THE TEMPTATION                                     *Plate 200*

Oil on canvas, 61×49.5 cm.

*Collection:* Giovannelli, Venice.

This work probably forms a series with a number of other paintings of 'piquant' subjects in a 'popular' context. A preliminary
drawing for the two women sewing is in the Museo Correr, no.
474 (Valcanover, 1956, 24) (Pl. 99).

*Literature:* Ravà, 1923, 99; Morassi, 1953, 55; Moschini, 1956, 24.

**Formerly KEIR, Lieut. Col. Stirling of Keir Collection**

THE PAINTER IN HIS STUDIO                          *Plate 49*

Oil on canvas, 38×51.5 cm.

*Collections:* Cavendish Bentinck, London; sold in 1891 (Graves, II,
no. 571); Sotheby 3.7.63.

This is the finest of several versions (in Ca' Rezzonico, Pl. 47;
Dublin, Pl. 48; formerly Paris, Kaufmann Collection). Datable to
between 1741 and 1744. Preliminary drawings in the Museo Correr,
no. 437, 439 (Pl. 45, 46).

*Literature:* Graves, 1921, 571; Pallucchini, 1951, 213; Moschini,
1956, 24.

**LONDON, Brinsley Ford Collection**

THE MILLINER                                       *Plate 105*

Oil on canvas, 60.5×51 cm.

*Collection:* Sir Charles Prescott, London.

A version similar to that in the Metropolitan Museum of Art,
New York (Pl. 103) but with a more brilliant palette and probably
later. The habit of repeating his subjects in almost identical versions is characteristic of Longhi's maturity.

**LONDON, Hallsborough Gallery**

THE CARD-PLAYERS                                   *Plates XX and 190*

Oil on canvas, 62×49 cm.

*Collections:* Gambardi, Florence; Freschi and Miari, Padua; Volpi,
Florence; Perera, New York. Sotheby 20.6.1964, no. 34.

In the Gallery listed as *The Visit.*
Datable to *c.* 1760. A drawing for the gentleman on the left is in
the Museo Correr, no. 491 (Valcanover, 1956, 25) (Pl. 189).

*Literature:* Ravà, 1923, 24; Moschini, 1956, 30.

**LONDON, Hallsborough Gallery**

COFFEE TIME                                        *Plate 187*

Oil on canvas, 62×49 cm.

*Collections:* Gambardi, Florence; Freschi and Miari, Padua; Volpi,
Florence; Perera, New York. Sotheby 24.6.1964, no. 31.

In the Gallery listed as *The Artist sketching an Elegant Company.*
The inclusion of a self-portrait by Longhi in the act of drawing,
to the left of the family group, makes the painting datable, with
the three following, to *c.* 1760. The closest among the prints
which portray Longhi are in fact those by Alessandro (1761) and
by an unknown hand (1766) (Pignatti, 1960, 178). The four family
groups from the Perera Collection mark the beginning of the conversation pieces of the 1760s which include some of the most
lively and most strongly characterised of Longhi's works. A study
for the figure of the painter is in the Museo Correr, no. 553.

*Literature:* Ravà, 1923, 31; Moschini, 1956, 30; Valcanover, 1956,
25 (Pl. 188).

**LONDON, Hallsborough Gallery**

FAMILY CONVERSATION                                *Plate 191*

Canvas, 61×49 cm.

*Collections:* Gambardi, Florence; Freschi and Miari, Padua; Volpi,
Florence; Perera, New York. Sotheby 24.6.1964, no. 32.

In the Gallery catalogue listed as *A Gentleman and his Wife taking
Chocolate.*

Like the others in this gallery, datable to *c.* 1760 (a difference of opinion from that of Arslan, who relates it to Faldoni's print of the Mira *Coffee-House*, engraved in 1748).

*Literature:* Ravà, 1923, 33; Arslan, 1943, 60; Moschini, 1956, 30.

## LONDON, Hallsborough Gallery

THE SPINET RECITAL                                     *Plate 192*

Oil on canvas, 62×49 cm.

*Collections:* Gambardi, Florence; Freschi and Miari, Padua; Volpi, Florence; Perera, New York. Sotheby 24.6.1964, no. 33.

In the Gallery listed as *A Musical Party*.
On the music can be read 'Sweet eyes' and on the wall is a painting of *The Daughters of Lot*.

*Literature:* Ravà, 1923, 33; Moschini, 1956, 30.

## LONDON, National Gallery (no. 5841)

THE EMBROIDERY WORKROOM                     *Plate 135*

Oil on canvas, 61.5×50.7 cm.

*Collections:* Cavendish Bentinck, London; Arthur James (where it is noted by Berenson).

In the Gallery catalogue listed as *A Lady Receiving a Cavalier*. Datable to the 1750s for the soft but dense quality of the colour. A drawing for the girls working is in the Museo Correr, no. 569 (Moschini, 1956, fig. 71) (Pl. 134).

*Literature:* Berenson, 1911, 112; Levey, 1956, 75.

## LONDON, National Gallery (no. 1100)

A FAMILY GROUP                                        *Plate 70*

Oil on canvas, 61.3×49.5 cm.

*Collections:* Oldofredi, Milan, and perhaps originally Gambardi, Florence.

In the Gallery catalogue listed as *An Interior with three Women and a Seated Man*. Stylistically related to *A Lady receives Visitors*, New York (Pl. 76) of 1746. The group is not easy to interpret. The old man in the foreground has been taken to be a servant, in which case the scene presents an act of charity on the part of the young ladies. The portrait of Gherardo Sagredo on the wall at the back suggests that it represents an event which took place in the home of that family. A preparatory drawing for the two girls is in the Museo Correr, no. 504 (Moschini, 1956, fig. 94) (Pl. 69).

*Literature:* Ravà, 1909, 70; Arslan, 1943, 60; Levey, 1956, 71.

## LONDON, National Gallery (no. 1334)

THE FORTUNE-TELLER                                *Plate 166*

Oil on canvas, 59.1×48.6 cm.

*Collection:* Cavendish Bentinck, London.

Signed 'Petrus Longhi'. On the pillar to the right can be read an inscription in praise of Doge Loredan, with the date 1753; on the wall is the name of Don Zuanne Farinato, a candidate for the parish of San Trovaso, with the date 1756. It is interesting that Farinato was not elected, and Don Francesco Comparato became the parish priest instead. As Levey observes, the probable date of the painting is therefore shortly after 1756, and this is confirmed by

its stylistic similarity to *The Quack* in Ca' Rezzonico (Pl. 160) of 1757.

*Literature:* Levey, 1956, 74.

## LONDON, National Gallery (no. 5852)

THE PROCURATORE PAYS A CALL                    *Plate 80*

Oil on canvas, 61.3×49.5 cm.

*Collections:* Cavendish Bentinck; Arthur James (where it is noted by Berenson).

In the Gallery catalogue listed as *A Nobleman kissing a Lady's Hand*. Comparable with the paintings of the late 1740s for its delicacy of line and the harmonious colouring of the interior. A study for the two servants is in the Museo Correr, no. 490 (Levey, 1956, 76) (Pl. 79).

*Literature:* Berenson, 1911, 102; Levey, 1956, 76.

## LONDON, National Gallery (no. 1101)

THE RHINOCEROS                                       *Plate 118*

Oil on canvas, 60.4×47 cm.

*Collections:* Oldofredi, Milan; perhaps Gambardi, Florence.

Datable, like the prototype in Ca' Rezzonico (Pl. 116) to *c.* 1751, this is a work of considerable pictorial subtlety. The rhinoceros caused a great stir when it was brought to Europe in 1741 by its captor, a certain Captain David Montvandermeer (Molmenti, 1908, III, 208). After being exhibited in Nuremberg, it arrived in Venice in 1751, when Longhi immediately painted it.

*Literature:* Levey, 1956, 72.

## LONDON, O'Nians Gallery

SHOOTING IN THE LAGOON                           *Plate 182*

Oil on canvas, 44×63.5 cm.

A version of the well-known painting at Venice (Pl. 180), corresponding to the sketch in the Museo Correr, no. 476 (Pl. 183). It is clear that Longhi worked on the two versions of the painting at the same time, although the dimensions of the two canvases vary considerably and the creative process is at work in each of them.

*Literature: Pietro Longhi*, 1967, XXXIII.

## LONDON, Private collection

THE DANCING GIRL                                     *Plate 106*

Oil on canvas, 61×49 cm.

*Collections:* Gambardi, Florence; Miari, Padua; Volpi, Florence; Perera, New York. Sotheby 19.4.1967.

The old man and the ballerina are the same as in *The Dancing Girl* of the Aldo Crespi collection, Milan, (Pl. 104), but the background is completely different, representing a gypsy encampment. It is probably of later date.

## LONDON, Private collection

NURSE WITH A BABY AND ITS PARENTS             *Plate 198*

Oil on canvas, 58×48 cm.

With *The Singing Test* (Pl. 198a) this painting is from the Sykes and Pakenham Collections, London, sold at Christie's 4.12.1964. It is clearly related to the series formerly in the Perera Collection and now at the Hallsborough Gallery, London.

*Literature: Pietro Longhi*, 1964, XLVII.

**LONDON, Private collection**

THE QUACK *Plate 254*

Oil on canvas, 61×49 cm.

*Collections:* Gambardi, Florence; Freschi and Miari, Padua; Volpi, Florence; Perera, New York. Sotheby 19.41.1967.

The inscription on the wall at the back praises Doge Pier Alvise Mocenigo, who was elected in 1763.

*Literature:* Moschini, 1956, 63.

**LONDON, Private collection**

THE QUACK *Plate 162*

Oil on canvas, 59.7×50.8 cm.

*Collections:* Pleydell Bouverie, sold at Christie's, 25.10.1957.

A replica, with some alterations, of *The Quack* in Ca' Rezzonico (Pl. 160).

**LONGLEAT (Wilts.), Marquess of Bath Collection**

THE MAN SELLING SALAD *Plate 89*

Oil on canvas, 61×50 cm.

*Collection:* Cavendish Bentinck, London.

Related to *The Woman selling Doughnuts* in Venice (Pl. 88) in tonality, it can be dated to the early 1750s. It is characteristic of this period that Longhi uses identical motives in several different paintings, in different arrangements. Here, for example, is one of the girls from the Ca' Rezzonico painting, and the seated figure playing the tambourine appears in many other works.

*Literature:* Graves, 1921, II, no. 570; Pallucchini, 1960, 181.

**MILAN, Alemagna collection**

THE HUNTER AND TWO PEASANT GIRLS *Plate 97*

Oil on canvas, 60×48 cm.

Longhi often repeats motives even after a lapse of some time. This is the case with the peasant woman carrying a cock in this painting, which is a reworking of the same subject in a painting at Bassano (Pl. 12). In this case, however, the work is of the 1750s and for its brilliance of colour is related to *The Temptation* at Hartford (Pl. 100). A drawing for the hunter and the sleeping boy is in the Museo Correr, no. 521 (Pl. 98).

*Literature:* Moschini, 1958, 22.

**MILAN, Aldo Crespi collection**

THE DANCING GIRL *Plate 104*

Oil on canvas, 61×49 cm.

*Collection:* Giovannelli, Venice.

One of a series with *The Seduction* (Pl. 102). The old man is to be seen again in the version formerly in the Perera Collection, now in London (Pl. 106).

*Literature:* Ravà, 1923, 103; Rosa, 1956, no. 38.

**MILAN, Aldo Crespi Collection**

THE LADY READS ALOUD *Plate 201*

Oil on canvas, 60×50 cm.

Shown at the *Kunstschätze der Lombardei* exhibition in 1948. Of the late 1750s or early 1760s, this painting, although similar in subject to *The Geography Lesson* (Pl. 126), probably represents a gathering of 'enlightened' patricians at an intellectual *salon*. The lady reading aloud is the same as in *The Visit from a Friar* (Pl. 208).

*Literature: Kunstschätze der Lombardei*, 1948, 290; Pallucchini, 1948, 170; Moschini, 1956, 26; Rosa, 1956, no. 35.

**MILAN, Aldo Crespi Collection**

MILORD'S SALAD *Plate 83*

Oil on canvas, 60×50 cm.

*Collection:* Giovannelli, Venice.

Another in the series of 'piquant' paintings, a gentleman waiting while his salad is prepared; it proclaims its affinity with others of the series also by the repetition of features such as the girl with the tambourine and the curious cage made of osiers which hangs from the ceiling. There are two preparatory drawings, one for a maidservant and one for the gentleman, in the Museo Correr, nos. 479 and 545 (Moschini, 1956, fig. 96) (Pl. 81, 82).

*Literature: Kunstschätze der Lombardei*, 1948, 290; Rosa, 1956, no. 36; Pallucchini, 1960, 181.

**MILAN, Aldo Crespi Collection**

THE SEDUCTION *Plate 102*

Oil on canvas, 60×50 cm.

*Collection:* Giovannelli, Venice.

One of the chief paintings of the 'piquant' series, it is undoubtedly of the 1750s. A drawing for the abbé and the old woman is in the Museo Correr, no. 452 (Pl. 101).

*Literature:* Ravà, 1923, 100; Rosa, 1956, no. 37.

**MILAN, Aldo Crespi Collection**

THE VISIT FROM A LADY *Plate 200*

Oil on canvas, 60×50 cm.

Exhibited at the *Kunstschätze der Lombardei* exhibition in 1948, and datable, like *The Lady reads aloud* in the same collection, to the late 1750s or early 1760s. The drawing in the Museo Correr, no. 509, mentioned by Moschini, although similar, is not closely related to this painting.

*Literature: Kunstschätze der Lombardei*, 1948, 290; Pallucchini, 1948, 170; Moschini, 1956, 26; Rosa, 1956, no. 34.

**MILAN, Heirs to the Senatore Mario Crespi Collection**

THE DANCER BINETTI *Plate 288*

Oil on canvas, 61×49 cm.

The identification of the subject of this unpublished work (to which attention has been drawn by Antonio Morassi) depends on the inscription beneath the engraving hanging on the wall. For a dating, it suggests comparison with works of the 1770s.

**MILAN, Heirs to the Senatore Mario Crespi Collection**

THE SPINET *Plate 133*

Oil on canvas, 44×36 cm.

An unpublished work, to which attention has been drawn by Antonio Morassi; probably of the early 1750s.

**MILAN, Count Gerli Collection**

THE BETROTHAL                                             *Plate 113*

Oil on canvas, 61×88 cm.

*Collections:* Duke of Newcastle; Sotheby, 1958.

Stylistically related to *The Friar's Sermon*, Bergamo (Pl. 114), with the same feeling of uncluttered space. The painting shows the young fiancée being presented to the old grandmother. In these large scenes Longhi uses a brilliant palette with strong chiaroscuro effects. A dating to the 1750s is probable.

*Literature: La Collezione Gerli*, 1963, 323.

**MILAN, Alessandro Orsi Collection**

PORTRAIT OF A GENTLEMAN IN GREEN          *Plate 259*

Oil on canvas, 81×65 cm.

This unpublished portrait is related in style to those of the Querini family, dated 1772 (Plates 256-58).

**MILAN, Alessandro Orsi Collection**

PORTRAIT OF A PAINTER                           *Plate 298*

Oil on canvas, 42×34 cm.

An unpublished painting, with an inscription '*Così si dipinge*' (Thus one paints) on the back. For its similarity to the *Portrait of a Painter* in Ca' Rezzonico (Plate 294) datable to *c.* 1781. It is not impossible that this is a portrait of Pietro Longhi himself, whose activity as an instructor in the Venetian Academy continued until 1780.

**MILAN, Alessandro Orsi Collection**

PORTRAIT OF A PRELATE                           *Plate 296*

Oil on canvas, 48×35.5 cm.

The sharp realism of the portraiture suggests that this work belongs to the painter's last period.

*Literature:* Martini, 1964, 108, note 244.

**MILAN, Alessandro Orsi Collection**

PORTRAIT OF A WRITER                            *Plate 295*

Oil on canvas, 48×36 cm.

A very late unpublished work, portraying an unidentified writer in the style of the portraits of *The Michiel Family* (Pl. 293).

**MILAN, Alessandro Orsi Collection**

THE TUTOR TO THE GRIMANI FAMILY          *Plate 292*

Oil on canvas, 55×38 cm.

An unpublished work, probably portraying the instruction of a young member of the Grimani family, since the painting was formerly in the possession of that family. It is possible that the abbé is Melchiorre Cesarotti, who was tutor to the Grimani family from 1760 to 1768. The painting, however, would appear to be of at least a decade later than that.

**MILAN, Private collection**

THE FRIAR'S SERMON                              *Plate 159*

Oil on canvas, 60×49 cm.

Reminiscent of the expressive manner of the *Sacraments* (Pl. 148-54) and thus datable to the end of the 1750s, as suggested by Arslan.

*Literature:* Arslan, 1946, 59.

**MILAN, Private collection**

A GIRL SPINNING                                 *Plate 19*

Oil on canvas, 62×50 cm.

*Collections:* Schaeffer, New York; Stanglino, Turin.

Datable to *c.* 1740 for the pale tones and the soft gradations of colour. The peasant girl reappears in the background of *The Polenta* at Zoppola (Pl. 26).

**MILAN, Private collection**

PORTRAIT OF A LADY                              *Plate 130*

Oil on canvas, 42×32 cm.

This painting, unpublished in its present state, is perhaps to be identified with that listed by Ravà (1923, 122) as 'whereabouts unknown', and if that is so this was before some restoration work. A second version, almost identical, is in the Paulucci Collection, Ferrara. The similarity of style and subject with the lady in *The Family Concert* in Ca' Rezzonico (Pl. 128) suggests a dating to the 1750s.

**MILAN, Galleria d'Arte Moderna**

THE CARD-PLAYERS                                *Plate 174*

Oil on canvas, 60×47 cm.

*Collections:* Papadopoli, Venice; Grassi, Milan.

Related to the paintings of the *Ridotto* group by the figures of the players and the mellow tonality of the colour, which suggests a dating to the end of the 1750s.

*Literature:* Ravà, 1909, 70; Nicodemi, 1962, 44; Pallucchini, 1960, 181.

**MILAN, Galleria d'Arte Moderna**

THE DRINKERS                                    *Plate 23*

Oil on canvas, 61×48 cm.

*Collections:* Papadopoli, Venice; Grassi, Milan.

The more velvety tonality and lively composition show Longhi's development as he approaches the period of his maturity, at the end of the 1740s.

*Literature:* Nicodemi, 1962, 34.

**MILAN, Galleria d'Arte Moderna**

THE WOMAN SELLING DOUGHNUTS                    *Plate 86*

Oil on canvas, 61×50 cm.

*Collection:* Grassi, Milan.

Almost identical with the painting in Ca' Rezzonico (Pl. 88), with the same inscription in favour of Padre Balischi, and thus datable to *c.* 1750.

*Literature:* Valsecchi, 1959, 72; Pignatti, 1960, 210; Nicodemi, 1962, 34.

## MILAN, Galleria di Brera

### THE FAMILY CONCERT

*Plate 117*

Oil on canvas, 50×62 cm.

*Collection:* Probably Gambardi, Florence.

Datable to the 1750s for the obvious advance it shows over the paintings in the Metropolitan Museum of Art, New York, which have the same provenance. Here Longhi appears to give more spaciousness to the composition, and soon after this painting begins the series of open-air scenes in which the lighting becomes more lively and natural. A certain similarity to Ceruti and Liotard, who was in Venice around 1745, has been noted, and this adds probability to the dating suggested by the style (Pallucchini, 1960, 182).

*Literature:* Modigliani, 1935, 57; Moschini, 1956, 22; Valcanover, 1956, 25.

## MILAN, Galleria di Brera

### THE TOOTH-DRAWER

*Plate 107*

Oil on canvas, 50×42 cm.

*Collection:* Probably Gambardi, Florence (Wehle, 1940, 293).

Signed 'Pietro Longhi'. The graffiti on the columns of the Doge's Palace refer to the reigning Doge Pietro Grimani (1741-52) and to the election of Antonio Poli to the parish of Sta Margherita, which took place in 1746 (Moschini, 1956, 60). The painting can thus be dated approximately, and its lively composition and limpid colour are typical of Longhi at the beginning of the 1750s. Pallucchini has drawn attention to the figure of the man selling vegetables on the left, reminiscent of Ceruti. A preparatory study for the dwarf is in the Museo Correr, no. 534 (Valcanover, 1956, 25) (Pl. 108). An engraving in reverse by Alessandro Longhi reproduces the scene with variations (Fig. 22).

*Literature:* Modigliani, 1935, 56; Pallucchini, 1960, 182.

*Fig. 22.* THE TOOTH-DRAWER. Engraving in reverse by Alessandro Longhi *(cf. pl. 107)*.

*Fig. 23.* THE MAN SELLING DOUGHNUTS. Engraving in reverse by Alessandro Longhi *(cf. pl. 87)*.

## Formerly MUNICH, H. Vollert Collection

### THE MAN SELLING DOUGHNUTS

*Plate 87*

Oil on canvas, 61×50 cm.

*Collection:* Conti di Collalto; exhibited at Rome in 1941. Sold Weinmüller, Munich, 30.6.1941.

It seems a companion to the painting at Longleat (Pl. 89). Apparently confiscated by the Allied Military Government in 1945 as part of the Goudstikker Collection, its present whereabouts are unknown. The inscription in the background mentions the Parish priest of Sta Maria Formosa, Don Piero Raimondi, which indicates a date of *c.* 1750, during the period of his service there (30 January 1733 to 18 May 1752). The considerable use of chiaroscuro which emphasizes the delicate colours of the figures in contrast with the areas of shadow is typical. A print of the painting, in reverse, was engraved by Alessandro (Fig. 23).

*Literature:* Morandotti, 1941, 49.

## NEW YORK, Robert Manning Collection

### PORTRAIT OF A VIOLINIST

*Plate 229*

Oil on copper, 10.2×8.3 cm.

Exhibited for the first time at the Venetian Exhibition, Detroit, 1952, this painting is datable to *c.* 1760 for the sharper portraiture

*Fig. 24.* THE MEETING OF THE PROCURATORE AND HIS WIFE. Engraving in reverse by C. Flipart *(cf. pl. 78)*.

which characterises the period during which Alessandro was working at his father's side and acquiring a manner of his own.

*Literature:* Richardson, 1952, 48; Morassi, 1953, 49.

**NEW YORK, Metropolitan Museum of Art (no. 14.32.2)**

A LADY RECEIVES VISITORS                          *Plate 76*

Oil on canvas, 60.9×49.5 cm.

*Collection:* Miari, Padua.

According to the catalogue of the Volpi sale, New York, 1917, it appears to have been one of a series of sales of works of art formerly in the Gambardi Collection, Florence (later dispersed to the National Gallery, London; Galleria di Brera, Milan; Miari Collection, Padua; Perera Collection, New York).

The signature 'Petrus Longhi 1746' establishes a firm date to which to attach a series of interiors executed towards the end of the 1740s. Comparison with the paintings of the *Concert* group (Pl. 37 *et al.*) shows a perceptible lightening of colour and an attempt to achieve a more translucent glazing to rival the effects of pastel. The portraiture is increasingly more penetrating, richer in humour, with a multiplicity of accessory characters — tutors, clerics, gallants — which well conveys the gossiping but shrewd character of Venetian society of the mid-eighteenth century. A preparatory drawing for the rear wall is in the Museo Correr, no. 547 (Valcanover, 1956, 25) (Pl. 77).

*Literature:* Ravà, 1923, 35; Wehle, 1940, 293.

*Fig. 25.* THE MEETING OF THE PROCURATORE AND HIS WIFE. Engraving by Hayd *(cf. pl. 78)*.

**NEW YORK, Metropolitan Museum of Art (no. 36.16)**

THE MEETING OF THE PROCURATORE AND HIS WIFE

*Plate 78*

Oil on canvas, 60.9×49.5 cm.

*Collections:* Gambardi, Florence; Miari, Padua.

Datable to *c.* 1746 for its similarities to *A Lady receives Visitors* in the same museum (Pl. 76). It is the prototype of a series of versions and copies which treat the 'piquant' subject of the Procuratore meeting his wife in a milieu frequented by masked couples (Moscow, Pushkin Museum; Venice, Casa Goldoni and Museo Correr; formerly Venice, Dal Zotto Collection). An engraving by Flipart reproduces the painting in reverse (Fig. 24); one by Hayd, in the same sense (Fig. 25). Cailleux mentions a derivation in an Italian private collection, attributing it to Gian Antonio Guardi (1967, p. 54).

*Literature:* Wehle, 1940, 294.

**NEW YORK, Metropolitan Museum of Art (no. 14.32.1)**

THE MILLINER                                      *Plate 103*

Oil on canvas, 60.9×49.5 cm.

*Collections:* Gambardi, Florence; Miari, Padua.

In the Museum catalogue listed as *The Letter*. By its subject this painting belongs to the *Temptation* series and is thus of a slightly

81

*Fig. 26.* THE MILLINER. Engraving by G. Cattini *(cf. p. 103)*.

*Fig. 27.* MILORD'S VISITOR. Engraving by Gutwein *(cf. pl. 84)*.

earlier date than the three other paintings by Longhi in this Museum, which are dated *c.* 1746. There is an engraving in the same sense by Cattini (Fig. 26) and an almost identical painting in the Brinsley Ford collection (Pl. 105).

*Literature:* Ravà, 1923, 98; Wehle, 1940, 293.

### NEW YORK, Metropolitan Museum of Art (no. 17.190.12)
MILORD'S VISITOR                                            Plate 84

Oil on canvas, 60.9×49.5 cm.

*Collections:* Gambardi, Florence; Miari, Padua.

In the Museum catalogue listed as *The Temptation*. Datable *c.* 1746 for its resemblance to the *Lady receives Visitors* (Pl. 76) in the same Museum. An engraving in the same sense was made from this painting by Gutwein with verses alluding specifically to the equivocal nature of the girl's visit to the milord, who is seen intent upon a meal. It is probably to this print that Longhi refers in a letter of 13 May 1749 to the printer Remondini (Document No. 6). The dating of the *Temptation* series to the 1740s can thus be confirmed. The painting on the wall at the back, in a style akin to that of Amigoni, is altered in Gutwein's engraving, where there is a copy of Amigoni's *Jupiter and Callisto* (Pilo, 1961, 34) (Fig. 27).

*Literature:* Ravà, 1923, 34; Wehle, 1940, 293.

### Formerly NEW YORK, Newhouse Gallery
PORTRAIT OF A LADY                                          Plate 178

Oil on canvas, 48.3×35.6 cm.

*Collection:* Gambara, Brescia.

Datable to the end of the 1750s, this is one of the series of small portraits which lead up to those of *Magrath the Giant* and *Pope Clement XIII Rezzonico* (Pl. 179 and 175) at Venice.

*Literature:* Richardson, 1952, no. 47; Morassi, 1953, 49.

### NORTHAMPTON (Mass.), Smith College Museum of Art
PEASANTS DANCING THE FURLANA                                Plate 93

Oil on canvas, 61.5×50 cm.

*Collection:* Schaeffer, New York.

This would appear to be the first version of a theme frequently treated by Longhi. Like the preceding works dated shortly after 1750, this painting shows the figures in an outdoor space with rustic ornamentation. The girl playing the tambourine appears again in other paintings of the series, as does the dancer and the figures in the background.

*Literature:* Hartt, 1947, 22.

### Formerly PADUA, Miari Collection
COFFEE TIME                                                 Plate 196

At presente the whereabouts of this painting are unknown, but by its provenance and on the grounds provided by Ravà's reproduction, it appears to belong to the series of conversation pieces formerly in the Perera Collection, and to be of *c.* 1760.

*Literature:* Ravà, 1923, 24.

## PADUA, Private collection

THE ADVOCATES                                               *Plate 271*

Oil on canvas, 60×48 cm.

The writing on the wall refers to Doge Alvise Mocenigo IV, whose reign was from 1763 to 1779. A date towards the end of this period, in the 1770s, seems indicated. The theme of the painting is not clear: 'From what straits did Fortune not liberate me?'. Perhaps the gentleman helped by Fortune has just been liberated from the clutches of the two men of law.

*Literature:* Morandotti, 1941, 54; Moschini, 1956, 38.

## PADUA, Museo Civico

THE GEOGRAPHY LESSON                                        *Plate 129*

Oil on canvas, 63×50 cm.

*Collection:* Piombin, Padua.

The painting in the background seems to portray the Blessed Gregorio Barbarigo, and this would suggest that the painting is of members of that family (Bortolini, 1954, 9). Datable to the 1750s for its similarity to the similar painting in Venice (Pl. 126).

*Literature:* Moschetti, 1938, 174; Arslan, 1943, 58; Grossato, 1957, 95.

## PARIS, Jean Cailleux Collection

PORTRAIT OF STEFANO QUERINI                                 *Plate 257*

Oil on canvas, 83×66.5 cm.

*Collection:* Rawdon Brown, London.

On the back an old label reads 'Stefano Querini, son of Pietro Antonio and Matilde da Ponte and brother of Alessandro. Portrait painted by Pietro Longhi in the year MDCCLXXII'. The portrait demonstrates the classicising tendency of Longhi in the 1770s, in comparison with the freer forms of the *Portrait of Guardi* (Plate 227). It forms a series with two other portraits of members of the same family, one now in Algiers (Pl. 256) and the other formerly in a Venetian collection (Pl. 258).

*Literature:* Valcanover, 1956, 362; Moschini, 1956, 60.

## Formerly PARIS, d'Atri Collection

LITERARY GENTLEMEN IN A LIBRARY                             *Plate 290*

Oil on canvas, 60×48 cm.

An example of the penetrating portraiture of Longhi's later period, in the style of the early 1770s.

*Literature:* Valcanover, 1956, 25.

## PARIS, Louvre

THE INTRODUCTION                                            *Plate 44*

Oil on canvas, 64×53 cm.

From the sale at the Hotel Drouot, 20.1.1941 (formerly Haberstock Gallery, Berlin).

One of the major works of the period of the Contarini paintings (Pl. 37, 38, 41, 42) in the Accademia, Venice, it is outstanding for the liveliness of the scene and the delicacy of the brushwork, almost in the French manner. A probable study for the lady is in the Museo Correr, no. 487 (Moschini, 1968, Pl. 16) (Pl. 43).

*Literature:* *Hôtel Drouot*, 1941; Moschini, 1956, 16.

## PETWORTH, Egremont Collection

THE SINGING LESSON                                          *Plate 282*

Oil on canvas, 54×71.7 cm.

Formerly attributed to Hogarth. On the music can be read 'La Serva Padrona' and on the spinet 'L.v.G.' There is a variant of this painting in the Pennsylvania Museum of Art, Philadelphia (Pl. 450). Datable to *c.* 1770.

*Literature:* Collins-Baker, 1920.

## PORT SUNLIGHT, Lady Lever Art Gallery

A POET RECITING HIS VERSES                                  *Plate 278*

Oil on canvas, 48×61 cm.

Reproduced by Watson with reference to the well-known drawing of the same subject in the Museo Correr (Fig. 28) attributed to A. Longhi (Byam Shaw, 1933, 60). Although there is the possibility of confusion between the small portraits executed by the young Alessandro Longhi in imitation of his father's style, and those by Pietro himself, this pleasant little picture can easily be related to Pietro's canvases of the 1770s such as The Advocates (Pl. 271) and *The Michiel Family* (Pl. 293).

*Literature:* Watson, 1964, IV, 17.

*Fig. 28.* A POET RECITING HIS VERSES. Drawing by Alessandro Longhi. Museo Correr *(cf. pl. 278)*.

**PROVIDENCE (Rh. I.), Rhode Island School of Design Museum of Art**

KISSING HANDS                                  *Plate 284*

Oil on canvas, 62×50.7 cm.

*Collection:* Giovannelli, Venice.

Among the finest works of the 1770s.

*Literature:* Rowe, 1935, 64; Arslan, 1943, 62; Moschini, 1956, 40; Valcanover, 1958, 686.

**PROVIDENCE (Rh. I.), Rhode Island School of Design Museum of Art**

A MEAL AT HOME                                 *Plate 132*

Pil on canvas, 62×51 cm.

*Collection:* Giovannelli, Venice.

Close in style to the patrician family groups, this work can be dated to the early 1750s. A drawing for the old man is in the Museo Correr, no. 487 verso (Pl. 131).

*Literature:* Richardson, 1953, no. 45; Morassi, 1953, 55; Valcanover, 1956, 24.

**ROME, Senatore Albertini Collection**

CONFESSION                                     *Plate 157*

Oil on canvas, 62×50 cm.

*Collection:* Possibly Cavendish Bentinck, London; Drake, London. Stylistically related to the canvases in the Pinacoteca Querini Stampalia (Pl. 154) and in the Uffizi (Pl. 156) datable to the 1750s.

*Literature:* Graves, 1921, II, no. 574; Modigliani, 1942, Pl. XXXIV.

**ROME, Morandotti Collection**

THREE MERRY FELLOWS                            *Plate 282*

Oil on canvas, 60×50 cm.

*Collection:* Brass, Venice.

Datable to *c.* 1740.

*Literature:* Pallucchini, 1946, 180.

**ROVIGO, Seminario Vescovile**

SHEPHERD BOY STANDING                          *Plate 13*

Oil on canvas, 60.7×45.4 cm.

Forms a series with the paintings in the Museo Civico, Bassano (Plates 7, 10, 11, 12) and datable to *c.* 1740.

*Literature:* Pallucchini, 1946, 180.

**SAN BARTOLOMEO DI CREMA, Paolo Stramezzi Collection**

THE BAGLIONI FAMILY                            *Plate 281*

Oil on canvas, 59×47.5 cm.

*Collection:* Conti Baglioni, Bergamo (according to the present owner).

Unpublished. Among the figures is one of a painter, clearly Pietro himself. On the grounds of the apparent age of this figure, supported by other considerations, the painting can be dated to the late 1770s, close in time to the portraits of Adriana Giustinian Barbarigo (1779) (Pl. 286-87).

**ST LOUIS (Mo.), City Art Museum**

THE RECEPTION IN THE COURTYARD                 *Plate 167*

Oil on canvas, 61×50.7 cm.

*Collection:* Papadopoli, Venice.

In the Museum Handbook listed as *Il Ridotto*. Close in date to *The Quack* in Ca' Rezzonico (Pl. 160). The two drawings, of a lady and of a gentleman, in the Kupferstichkabinett, indicated by Moschini (1956, 28-30), have no direct relation to this painting.

*Literature:* *City Art Museum Bulletin*, 1939, XXIV, 4; Morassi, 1953, 56; Moschini, 1956, 28.

**SAN FRANCISCO (Cal.), California Palace of the Legion of Honor**

THE MUSIC LESSON                               *Plate 54*

Oil on canvas, 53×42 cm.

Gift of C. Leventritt. In the Museum Handbook listed as *The Bird Cage*. Acquired by the gallery in 1952, it has hitherto been unknown to students of Longhi. A work of great chromatic beauty, with thick impasto and rich effects of light, it belongs to the 1740s and is close in date to the paintings in the Accademia, Venice (Pl. 37, 38, 41, 42). A preparatory drawing for the cage and the violinist is in the Museo Correr, no. 447 (Pl. 52).

*Literature:* *Inaugural Exhibition*, 1954, no. 54.

**SAN PELLEGRINO, Parish church**

ST PELLEGRINO CONDEMNED TO DEATH               *Plate 1*

Oil on canvas, 400×340 cm.

Dated by Galizzi to between 1729 and 1732 on the evidence of the register of the Scuola del SS. Sacramento, which undertook the payment of the stucco work of the altar, concluded in 1729 by Francesco Camizzi. The altarpiece was 'brought from Venice' and the document states that the work was 'thought to be of great value by Rizzi and Tiepoletto'. According to Valcanover it is a typical example of the work of Longhi in his thirties, by now a 'famous painter' as he is called in the document published by Galizzi. Apart from what he had learnt from Balestra, evident in the anatomical foreshortening and the elaborate lines of the composition, Longhi appears to be making use of ideas from Ricci and Tiepolo. Valcanover denies any Bolognese influence here, and he is thus driven to place that decisive period in the artist's formation between 1732, when the San Pellegrino altarpiece was completed, and 1734, the latest date for the Sagredo frescoes.

*Literature:* Galizzi, 1942; Valcanover, 1951, 169.

**SEGROMIGNO MONTE, Heirs to the Salom collection**

BORGOGNA'S SHOW                                *Plate 253*

Oil on canvas, 75×58 cm.

It seems reasonable to attribute this painting to the period of *The Lion Show* in the Pinacoteca Querini Stampalia (Pl. 252), although earlier dates have been suggested (Arslan, *c.* 1745). The existence of a print engraved in reverse by Alessandro, executed after 1760, adds confirmation (Fig. 29).

*Literature:* Ravà, 1923, 54; Arslan, 1943, 60; Moschini, 1956, 32.

*Fig. 29.* BORGOGNA'S SHOW. Engraving in reverse by Alessandro Longhi *(cf. pl. 253)*.

**SEGROMIGNO MONTE, Heirs to the Salom collection**

THE COSMORAMA                                              *Plate 163*

Oil on canvas, 64×54 cm.

The usual young women concealed by their masks and cloaks beneath the arcades of the Doge's palace. In the background is the Cosmorama ('The New World'). Datable to the end of the 1750s for its similarity to *The Quack* in Ca' Rezzonico (Pl. 160).

*Literature:* Ravà, 1923, 62.

**SEGROMIGNO MONTE, Heirs to the Salom collection**

THE ELEPHANT                                              *Plate 255*

Oil on canvas, 66×53 cm.

The inscription says 'True depiction of the Elephant brought to Venice in 1774, painted by Pietro Longhi by request of the Noble Lady Marina Sagredo Pisani'.

*Literature:* Ravà, 1923, 58; Arslan, 1943, 60; Moschini, 1956, 38.

**SEGROMIGNO MONTE, Heirs to the Salom collection**

THE FAINT                                              *Plate 211*

Oil on canvas, 70×54 cm.

Like *The Game of the Cooking-Pot* in the same collection (Pl. 212) this is a later replica of the painting formerly in the Giovannelli collection, now in Washington (Pl. 67). The *sfumatura* effects and a characteristic diminishing of the size of the figures relative to the proportions of their surroundings suggest a dating to *c.* 1760.

*Literature:* Ravà, 1923, 20; Arslan, 1943, 60.

**SEGROMIGNO MONTE, Heirs to the Salom collection**

FAMILY GROUP                                              *Plate 220*

Oil on canvas, 80×98 cm.

A family group of the 1760s, similar to that of the Albrizzi in Venice (Pl. 218). In the background is a portrait of Doge Seba-

stian Venier. A preparatory study for the nurse is in Museo Correr, no. 483 (Moschini, 1956, fig. 169) (Pl. 219).

*Literature:* Ravà, 1923, 32; Arslan, 1943, 60; Moschini, 1956, 30.

**SEGROMIGNO MONTE, Heirs to the Salom collection**

THE GAME OF THE COOKING-POT                    *Plate 212*

Oil on canvas, 68×56 cm.

Like *The Faint* in the same collection, it is a later version of the painting formerly in the Giovannelli collection now in Washington (Pl. 68). Datable to *c.* 1760.

*Literature:* Ravà, 1923, 20; Arslan, 1943, 60.

**SEGROMIGNO MONTE, Heirs to the Salom collection**

THE QUACK                                              *Plate 161*

Canvas, 64×54 cm.

An unpublished version of the subject already treated in the painting now in Ca' Rezzonico (Pl. 160), and to be dated to about the same year, 1757.

**SEGROMIGNO MONTE, Heirs to the Salom collection**

THE RIDOTTO                                              *Plate 168*

Oil on canvas, 56×67 cm.

This shows the Ridotto in Ca' Giustinian before Maccaruzzi's restoration in 1768, and certainly derives from the painting attributed to Francesco Guardi now in Ca' Rezzonico, datable to *c.* 1750. Alessandro engraved this painting, in reverse, in *c.* 1760, so that this provides an approximate date for this work (Fig. 30). A drawing in Berlin which is related to the painting (Moschini, 1956, fig. 142) is a study of two figures in the background: the masked figure gesticulating in conversation on the right (only the upper part of the figure can be seen); and the domino leaning on a bench in the little room at the back on the right (Pl. 169).

*Literature:* Ravà, 1909, 97; Valcanover, 1956, 25; Moschini, 1956, 28.

*Fig. 30.* THE RIDOTTO. Engraving in reverse by Alessandro Longhi *(cf. pl. 168)*.

85

**STANFORD (Cal.), Stanford University Museum**

CONVERSATION *Plate 193*

Oil on canvas, 61×51 cm.

*Collections:* Lord Winbourne, London; Mortimer C. Leventritt.

A date in the 1750s is suggested for this work by the probable self-portrait in the third figure from the right in the background, similar to that in *Coffee Time* in the Hallsborough Gallery (Pl. 187). The old man seated on the left appears in the *Coffee Time* (Pl. 196) formerly in the Miari collection. There are two interesting pieces of *chinoiserie* on the lacquered commode in the background.

*Literature:* Davis, 1946, 60.

**STANFORD (Cal.), Stanford University Museum**

THE PAINTER IN HIS STUDIO *Plate 194*

Oli on canvas, 61×51 cm.

*Collection:* Lord Winbourne, London.

Related to the group of paintings from the Papadopoli Collection, later Perera Collection.

Datable to the 1750s for the pastel-like tonality.

A preliminary drawing for the painter is in the Museo Correr, no. 438 (Pl. 195).

*Literature:* Davis, 1946, 60.

**TREVISO, Museo Civico**

PORTRAIT OF A GENTLEMAN *Plate 260*

Oil on canvas, 90×73 cm.

*Collection:* Sernagiotto Cerato.

Identified as by Longhi by Moschini. There is no reason for doubting that this is a fine example of a Longhi portrait of the mid 1770s, close in date to those of the Querini family (Pl. 256, 257, 258).

**TURIN, Private collection**

THE QUINTET *Plate 289*

Oil on canvas, 61×49 cm.

An unpublished work of Longhi's last period (communicated by Antonio Morassi). The marked characterization is typical of the 'bourgeois portrait' phase of Longhi's career.

**UDINE, Museo Civico**

THE PROCURATORE LUDOVICO MANIN *Plate 230*

Oil on canvas, 244×155 cm.

*Collection:* Manin, Passerieno.

Signed on the back 'P. Longhi fecit 1764'. An engraving was made by Orsolini in the same year. There has been some uncertainty about this attribution, particularly suggesting that the work was done in collaboration with Alessandro. However, although damaged and partially repainted along the edges of the canvas, it seems undoubtedly the work of Pietro. As Moschini points out, it is mentioned by the diarist Pietro Gradenigo on 30 April 1764, and ascribed by him to Pietro Longhi alone.

*Literature:* Someda, 1956, 42; Moschini, 1956, 63; Valcanover, 1958, 686; Pallucchini, 1960, 185; Rizzi, 1965, 108.

**VENICE, Ca' Rezzonico (no. 1200)**

THE ALCHEMISTS *Plate 176*

Oil on canvas, 61×50 cm.

*Collection:* Morosini, Venice.

Probably a triple portrait of well-known persons. The activities of the three experimenters in search of the 'quintessence', following the instructions of the treatise of Ramón Lull, which the friar has under his arm, are treated with a suggestion of caricature. The silvery-brown tones of the painting are reminiscent of *The Quack* in the same gallery (Pl. 160) whose date, 1757, can be taken as an a approximate date for this work also. A later version, probably of 1779, is in the Cagnola collection at Gazzada (Varese), Pl. 269.

*Literature:* Ravà, 1923, 92; Valcanover, 1956, 25; Pignatti, 1960, 192.

**VENICE, Ca' Rezzonico (no. 1300)**

IN THE ESTUARY GARDENS *Plate 186*

Oil on canvas, 62×50 cm.

*Collection:* Morosini, Venice.

One of the chief paintings to show natural surroundings, using a particular range of *sfumatura* effects. The island of the estuary depicted is probably one of those between the Certosa and the Vignole (market-gardens): in the background can be seen the Forte Sant'Andrea and the church of San Nicolò. As Moschini has suggested, this painting is probably of *c*. 1759, the date of *The Tooth-Drawer* (Pl. 184) in the Ravà collection, Venice with a similar setting. A study for the woman on the left is in the Museo Correr, no. 1445 (Valcanover, 1956, 25) (Pl. 185).

*Literature:* Ravà, 1923, 80; Pallucchini, 1951-52, II, 62; Moschini, 1956, 30; Pignatti, 1960, 194.

**VENICE, Ca' Rezzonico (no. 1311)**

THE FAMILY CONCERT *Plate 128*

Oil on canvas, 62×50 cm.

*Collection:* Morosini, Venice.

Painted in suggestive, velvety tones of green, pink and brown, this family scene is full of a Goldoni type humour. It belongs to the time of *The Fortune-Teller* (Pl. 95), not long after 1752. A study for the guitarist is in the Museo Correr, no. 443 (Valcanover, 1956, 25) (Pl. 127).

*Literature:* Ravà, 1923, 38; Arslan, 1943, 60; Moschini, 1956, 24; Pignatti, 1960, 207.

**VENICE, Ca' Rezzonico (no. 1303)**

THE FORTUNE-TELLER *Plate 95*

Oil on canvas, 62×50 cm.

*Collection:* Morosini, Venice.

The inscription on the wall in the background celebrates the election of the parish priest of San Trovaso, Franco Comparato, in 1752; another, on the column, mentions Doge Loredan (1752-62). It is therefore probable that the painting was executed in *c*. 1752, especially since the similar painting in the National Gallery, London (Pl. 166) bears the date 1753 beneath the name of the Doge; and there the Parish priest is Don Zuanne Farinato, with the date 1756 (Levey, 1956, 74). The comparatively precise dating makes this *Fortune-Teller* the pointer for a group of paintings of social customs which span the 1750s. The silvery tones and *sfumatura* effects of Longhi's palette are characteristic of this period.

*Literature:* Ravà, 1923, 49; Pallucchini, 1951-52, II, 67; Pignatti, 1960, 206.

### VENICE, Ca' Rezzonico (no. 128)
THE HAIRDRESSER                                    *Plate 206*

Oil on canvas, 63×51 cm.

*Collection:* Teodoro Correr, Venice.

A work of the end of the 1750s, close in date to *A Visit from a Domino* (Pl. 203). The portrait on the wall is of Doge Ruzzini (d. 1735), probably an ancestor of the lady whose hair is being dressed. Drawings for the hairdresser and for the nurse are in the Museo Correr, nos. 441 and 539 (Valcanover, 1956, 25) (Pl. 204, 205).

*Literature:* Lazari, 1889, 24; Ravà, 1923, 10; Moschini, 1956, 90; Pignatti, 1960, 166.

### VENICE, Ca' Rezzonico (no. 1310)
THE LADY AT THE DRESSMAKER'S                       *Plate 209*

Oil on canvas, 61×52 cm.

*Collection:* Morosini, Venice.

Its similarity to *The Toilet* (Pl. 210) suggests that this painting can be dated to the 1750-1760s.

*Literature:* Ravà, 1923, 8; Pallucchini, 1951-52, II, 67; Moschini, 1956, 24; Pignatti, 1960, 206.

### VENICE, Ca' Rezzonico (no. 132)
THE LADY'S HAIR IS DRESSED                         *Plate 213*

Oil on canvas, 62×50 cm.

*Collection:* Teodoro Correr, Venice.

Although by its subject this painting belongs to the group of *The Toilet*, of the late 1750s and early 1760s, its darker tonality and the rather loose brushwork show affinity with the *Portrait of Magrath the Giant* (Pl. 179), of 1757.

*Literature:* Lazari, 1859, 25; Lorenzetti, 1951, 10; Pignatti, 1960, 171.

### VENICE, Ca' Rezzonico (no. 1313)
MEETING OF DOMINOES                         *Plates XIX and 173*

Oil on canvas, 62×51 cm.

*Collection:* Morosini, Venice.

It is difficult to fix a date for this work, very carefully painted as to detail, and exquisite as to colour. It is perhaps of the late 1750s, to be placed in the series of masked subjects. It has already been observed that these paintings are apparently in the nature of 'portraits', suggestive of Nazzari and Alessandro Longhi and typical of a certain attitude of the artist towards such themes in *c.* 1760.

*Literature:* Ravà, 1923, 48; Pignatti, 1960, 210.

### VENICE, Ca' Rezzonico (no. 1302)
THE MOOR'S LETTER                                  *Plates X, 119*

Oil on canvas, 62×50 cm.

*Collection:* Morosini, Venice.

Outstanding for its pale, luminous palette, applied with fluent, felicitous brushwork. The date must be close to that of *The Rhinoceros* of 1751 (Pl. 116). In the background is a small Zuccarelli.

*Literature:* Ravà, 1923, 34; Arslan, 1943, 60; Pallucchini, 1951-52, II, 67; Valcanover, 1956, 25; Moschini, 1956, 24; Pignatti, 1960, 195.

### VENICE, Ca' Rezzonico (no. 142)
THE MORNING CUP OF CHOCOLATE              *Plates XXIII, 279*

Oil on canvas, 60×47 cm.

*Collection:* Teodoro Correr, Venice.

An outstanding work of gentle domestic humour, painted some time between the *Portrait of Benedetto Ganassoni* (Pl. 261) of 1774 and *The Michiel Family* (Pl. 293) of *c.* 1780. As sometimes occurs in these later works, the palette is luminous but the brushwork seems hesitant and returns several times in the course of the painting to outline the figures.

*Literature:* Lazari, 1859, 29; Ravà, 1923, 5; Valcanover, 1956, 25; Pignatti, 1960, 175.

### VENICE, Ca' Rezzonico (no. 1302)
THE NEEDLEWORK SCHOOL                              *Plate 96*

Oil on canvas, 62×50 cm.

*Collection:* Morosini, Venice.

The silvery colours, applied fluently, recall *The Fortune-Teller* (Pl. 95) of *c.* 1752. The wax head on the shelf wears a lady's headpiece.

*Literature:* Ravà, 1923, 97; Pallucchini, 1951-52, II, 67; Valcanover, 1956, 24; Pignatti, 1960, 195.

### VENICE, Ca' Rezzonico (no. 135)
THE NURSE                                          *Plate 64*

Oil on canvas, 52×41 cm.

*Collection:* Teodoro Correr, Venice.

A companion to *The Sick Lady* in the same gallery (Pl. 66). Owing to the bad state of preservation the painting remained unidentified for a long time and only recently, after a successful restoration, has it been recognised as an early work of Longhi, datable to the period 1741-44.

*Literature:* Ravà, 1923, 12; Valcanover, 1956, 25; Moschini, 1956, 54; Pignatti, 1960, 173.

### VENICE, Ca' Rezzonico (no. 133)
THE PAINTER IN HIS STUDIO                     *Plates IV and 47*

Oil on canvas, 44×53 cm.

*Collection:* Teodoro Correr, Venice.

A slightly larger version of the painting formerly in the collection of Lieut. Col. Keir of Stirling (Pl. 49). Preliminary drawings for the gentleman and the painter are in the Museo Correr, nos. 437 and 439 (Valcanover, 1956, 24). Datable to 1741-44 (Pl. 45, 46).

*Literature:* Ravà, 1923, 47; Pallucchini, 1951, 213; Moschini, 1956, 24; Pignatti, 1960, 172.

## VENICE, Ca' Rezzonico (no. 126)
A PATRICIAN FAMILY *Plate 123*

Oil on canvas, 62×50 cm.

Comparison with *The Sagredo Family* in the Pinacoteca Querini Stampalia (Pl. 120) suggests a dating after 1752. This is an outstanding work for the lively palette and firm linear technique of the witty portraits. Two preliminary drawings, for the seated gentleman and for the man leaning on the chair, are in the Museo Correr, nos. 440 and 463 (Valcanover, 1956, 25) (Pl. 121, 122).

*Literature:* Ravà, 1923, 124; Arslan, 1943, 60; Pallucchini, 1951-52, II, 66; Moschini, 1956, 26; Pignatti, 1960, 163.

## VENICE, Ca' Rezzonico (no. 1314)
PEASANTS DANCING THE FURLANA *Plate 92*

Oil on canvas, 62×51 cm.

*Collection:* Morosini, Venice.

Another treatment of the subject of the painting in Northampton (Pl. 93), with variations in the figure of the male dancer and the proportional size of the figures. There is another version in the Pinacoteca Querini Stampalia (Pl. 94).

*Literature:* Ravà, 1923, 97; Pallucchini, 1951-52, II, 67; Valcanover, 1956, 24; Pignatti, 1960, 210.

## VENICE, Ca' Rezzonico (no. 127)
THE PERFUME-SELLER *Plate 164*

Oil on canvas, 61×51 cm.

*Collection:* Teodoro Correr, Venice.

The brown tonality suggests a dating close to that to *The Quack* (Pl. 160), and the masked figures are related to those of the *Ridotto* paintings in the Pinacoteca Querini Stampalia (Pl. 170, 171).

*Literature:* Lazari, 1859, 24; Arslan, 1943, 58; Valcanover, 1956, 26; Pignatti, 1960, 165.

## VENICE, Ca' Rezzonico (no. 578)
PORTRAIT OF BENEDETTO GANASSONI *Plates XXII, 261*

Oil on canvas, 42×26 cm.

*Collection:* Teodoro Correr, Venice.

Signed and dated on the back 'P.L. 1774'. Recently identified as a portrait of Benedetto Ganassoni, Bishop of Feltre. There is a portrait of him in the Seminary at Feltre (Fig. 31) in which the features resemble this picture, which is signed by Alessandro Longhi and dated 1774 (Valcanover, 1954, no. 135). It is not likely that the Ca' Rezzonico painting is, as Valcanover and Moschini suggest, a kind of sketch made to facilitate his son's work, but rather, as Pallucchini suggests, that Pietro has perhaps learned from the freer portrait technique of Alessandro.

*Literature:* Lorenzetti, 1936, 58; Arslan, 1943, 63; Pallucchini, 1951-52, II, 73; Valcanover, 1956, 25; Moschini, 1956, 38; Pignatti, 1960, 184.

*Fig. 31.* PORTRAIT OF BENEDETTO GANASSONI, by Alessandro Longhi. Feltre Seminary *(cf. pl. 261).*

## VENICE, Ca' Rezzonico (no. 136)
PORTRAIT OF ADRIANA GIUSTINIAN BARBARIGO
*Plate 287*

Oil on canvas, 58×45 cm.

*Collection:* Teodoro Correr, Venice.

A variant of the painting of the same subject, whose present whereabouts is unknown, dated 1779, which includes a portrait of her son, Gerolamo Ascanio.

*Literature:* Lazari, 1859, 25; Pignatti, 1960, 175.

## VENICE, Ca' Rezzonico (no. 868)
PORTRAIT OF WILLIAM GRAHAM (GRAEME), SECOND DUKE OF MONTROSE *Plate 142*

Oil on canvas, 62×50 cm.

*Collection:* Paravia, Venice.

On the back is an inscription identifying the subject as the Scottish general, William Graham, or Graeme (Commander-in-Chief of the Venetian forces) with his aide Moser de Filsek. Graeme came to Venice in 1755, and this could be the date of the painting. It is interesting that this is Longhi's first attempt to portray a real landscape in the manner of the 'battle-painters' such as Simonini.

*Literature:* Lorenzetti, 1936, 52; Arslan, 1943, 60; Pallucchini, 1951-52, 69; Valcanover, 1956, 25; Moschini, 1956, 28; Pignatti, 1960, 189.

## VENICE, Ca' Rezzonico (no. 761)
PORTRAIT OF FRANCESCO GUARDI     *Plates XXI and 227*

Oil on canvas, 132 × 100 cm.

*Collection:* Teodoro Correr, Venice.

Signed on the back 'Fran.º de Guardi Pietro Longhi Pr. 1764' (Fig. 32). This work is of great interest not only because portraits by Longhi are rare, but also for the sitter, of whom this is the only known portrait. The date 1764 provides a sound basis for dating other portraits of the 1760s, characterised by delicate but constructive brushwork and seeming to be rather 'enlargements' of the smaller, more typical paintings (in the Trucchi collection, Genoa, Pl. 231; Brass collection, Venice, Pl. 232). Guardi is shown painting a view of the Doge's palace from San Giorgio, similar to one, recently destroyed, in the Museum at Strasbourg.

*Literature:* Yriarte, 1878, 176; Pignatti, 1947, 294; Valcanover, 1956, 25; Moschini, 1956, 32; Pignatti, 1960, 187; Cailleux, 1967, 51.

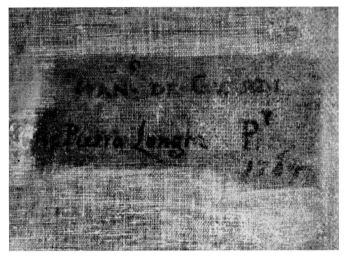

*Fig. 32.* Signature of Pietro Longhi on the back of his portrait of Francesco Guardi *(cf. pl. 227).*

## VENICE, Ca' Rezzonico (no. 1289)
PORTRAIT OF MAGRATH THE GIANT     *Plate 179*

Canvas, 61 × 50.

*Collection:* Morosini, Venice.

The inscription on the wall says 'True portrait of the Irish Giant Cornelius Magrat, who came to Venice in 1757; born on 1 January 1737, 7 foot high and weighing 420lb. Painted by command of the Nobleman Giovanni Grimani dei Servi, Patrician of Venice'. This is the same gentleman, amateur of curiosities, who in 1751 commissioned Longhi to paint the *Rhinoceros* (Pl. 116). The particular brown tones of the palette and the use of impasto herald

the characteristic style of Longhi's work in the 1760s, culminating in the *Shooting in the Valley* series.

*Literature:* Ravà, 1923, 60; Valcanover, 1956, 25; Moschini, 1956, 28; Pallucchini, 1960, 184; Pignatti, 1960, 190.

## VENICE, Ca' Rezzonico (no. 231)
PORTRAIT OF A PAINTER     *Plate 294*

Oil on canvas, 42 × 33 cm.

*Collection:* Teodoro Correr, Venice.

Signed 'P.L. 1781', this painting provides a pointer for dating the last works of the painter, who died in 1785. Contrary to what has been believed, this is not a self-portrait but, given the estimated age of the sitter, and with the evidence of the etchings in the *Vite*, it is at least a tenable theory that the subject is Alessandro Longhi (Moschini, 1956, 40).

## VENICE, Ca' Rezzonico (no. 403)
PORTRAIT OF POPE CLEMENT XIII REZZONICO     *Plate 175*

Oil on canvas, 52 × 50 cm.

*Collection:* Teodoro Correr, Venice.

A portrait of the Venetian Pope, Clement XIII, with his nephews Carlo and Ludovico and the wife of the latter, Faustina Savorgna. Since the election of the Pope was in 1758 and in 1762 Ludovico became Procuratore, obviously after the painting was executed, since he does not appear as such, the portrait must have been made between these dates. The accuracy of the portraiture and the softening of the palette, with a tendency to brownish tones, is typical of Longhi in the 1760s.

*Literature:* Lorenzetti, 1951, 49; Valcanover, 1956, 15; Pignatti, 1960, 183.

## VENICE, Ca' Rezzonico (no. 568)
PORTRAIT OF PIERO RINALDI     *Plate 299*

Oil on canvas, 51 × 38 cm.

*Collection:* Teodoro Correr, Venice.

At the bottom of the picture is the name of the sitter 'Piero Rinaldi, Ship's Captain'. Datable by analogy with the *Portrait of a Painter*, of 1781.

## VENICE, Ca' Rezzonico (no. 359)
PORTRAIT OF EUGENE OF SAVOY     *Plate 145*

Oil on canvas, 62 × 51 cm.

*Collection:* Teodoro Correr, Venice.

A portrait *in memoriam* of the famous general of the Battle of Belgrade (1717), probably of similar date to *The Tooth-Drawer* of 1759 (Pl. 184), which it resembles in the background and in the rather thread-like application of colour.

*Literature:* Ravà, 1923, 83; Pallucchini, 1951-52, II, 70; Pignatti, 1960, 179.

## VENICE, Ca' Rezzonico (no. 129)
THE QUACK     *Plates XIV, XV and 160*

Oil on canvas, 62 × 50 cm.

*Collection:* Teodoro Correr, Venice.

Signed 'Longhi Pin.t 1757'. A corner-stone of Longhi chronology, this work, with its use of denser colour lightly applied, heralds a more flowing style and less graphic control which are typical of the 1760s. The theme of masked figures in the *bauta*, or domino, is treated many times by Longhi in a series of paintings depicting the arcades of the Doge's palace or the *Ridotto* and casinos of the city.

*Literature:* Lazari, 1859, 24; Ravà, 1923, 51; Arslan, 1943, 60; Valcanover, 1956, 25; Moschini, 1956, 62; Pallucchini, 1960, 184; Pignatti, 1960, 168.

## VENICE, Ca' Rezzonico (no. 1312)

THE RHINOCEROS                                        *Plate 116*

Oil on canvas, 62×50 cm.

*Collection:* Morosini, Venice.

The inscription says 'True portrait of a Rhinoceros brought to Venice in the year 1751, painted by Pietro Longhi by command of the Nobleman Giovanni Grimani dei Servi, Venetian Patrician'. This is one of Longhi's masterpieces, showing how his brushwork freed from certain early mannerisms which are now absorbed and diffused harmoniously into the work as a whole. A similar painting, but lacking an inscription, is in the National Gallery, London (Pl. 118). Alessandro Longhi made an engraving in reverse of this *Rhinoceros* (Fig. 33).

*Literature:* Berenson, 1894, 104; Ravà, 1923, 50; Valcanover, 1956, 25; Moschini, 1956, 26; Levey, 1956, 73; Pallucchini, 1960, 182; Pignatti, 1960, 210.

*Fig. 33.* THE RHINOCEROS. Engraving in reverse by Alessandro Longhi (*cf. pl. 116*).

## VENICE, Ca' Rezzonico (no. 256)

THE RIDE                                *Plates XVII and 144*

Oil on canvas, 62×58 cm.

*Collection:* Tironi, Venice.

The similarity of style to that of the *Portrait of William Graham* (Pl. 142) suggests that the date of this painting is *c.* 1755. The masterly execution of the animals and the misty landscape are reminiscent of the series of *Shooting in the Valley*, painted in the following decade.

*Literature:* Ravà, 1923, 81; Arslan, 1943, 60; Pallucchini, 1951-52, II, 67; Valcanover, 1956, 25; Moschini, 1956, 28; Pignatti, 1960, 179.

## VENICE, Ca' Rezzonico (no. 1307)

SCENES OF PEASANT LIFE - THE MERRY COUPLE
                                                        *Plate 17*

Oil on canvas, 61×50 cm.

With the three following canvases and the four now at Zoppola (Plates 25, 26, 27, 31), from the Gambara Collection, Venice (Rizzi, 1962, 169). Critics are divided as to the dating of these peasant subjects, inspired by typical themes of the Bolognese school.

An early dating seems most generally accepted (Arslan), of *c.* 1740, by comparison with other treatments of similar subjects in the 1750s and 1760s (Moschini).

*Literature:* Ravà, 1909, fig. 118; Pignatti, 1960, 201.

## VENICE, Ca' Rezzonico (no. 1308)

SCENES OF PEASANT LIFE - A GIRL SPINNING   *Plate 15*

Oil on canvas, 61×50 cm.

*Collection:* Gambara, Venice.

A drawing in the Museo Correr, no. 557, reproduces exactly the figure of the mandoline player, but the late dating of this drawing, in the 1760s, is by no means certain; on the contrary, its heavy line and careful detail suggest that it belongs to the drawings of Longhi's youth, and this would agree with the early date of the painting (Valcanover, 1956, 25) (Pl. 14).

*Literature:* Ravà, 1909, fig. 117; Arslan, 1943, 52; Pallucchini, 1945, 133; Valcanover, 1956, 24; Pignatti, 1960, 20.

## VENICE, Ca' Rezzonico (no. 1306)

SCENES OF PEASANT LIFE - THE WASHERWOMEN
                                                        *Plate 16*

Wood, 61×50 cm.

*Collection:* Gambara, Venice.

Signed 'Longhi P.' on the washtub. It is not known why this painting was made on wood, and the existence of an unsigned copy in the Museo Civico, Padua, does not help to suggest a reason (Grossato, 1957, 96).

*Literature:* Ravà, 1909, fig. 117; Pignatti, 1960, 201.

## VENICE, Ca' Rezzonico (no. 1305)

SCENES OF PEASANT LIFE - THE POLENTA      *Plate 18*

Oil on canvas, 61×50 cm.

*Collection:* Gambara, Venice.

Forms a series with the preceding works.

*Literature:* Ravà, 1909, fig. 117; Pignatti, 1960, 201.

**VENICE, Ca' Rezzonico (no. 134)**

THE SICK LADY                                              *Plate 66*

Oil on canvas, 52×41 cm.

*Collection:* Teodoro Correr, Venice.

There is an evident similarity between the figure of the doctor in this painting and that of the viola player in *The Concert* in the Accademia (Pl. 37), dated 1741. and between the lady here and the subject of *The Faint* in Washington (Pl. 67), which is datable to *c.* 1744. The painting, lively in colour and rich in *sfumatura* effects, belongs probably between these dates. The differing opinions of Valcanover (*c.* 1762-72) and of Moschini (a workshop production, like *The Nurse*, Pl. 64) were probably affected by the bad state of the painting, which has only recently been restored. A study for the doctor is in the Museo Correr, no. 435 (Pl. 65).

*Literature:* Ravà, 1923, 21; Valcanover, 1956, 25; Moschini, 1956, 54; Pignatti, 1960, 173.

**VENICE, Ca' Rezzonico (no. 131)**

THE TOILET                                                *Plate 210*

Oil on canvas, 61×50 cm.

*Collection:* Teodoro Correr, Venice.

The brilliant, rather sharp palette of this painting suggest a dating close to that of *The Visit from a Domino* (Pl. 203) and *The Hairdresser* (Pl. 206), at the end of the 1750s.

*Literature:* Lazari, 1859, 25; Ravà, 1923, 7; Arslan, 1943, 58; Valcanover, 1956, 25; Pignatti, 1960, 170.

**VENICE, Ca' Rezzonico (no. 2251)**

THE VISIT TO THE CAPUCHIN CONVENT          *Plate 262*

Oil on canvas, 61×50 cm.

This painting shows the same acute characterisation of features as the Ganassoni portrait (Pl. 261) and so can be dated to *c.* 1774. The heraldic bearing on the wall is that of the Capuchin Order. The brownish impasto and the colour somewhat lacking in body are characteristic of a group of later works by Longhi whose attribution to him has sometimes been doubted by critics (Moschini, 1956, 54).

*Literature:* Lorenzetti, 1936, 55; Pignatti, 1960, 213.

**VENICE, Ca' Rezzonico (no. 2252)**

THE VISIT FROM A DOMINO                        *Plate 203*

Oil on canvas, 62×50 cm.

A painting of the late 1750s or early 1760s. This painting, as Moschini remarks, differs slightly from the series of conversation pieces such as the works formerly in the Perera Collection (Pl. 199, 200, 201) in the sharp luminosity of the colour, more piercing and even acid. A drawing for the seated gentleman is in the Museo Correr, no. 555 (Moschini, 1956, fig. 161).

*Literature:* Ravà, 1923, 35; Moschini, 1956, 30; Pignatti, 1960, 215.

**VENICE, Ca' Rezzonico (no. 1303)**

THE VISIT FROM A FRIAR                           *Plate 208*

Oil on canvas, 61×50 cm.

*Collection:* Morosini, Venice.

Datable to *c.* 1760 for its resemblance to the Perera collection paintings and to *The Lady reads aloud* (Pl. 201), of which the figure of the lady is repeated here. A study for the friars is in the Museo Correr, no. 494 (Moschini, 1956, fig. 79) (Pl. 207).

*Literature:* Ravà, 1923, 17; Pignatti, 1960, 197.

**VENICE, Ca' Rezzonico (no. 401)**

THE VISIT TO THE INVALID                         *Plate 263*

Oil on canvas, 60×47 cm.

*Collection:* Teodoro Correr, Venice.

The greenish-brown tonality and sharp characterisation are reminiscent of *The Visit to the Convent*, datable to *c.* 1774. In Moschini's opinion, a workshop production.

*Literature:* Lorenzetti, 1936, 51; Valcanover, 1956, 25; Moschini, 1956, 54; Pignatti, 1960, 182.

**VENICE, Ca' Rezzonico (no. 1304)**

THE WOMAN SELLING DOUGHNUTS              *Plate 88*

Oil on canvas, 62×51 cm.

*Collection:* Morosini, Venice.

The inscription 'P. Lorenzo Balischi for parish priest in San Baseggio' indicates a date *c.* 1750 (Moschini, 1956, 61). This provides another useful chronological pointer which helps to group many paintings of popular subjects of the early 1750s. The clear palette and subtle use of *sfumato* effects mark a new tendency which was to be developed throughout the 1750s (Pallucchini, 1951-52, II, 63). A replica is in the Galleria d'Arte Moderna, Milan (Pl. 86).

*Literature:* Ravà, 1923, 101; Valcanover, 1956, 25; Pignatti, 1960, 199.

**VENICE, Ca' Sagredo**

THE FALL OF THE GIANTS                          *Plates 3, 5, 6*

Fresco.

The date 1734 at the base of the frescoes which decorate the main staircase is that of the completion of the work, probably after the artist's return from Bologna. Valcanover has pointed out that his stay in Bologna, of great importance in his artistic formation, must have lasted from 1732, the final date for the San Pellegrino altarpiece (showing no trace of Bolognese elements) and 1734, that of the Sagredo frescoes (which are over-burdened with them). Pallucchini, however, denies that Bolognese influence is evident, and sees the preponderant influence as that of Dorigny. Moreover, Longhi was in his native city on 28 September 1732 for his marriage to Caterina Maria Rizzi; and it is quite possible that the frescoes were in fact begun in 1732. A study for a detail of *The Fall of the Giants* is in the Museo Correr, no. 514 verso (Pl. 4).

*Literature:* Ravà, 1909, 16; Valcanover, 1951, 170; figs. 4-5) (Moschini, 1956, Pallucchini, 1960, 177.

**VENICE, Church of San Pantalon**

THE VIRGIN AND CHILD WITH SAINTS AND ANGELS

*Plates V and 71-75*

Fresco.

After the S. Pellegrino altarpiece and the Sagredo staircase, these frescoes in the chapel of the Holy House of Loreto are the most notable works of Longhi as a history-painter, and their recent discovery is of outstanding importance. The painter decorated the whole of the small chapel, with a starry sky on the ceiling and on the mock-brick walls the sacred figures enclosed by hazel-grey clouds: the Virgin of Loreto, saints and angels. In 1954, in spite of the disapproval of the *Soprintendenza*, the background of mock brick around the figures was scraped away, and they now appear isolated against the plaster of the wall, resulting in the destruction of the chromatic unity of the chapel, which had previously been reminiscent of the domestic scenes characteristic of Longhi. The photographs reproduced here show the state of the frescoes before this deed was perpetrated. The discovery of a book published by Groppi in Venice in 1756, which describes the work done on the walls of the chapel between 6 May 1744 and 25 March 1745 gives a precise date for the work. Valcanover has shown that the frescoes of San Pantalon mark a phase in which Longhi's palette approaches that of the most delicate work being done in Venice at that time, in the manner of Amigoni and Rosalba Carriera. A drawing in the Museo Correr, no. 1201, attributed to Jacopo Marieschi, reproduces the wall with a female martyr, Joseph and the Virgin (Fig. 34).

*Literature:* Valcanover, 1956, 21.

*Fig. 34.* THE VIRGIN AND CHILD WITH JOSEPH AND A FEMALE MARTYR. Drawing by Jacopo Marieschi. Museo Correr *(cf. pls. 71-75)*.

**VENICE, Barnabò Collection**

FAMILY GROUP

*Plate 199*

Oil on canvas, 61×49 cm.

*Collection:* Brass, Venice.

Datable to *c.* 1760 for its similarity to the paintings formerly in the Perera Collection, particularly in the use of pale colours and the delicacy of tonal values.

*Literature:* Morandotti, 1941, 43.

**Formerly VENICE, Nicolò Barozzi Collection**

THE USURERS

*Plate 291*

Oil on canvas, 65×50 cm.

Closely related to *The Advocates* at Padua (Pl. 271), of the late 1770s.

*Literature:* Ravà, 1923, 27.

**Formerly VENICE, Brass Collection**

ORIENTAL SCENE

*Plate 275*

Oil on canvas, 62×48 cm.

A curious painting, alluding to a voyage in the East undertaken by the gentleman in the foreground. The inscription on the architrave of the mosque says: 'If Mecca is sacred, you know the reason why'. Datable to the end of the 1770s, the portraits of the gentleman and the priest being very similar in style to those of *The Advocates* in Padua (Pl. 271).

*Literature:* Ravà, 1923, 64; Morandotti, 1941, 52.

**VENICE, Brass Collection**

PORTRAIT OF A POLISH GENTLEMAN

*Plate 232*

Oil on canvas, 104×75 cm.

Although there is some doubt whether this painting should not be attributed to Alessandro Longhi (Moschini, 1932, 126), it is more probably the work of Pietro, of *c.* 1764, the year in which he painted the portrait of Francesco Guardi (Pl. 227). The composition here is precise and careful in detail and gradations of colours, as in the best of Longhi's conversation pieces.

*Literature:* Ravà, 1923, 218.

**Formerly VENICE, Emilia Charmet Padoan Collection**

PORTRAIT OF MARINA QUERINI BENZON

*Plate 258*

Oil on canvas, 83×66 cm.

Exhibited at the exhibition of Italian Portraits, Florence, 1922 (218). As in the similar portraits in Paris and Algiers (Pl. 256 and 257), a label on the back gives the name of the sitter and the date 1772.

*Literature:* Ravà, 1923, 115.

**VENICE, Curtis Collection**

THE VISIT TO GRANDMAMA

*Plate 283*

Oil on canvas, 60×48 cm.

Similar to the *Portrait of Adriana Giustinian Barbarigo* (Pl. 287) of 1779. In the background is a painting of Doge Marcantonio Memmo (elected in 1512), possibly an ancestor of the family portrayed.

*Literature:* Bassi, 34; Pallucchini, 1950, 171.

**Formerly VENICE, Adele Fornoni Bisacco Collection**

A GIRL SPINNING

*Plate 265*

Oil on canvas, 60×49 cm.

Signed 'P. Longhi 1779'. A variant of the painting of an earlier period in the castle at Zoppola (Pl. 27), showing the impasto and brown tones typical of his late works.

*Literature:* Ravà, 1923, 104; Moschini, 1956, 36; Valcanover, 1958, 681; Pallucchini, 1960, 186.

**Formerly VENICE, Adele Fornoni Bisacco Collection**

PEASANTS DANCING THE FURLANA            *Plate 268*

Oil on canvas, 49×68 cm.

A late variant of the *Furlana* in Ca' Rezzonico (Pl. 92). These compositions of reassembled motives are characteristic of the last decade of Longhi's active life.

*Literature:* Ravà, 1923, 106; Moschini, 1956, 36; Valcanover, 1958, 686; Pallucchini, 1960, 186.

**Formerly VENICE, Adele Fornoni Bisacco Collection**

THE POLENTA            *Plate 266*

Oil on canvas, 60×49 cm.

Like the *Girl spinning* in the same collection, this scene of peasant life is of the late 1770s.

*Literature:* Ravà, 1923, 105; Moschini, 1956, 36; Valcanover, 1958, 686; Pallucchini, 1960, 186.

**Formerly VENICE, Adele Fornoni Bisacco Collection**

THE QUACK            *Plate 267*

Oil on canvas, 49×68 cm.

A later variant of the famous subject already treated several times and closest to that reproduced in Plate 162. The date may be close to 1779, the year of the *Girl spinning* in the same collection.

*Literature:* Ravà, 1923, 55; Moschini, 1956, 36; Valcanover, 1958, 686; Pallucchini, 1960, 186.

**Formerly VENICE, Papadopoli Collection**

THE MANDOLINE RECITAL            *Plate 197*

Oil on canvas, 60×47 cm.

A painting at present lost sight of, which, on the basis of the reproduction published by Ravà, may belong to the group of conversation pieces formerly in the Perera Collection, of *c.* 1760.

*Literature:* Ravà, 1923, 38; Longhi, 1953, 116.

**Formerly VENICE, Heirs to the Ravà Collection**

THE TOOTH-DRAWER            *Plate 184*

Oil on canvas, 63×50 cm.

Signed and dated on the back 'Pietro Longhi 1759'. One of the few paintings by Longhi which show an interest in the scenery of the Venetian lagoon. Sold by auction in the Ravà sale, Venice, 16.5.1967.

**VENICE, Barone Rubin de Cervin Albrizzi Collection**

THE ALBRIZZI FAMILY            *Plate 218*

Oil on canvas, 115×160 cm.

*Collection:* Albrizzi, Venice.

This patrician family group, of unusual proportions, must certainly belong to the 1780s, both for the dark tonality and for the spatial composition, in which the figures are small in porportion to their surroundings, both characteristics of this period. A preliminary drawing for the children is in the Museo Correr, no. 488 (Moschini, 1956, fig. 165) (Pl. 217).

*Literature:* Ravà, 1909, 130; Moschini, 1956, 30.

**VENICE, Barone Rubin de Cervin Albrizzi Collection**

THE SLEEPER TICKLED            *Plate 214*

Oil on canvas, 60×48 cm.

This unpublished painting is a delicate reworking of the theme treated in Longhi's early years (Pl. 53). Here the palette is light and muted, as the paintings formerly in the Perera Collection. A study for the sleeping man is in the Kupferstichkabinett, Berlin (Pl. 215).

**VENICE, Gallerie dell'Accademia (no. 467)**

THE APOTHECARY            *Plates IX and 112*

Oil on canvas, 60×48 cm.

*Collection:* Contarini, Venice.

By analogy with *The Fortune-Teller* (Pl. 109) datable to *c.* 1752. Signed on the back 'Pietro Longhi'. A work of Longhi's best period which combines the acute characterisation of his portraits 'which seek the truth' with the delicate palette of his Venetian contemporaries, in spite of the obvious French influence. The *Nativity* on the wall at the back is a copy of a work by Balestra which is now in a private collection in Venice, identified by Mario Abis (Pilo, 1961, 32).

*Literature:* Ravà, 1923, 22; Moschini, 1956, 32.

**VENICE, Gallerie dell'Accademia (no. 466)**

THE CONCERT            *Plates II and 37*

Oil on canvas, 60×48 cm.

*Collection:* Contarini, Venice.

Signed on the back 'Petrus Longhi 1741'. The date provides a milestone in tracing the development of the painter's work, offering evidence for dating to the early 1740s the beginning of the 'small figures, conversation pieces, *Ridotto* interiors, dominoes, convent parlours' to which Guarienti refers in his 1753 edition of Orlandi's *Abecedario Pittorico*. Longhi's pictorial style in 1741 shows the plasticity of the Bologna school being superseded by a style which is graphically detailed but with a very subtle use of colour. The use of space in the composition reveals a study of the French illustrators.

*Literature:* Ravà, 1909, 27; Moschini, 1956, 14.

**VENICE, Gallerie dell'Accademia (no. 465)**

THE DANCING LESSON            *Plate 41*

Oil on canvas, 60×49 cm.

*Collection:* Contarini, Venice.

Painted about 1741, the year of *The Concert* (Pl. 37). It is generally agreed that the painting derives from an original ascribed to Crespi now in the Alte Pinakothek, Munich, although Cailleux assumed that the Munich painting was the derivation, which he ascribed to Gian Antonio Guardi. Longhi, however, makes changes in the proportions and gives special attention, according to his own manner, to a delicate harmony of colour. The preliminary drawing for the dancing master is in the Museo Correr, no. 252 (Valcanover, 1956, 25) (Pl. 40). Flipart made an engraving, in reverse except for

*Fig. 35.* THE DANCING LESSON. Engraving in reverse by C. Flipart *(cf. pl. 41)*.

*Fig. 36.* THE DANCING LESSON. Engraving by Hayd *(cf. pl. 41)*.

the violinist, who still holds his instrument in his left hand (Fig. 35). Hayd also made an engraving (Fig. 36), in the same sense as the painting, as was his custom, but it is curious that the violinist is reversed, and holds the violin in his right hand, which seems to prove that Hayd's print derives from that of Flipart. Cailleux mentions a derivation in a private collection in Italy, attributing it to Gian Antonio Guardi.

*Literature:* Ravà, 1909, 66; Moschini, 1956, 14; Cailleux, 1967, 54.

### VENICE, Gallerie dell'Accademia (no. 468)

THE FORTUNE-TELLER                                     *Plate 109*

Oil on canvas, 60×49 cm.

*Collection:* Contarini, Venice.

Signed on the back 'Pietro Longhi'. This work belongs to the period of *The Tooth-Drawer* in Milan (Pl. 107) and so is somewhat later than the other paintings of the same provenance, which are related to *The Concert* (Pl. 37). Two drawings in the Museo Correr are studies for the figure of a gentleman (no. 492) and the peasant who is listening to the predictions (no. 6058) (Valcanover, 1956, 24) (Pl. 110, 111).

*Literature:* Ravà, 1923, 56; Moschini, 1956, 22.

### VENICE, Gallerie dell'Accademia (no. 479)

THE PHILOSOPHER PYTHAGORAS                             *Plate 226*

Oil on canvas, 130×91 cm.

Pietro Longhi's reception piece for the Accademia Veneta in 1762 (Fogolari, 1913, 260). Signed 'Pietro Longhi'. Engraved in reverse by his son Alessandro (Fig. 37).

*Literature:* Zanetti, 1771, p. 483; Moschini, 1956, 63; Pallucchini, 1960, 185.

### VENICE, Gallerie dell'Accademia (no. 469)

THE TAILOR                                             *Plate 38*

Oil on canvas, 60×49 cm.

*Collection:* Contarini, Venice.

Datable to *c.* 1741, the year of *The Concert* (Pl. 37).

*Literature:* Ravà, 1909, 64; Moschini, 1956, 16.

### VENICE, Gallerie dell'Accademia (no. 464)

THE TOILET                                             *Plate 42*

Oil on canvas, 60×49 cm.

*Collection:* Contarini, Venice.

Datable to *c.* 1741 for its similarity to *The Concert* (Pl. 37). Here

94

*Fig. 37.* THE PHILOSOPHER PYTHAGORAS. Engraving in reverse by Alessandro Longhi *(cf. pl. 226).*

Longhi shows a liking for a wide surface of brocade with splendid effects of colour. The sumptuous silk crinoline of the lady is painted with raised accents of paint on a clearly marked design.

*Literature:* Ravà, 1909, 65; Moschini, 1956, 14.

## VENICE, Museo Correr (no. 130)
### THE DOGE PIETRO GRIMANI GIVING AUDIENCE
*Plate 139*

Oil on canvas, 61×50 cm.

*Collection:* Teodoro Correr, Venice.

The Doge is shown towards the end of his reign, and his features are here considerably older than in the Nazzari-Orsolini print of 1744, closer to those of the Cattini print of 1752. A preparatory drawing for the senators is in the Museo Correr, no. 574 (Valcanover, 1956, 24) (Pl. 140). Another portrait of the Doge is in a private collection in Bergamo (Pl. 141).

*Literature:* Lazari, 1859; Moschini, 1956, 60; Pignatti, 1960, 168.

## VENICE, Pinacoteca Querini Stampalia
### THE COSMORAMA
*Plate 165*

Oil on canvas, 61×49 cm.

*Collection:* Donà delle Rose, Venice.

A variant of the *Cosmorama* at Segromigno Monte (Pl. 163), but more lively. The inscription on the column mentions Doge Loredan, who reigned 1752-62, and the painting is certainly of that period.

*Literature:* Lorenzetti-Planiscig, 1934, 28; *Itinerario*, 1946, 23; Valcanover, 1956, 25.

## VENICE, Pinacoteca Querini Stampalia
### THE GEOGRAPHY LESSON
*Plates XI and 126*

Oil on canvas, 62×41.5 cm.

Comparison with *The Sagredo Family* suggests a dating to *c.* 1752. This is another family group, depicting an occasion typical of the century of enlightenment in which Algarotti's *Newtonianismo per le dame* was available to read. Drawings for the maid and for the gentleman hearing the lesson are in the Museo Correr, no. 450 recto and verso (Valcanover, 1956, 24) (Pl. 124, 125).

*Literature:* Ravà, 1923, 16; Arslan, 1943, 56; *Itinerario*, 1946, 25.

## VENICE, Pinacoteca Querini Stampalia (no. 47.280)
### A GIRL SPINNING
*Plates VI and 32*

Oil on canvas, 69×49 cm.

Very similar to the painting at Zoppola (Pl. 27), with delicate and lively effects of light, probably datable to the end of the 1740s.

*Literature:* *Catalogo*, 1925, 41; Moschini, 1956, 36; Pallucchini, 1960, 178.

## VENICE, Pinacoteca Querini Stampalia (no. 48.281)
### GIRLS SPINNING
*Plate 33*

Oil on canvas, 60×49 cm.

Moschini has suggested a date as late as the 1760s for this painting, because of its vivid luminosity. While it certainly shows a marked advance over the popular scenes in Ca' Rezzonico, it does not however seem to belong to a phase later than the 1740s. A drawing in the Museo Civico, Bassano, in reverse, with two cows, is likely to derive from Alessandro Longhi's engraving made from this painting (Fig. 38).

*Literature:* *Catalogo*, 1925, 41; Moschini, 1956, 36; Pallucchini, 1960, 178.

## VENICE, Pinacoteca Querini Stampalia (no. 20.274)
### THE LION SHOW
*Plate 252*

Oil on canvas, 61×50 cm.

The inscription at the bottom of the picture says 'The Lion show seen at Venice, Carnival 1767. Painted from life by Pietro Longhi'. The date is confirmed by the probability that the first figure next to the little door through which the performing dog is passing is Alessandro Longhi. He is identical with the portrait etched in his *Vite* (1761).

*Literature:* *Catalogo*, 1925, 41; Moschini, 1956, 32; Pallucchini, 1960, 184.

*Fig. 38.* GIRLS SPINNING. Engraving in reverse by Alessandro Longhi *(cf. pl. 33)*.

## VENICE, Pinacoteca Querini Stampalia

THE MICHIEL FAMILY    *Plates XXIV and 293*

Oil on canvas, 49×61 cm.

*Collection:* Donà delle Rose, Venice.

This work portrays the family of Marcantonio Michiel with his mother, Elena Corner, in the centre, his wife Giustina Renier Michiel (the celebrated authoress of the *Feste Veneziane*) to one side, with two of their children, and his two sisters, Elena and Cecilia. On the basis of the ages of the sitters a date of *c.* 1780 can be given.

*Literature:* Ravà, 1923, 125; Lorenzetti-Planiscig, 1934, 25; Moschini, 1956, 40; Valcanover, 1956, 25; Pallucchini, 1960, 186.

## VENICE, Pinacoteca Querini Stampalia (no. 21.275)

MONKS, CANONS, AND FRIARS OF VENICE    *Plate 221*

Oil on canvas, 61×49 cm.

Signed on the back 'Petrus Longhi pint. 1761'. An old sheet of paper stuck to the back gives a satirical description of the religious orders portrayed, in an eighteenth-century hand. The Franciscan in the right foreground has been identified by Pallucchini as Fr. Lodoli, a well-known expert on aesthetic matters. It is a work of fundamental importance, showing Longhi at the beginning of the 1760s embarking on a work of somewhat ironical portraiture.

The colour, in typical subdued tones, is sharpened here and there by sudden touches of light.

*Literature:* Ravà, 1909, 127; Pallucchini, 1951-52, II, 72; Moschini, 1956, 32.

## VENICE, Pinacoteca Querini Stampalia

PEASANTS DANCING THE FURLANA    *Plate 94*

Oil on canvas, 61×49.5 cm.

*Collection:* Donà delle Rose, Venice.

Another treatment, with some notable variations in the background figures, of the painting in Ca' Rezzonico (Pl. 92). It is not impossible that a stronger characterization and a tendency to monochrome may indicate a rather later date.

*Literature: Itinerario,* 1946, 23.

## VENICE, Pinacoteca Querini Stampalia

PEASANTS AT AN INN    *Plate 244*

Oil on canvas, 60×49 cm.

*Collection:* Donà delle Rose, Venice.

Close in style to the *Shooting in the Valley* series, this work can be dated to the mid 1760s. It is the painting for which most preparatory drawings are known; there are five of them in the Museo Correr, nos. 466-69, 471 (Valcanover, 1956, 25) (Pl. 243-248).

*Literature:* Ravà, 1909, 115; Lorenzetti-Planiscig, 1934, 27; Moschini, 1956, 34.

## VENICE, Pinacoteca Querini Stampalia (no. 19.273)

THE RIDOTTO    *Plate 171*

Oil on canvas, 61×49 cm.

The two figures in the foreground are identical with those in *The Quack* in Ca' Rezzonico (Pl. 160), so that a dating to *c.* 1757 is probable for this painting and for others of similar subjects. The *Ridotto* is the casino of Ca' Giustinian, San Marco, immortalized in the famous painting in Ca' Rezzonico by Francesco Guardi, of *c.* 1750.

*Literature: Catalogo,* 1925, 41; *Itinerario,* 1946, 25; Valcanover, 1956, 23; Moschini, 1956, 28.

## VENICE, Pinacoteca Querini Stampalia

THE RIDOTTO    *Plate 170*

Oil on canvas, 60×47 cm.

*Collection:* Donà delle Rose, Venice.

A version with slight alterations of the other *Ridotto* in the same gallery, (Pl. 171), datable to *c.* 1575.

*Literature:* Lorenzetti-Planiscig, 1934, 27; *Itinerario,* 1946, 23.

## VENICE, Pinacoteca Querini Stampalia (no. 11.265)

THE SACRAMENTS - BAPTISM    *Plate 148*

Oil on canvas, 60×49 cm.

The seven canvases representing the Sacraments are the outstanding works of Longhi's maturity. Iconographically, they derive from the series by G.M. Crespi, and they have sometimes been dated to *c.* 1740 (Arslan) or before 1751 (Valcanover). The later dates suggested by Moschini and Pallucchini seem however more probable, and the whole series should be ascribed to the 1740s, bearing in mind the mature use of colour, with the soft gradations of tone found in the paintings between *The Fortune-Teller* (Pl. 95) and *The Quack* (Pl. 160) in Ca' Rezzonico. In the opinion of Pallucchini the series does not constitute a unity, since there are stylistic differences between the individual works. It is known that Goldoni, in the dedication of his *Il Frappatore* (Vol. X of his *Commedie* published in Florence by Paperini) to Pitteri, mentions that the engraver had begun the reproduction of Longhi's *Sacraments*. This particular volume bears the date 1755 (not 1757, as the other volumes) and there is no evidence to suggest that this earlier date may have been printed in error, as Moschini suggests (1956, 62) on the basis of the unsupported opinion expressed by Ortolani in his edition of Goldoni's works (Venice, 1908, 13). Accordingly the date *ante quem* for the *Sacraments* must be put two years earlier. Francesco Guardi reproduced the paintings in a series of drawings, now in the Museo Correr, made from the engravings of Pitteri (Pallucchini, 1943, 59) (Figs. 39-52).

*Literature:* *Catalogo*, 1925, 41; Arslan, 1943, 11; Pallucchini, 1951-52, II, 68; Valcanover, 1956, 24; Moschini, 1956, 26; Pallucchinl, 1968, 183.

**VENICE, Pinacoteca Querini Stampalia (no. 14.268)**

THE SACRAMENTS - COMMUNION                    *Plate 150*

Oil on canvas, 60×49 cm.

There is a print by Pitteri in the same sense (Fig. 41).

*Literature:* As for *Baptism.*

**VENICE, Pinacoteca Querini Stampalia (no. 13.267)**

THE SACRAMENTS - CONFESSION                    *Plate 154*

Oil on canvas, 60×49 cm.

This subject offered itself for a variety of treatments, now to be seen in the Uffizi (Pl. 156) and in Rome (Pl. 157). Moschini (1956, 28) maintains that this painting may well have been the first executed of the series, and cites a drawing in the Museo Correr, which however appears to refer only to the version in the Uffizi. There is a print by Pitteri in the same sense (Fig. 45).

*Literature:* As for *Baptism.*

**VENICE, Pinacoteca Querini Stampalia (no. 12.266)**

THE SACRAMENTS - CONFIRMATION                    *Plate 149*

Oil on canvas, 60×49 cm.

There is a print by Pitteri in the same sense (Fig. 43).

*Literature:* As for *Baptism.*

*Fig. 39.* THE SACRAMENTS - BAPTISM. Engraving by Pitteri *(cf. pl. 148)*.

*Fig. 40.* THE SACRAMENTS - BAPTISM. Drawing by Francesco Guardi. Museo Correr *(cf. pl. 148)*.

*Fig. 41.* THE SACRAMENTS - COMMUNION. Engraving by Pitteri *(cf. pl. 150)*.

*Fig. 43.* THE SACRAMENTS - CONFIRMATION. Engraving by Pitteri *(cf. pl. 149)*.

*Fig. 42.* THE SACRAMENTS - COMMUNION. Drawing by Francesco Guardi. Museo Correr *(cf. pl. 150)*.

*Fig. 44.* THE SACRAMENTS - CONFIRMATION. Drawing by Francesco Guardi. Museo Correr *(cf. pl. 149)*.

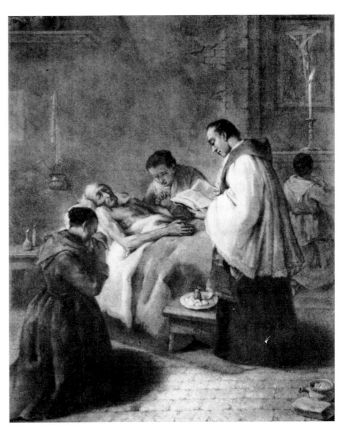

Fig. 45. THE SACRAMENTS - CONFESSION. Engraving by Pitteri *(cf. pl. 154)*.

Fig. 47. THE SACRAMENTS - EXTREME UNCTION. Engraving by Pitteri *(cf. pl. 152)*.

Fig 46. THE SACRAMENTS - CONFESSION. Drawing by Francesco Guardi. Museo Correr *(cf. pl. 154)*.

Fig. 48. THE SACRAMENTS - EXTREME UNCTION. Drawing by Francesco Guardi. Museo Correr *(cf. pl. 152)*.

*Fig. 49.* THE SACRAMENTS - HOLY ORDERS. Engraving by Pitteri *(cf. pl. 153)*.

*Fig. 51.* THE SACRAMENTS - MATRIMONY. Engraving by Pitteri *(cf. pl. 151)*.

*Fig. 50.* THE SACRAMENTS - HOLY ORDERS. Drawing by Francesco Guardi. Museo Correr *(cf. pl. 153)*.

*Fig. 52.* THE SACRAMENTS - MATRIMONY. Drawing by Francesco Guardi. Museo Correr *(cf. pl. 151)*.

**VENICE, Pinacoteca Querini Stampalia (no. 15.269)**

THE SACRAMENTS - EXTREME UNCTION  *Plate 152*

Oil on canvas, 61×50 cm.

There is a print by Pitteri in the same sense (Fig. 47).

*Literature:* As for *Baptism.*

**VENICE, Pinacoteca Querini Stampalia (no. 16.270)**

THE SACRAMENTS - HOLY ORDERS  *Plate 153*

Oil on canvas, 61×49 cm.

There is a print by Pitteri in the same sense (Fig. 49).

*Literature:* As for *Baptism.*

**VENICE, Pinacoteca Querini Stampalia (no. 17.271)**

THE SACRAMENTS - MATRIMONY  *Plates XIII and 153*

Oil on canvas, 62×50 cm.

There is a print by Pitteri in the same sense (Fig. 51).

*Literature:* As for *Baptism.*

**VENICE, Pinacoteca Querini Stampalia**

THE SAGREDO FAMILY  *Plates XII and 120*

Oil on canvas, 61×50 cm.

*Collection:* Donà delle Rose, Venice.

One of Longhi's greatest works. The researches of Rodolfo Gallo
have identified the sitters and obtained a dating of *c.* 1752 (Pallucchini, 1947, 54). As the inscription at the bottom of the picture
indicates, the figures portrayed are Cecilia Grimani Calergi Sagredo
with her two daughters, Marina (on the left) and her grandson
Almorò II Pisani, and Caterina (on the right) with her granddaugh-
ters Cecilia and Contarina Barbarigo. Longhi undertook this kind
of portraiture many times in the 1750s, painting 'conversation
pieces' in the English tradition. Valcanover suggests that a drawing in the Brinsley Ford Collection, London, is a study for this
painting (1956, 25), but the similarity is not convincing (Pl. 308).

*Literature:* Ravà, 1923, 31; Lorenzetti-Planiscig, 1934, 24; *Itinerario,* 1946, 35; Moschini, 1956, 26.

**VENICE, Pinacoteca Querini Stampalia**

SHOOTING HARES  *Plate 147*

Oil on canvas, 56×72.5 cm.

*Collection:* Donà delle Rose, Venice.

Datable to the end of the 1750s, after *The Ride* (Pl. 144) in Ca'
Rezzonico. The landscape background seems to have been suggested to Longhi by paintings by Marco Ricci or Zais. A study
for the lady and a hunter is in the Museo Correr, no. 489 (Moschini,
1956, fig. 183) (Pl. 146).

*Literature:* Ravà, 1909, 76; Lorenzetti-Planiscig, 1934, 26; Arslan,
1943, 60; *Itinerario,* 1946, 7.

**VENICE, Pinacoteca Querini Stampalia**

SHOOTING IN THE LAGOON  *Plates XVIII and 180*

Oil on canvas, 57×74 cm.

*Collection:* Donà delle Rose, Venice.

This is the best of Longhi's landscape series, and can be dated to
*c.* 1760. According to Lorenzetti, this contains the portrait of a
member of the Barbarigo family. Note that the hunter is not using
bow and arrow, but a rather rare type of bow using pellets of
terracotta (the ammunition can be seen in a basket in the prow of
the *caorlina*. A sketch is in the Museo Correr, no. 475 (Pl. 181). A
similar painting has recently been discovered (Pl. 182) which
corresponds to another sketch in the Museo Correr, no. 489.

*Literature:* Ravà, 1909, 35; Lorenzetti, 1934, 27; Arslan, 1943, 60;
*Itinerario,* 1946, 27; Pallucchini, 1951-52, II, 69; Valcanover, 1956,
25; Moschini, 1956, 34.

**VENICE, Pinacoteca Querini Stampalia**

SHOOTING IN THE VALLEY - THE MASTER'S ARRIVAL
*Plate 233*

Oil on canvas, 62×50 cm.

*Collection:* Donà delle Rose, Venice, (with the following six works).

There is some controversy over the dating of these paintings, commissioned by the Barbarigo family. A fairly early date has been
suggested by some (Arslan, *c.* 1740) but critics now tend to favour
a dating to the artist's maturity, after *Magrath the Giant* (Pl. 179,
1757) and *The Tooth-Drawer* (Pl. 184, 1759). In the opinion of the
present writer, the strong chiaroscuro is suggestive of a tendency

*Fig. 53.* SHOOTING IN THE VALLEY - THE MASTER'S ARRIVAL. Etching
by Pitteri (*cf. pl. 233*).

to emulate some effects of Rembrandt which was fashionable at that period, as can be seen in the works of Nogari and others. The series, with the exception of *The Departure of the Hunters*, was very successfully etched by Pitteri, with care for the effects of graduated deep tones (Figs. 53-58). A drawing for *The Master's Arrival* is in the British Museum, no. 1938-3-12-1 (information kindly supplied by John Gere) (Pl. 234).

*Literature:* Ravà, 1909, 106; Lorenzetti-Planiscig, 1934, 25; Arslan, 1943, 55; Pallucchini, 1951-52, II, 70; Valcanover, 1956, 25; Moschini, 1956, 34.

### VENICE, Pinacoteca Querini Stampalia
### SHOOTING IN THE VALLEY - PREPARING THE GUNS
*Plates XVI and 235*

Oil on canvas, 61×50 cm.

*Literature:* Ravà, 1909, 109.

### VENICE, Pinacoteca Querini Stampalia
### SHOOTING IN THE VALLEY - UNLOADING SHOOTING EQUIPMENT
*Plate 236*

Oil on canvas, 61×50 cm.

*Literature:* Ravà, 1909, 107.

*Fig. 55.* SHOOTING IN THE VALLEY - UNLOADING SHOOTING EQUIPMENT. Etching by Pitteri *(cf. pl. 236)*.

*Fig. 54.* SHOOTING IN THE VALLEY - PREPARING THE GUNS. Etching by Pitteri *(cf. pl. 235)*.

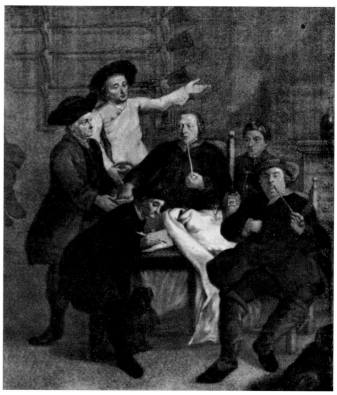

*Fig. 56.* SHOOTING IN THE VALLEY - THE HUNTERS DRAW LOTS. Etching by Pitteri *(cf. pl. 238)*.

*Fig. 57.* SHOOTING IN THE VALLEY - SHOOTING POSITION IN A BARREL. Etching by Pitteri *(cf. pl. 241)*.

*Fig. 58.* SHOOTING IN THE VALLEY - COUNTING THE BAG. Etching by Pitteri *(cf. pl. 242)*.

**VENICE, Pinacoteca Querini Stampalia**

SHOOTING IN THE VALLEY - THE HUNTERS DRAW LOTS                                            *Plate 238*

Oil on canvas, 61×49 cm.

A preparatory drawing for the figure on the right is in the Museo Correr, no. 536 (Valcanover, 1956, 25) (Pl. 237).

*Literature:* Ravà, 1909, 108.

**VENICE, Pinacoteca Querini Stampalia**

SHOOTING IN THE VALLEY - THE DEPARTURE OF THE HUNTERS                                        *Plate 239*

Oil on canvas, 61×50 cm.

*Literature:* Ravà, 1909, 112.

**VENICE, Pinacoteca Querini Stampalia**

SHOOTING IN THE VALLEY - SHOOTING POSITION IN A BARREL                                         *Plate 241*

Oil on canvas, 61×49.5 cm.

A preliminary drawing for the shooters is in the Museo Correr, no. 427 (Valcanover, 1956, 25) (Pl. 240).

*Literature:* Ravà, 1909, 111.

**VENICE, Pinacoteca Querini Stampalia**

SHOOTING IN THE VALLEY - COUNTING THE BAG                                            *Plate 242*

Oil on canvas, 61×50 cm.

*Literature:* Ravà, 1909, 113.

**VENICE, Pinacoteca Querini Stampalia (no. 46.279)**

THE SLEEPING PEASANT GIRL                                      *Plate 34*

Oil on canvas, 61×50 cm.

This painting, together with the *Girls spinning* (Pl. 33), is probably of the late 1740s, suggested by the liveliness of touch and colour.

*Literature: Catalogo*, 1925, 41; Moschini, 1956, 36; Pallucchini, 1960, 244.

**VENICE, Pinacoteca Querini Stampalia (no. 18.272)**

THE TEMPTATIONS OF ST ANTHONY                             *Plate 225*

Oil on canvas, 60×50 cm.

A strange painting, in which only the female figures betray a glimpse of Longhi's usual manner. In fact several academic temptations beset Longhi himself during these years, between teaching in the Accademia (post 1756) and teaching in the school set up

*Fig. 59.* THE TEMPTATIONS OF ST ANTHONY. Engraving by Alessandro Longhi *(cf. pl. 225)*.

by the Pisani family in their house (1763-66). A print of a similar subject by Alessandro Longhi, dated 1761, draws on motives from this painting, which is therefore slightly earlier (Fig. 59).

*Literature:* Catalogo, 1925, 42; Moschini, 1956, 63.

## VENICE, Scuola di San Giovanni Evangelista

ADORATION OF THE MAGI                    *Plate 2*

Oil on canvas, 190×150 cm.

This is probably the painting formerly described by Zanetti as being in the principal chapel of Sta Maria Materdomini. Lost sight of after 1819, it was found in its present situation by Martini, who is however entirely certain of the identification. Comparison with the altarpiece of San Pellegrino, presumably of the same period, confirms the attribution to Pietro Longhi, in the years preceding the Ca' Sagredo frescoes. Typical of this period is the influence of Balestra, evident in both composition and palette. As Martini observes, the powers of characterisation of Pietro Longhi are already visible in the little page in the centre, a forerunner of the *Shepherd Boys* at Rovigo and Bassano, painted not long after.

*Literature:* Zanetti, 1733, 443; Martini, 1964, 262, no. 239.

## VERONA, Museo di Castelvecchio

FAMILY GROUP                    *Plate 216*

Oil on canvas, 43×60 cm.

*Collection:* Galleria Pompei, Venice.

Recently removed from the reserve collection of the Museum, where it had lain unrecognised, and exhibited with an attribution to Pietro Longhi by Licisco Magagnato. The light and luminous colours relate this work to the paintings of similar subjects, such as *The Family Concert* at Milan (Pl. 117), but the sharper characterisation and the strange diminution of the figures suggest a rather later date, after 1760.

*Literature:* Galleria Pompei, 1865, 48.

## WASHINGTON, National Gallery of Art (Kress Collection)

THE FAINT                    *Plates III and 67*

Oil on canvas, 49×61 cm.

*Collection:* Giovannelli, Venice.

Like the following work, datable to 1744. A later version is in the Salom Collection (Pl. 211).

*Literature:* National Gallery Preliminary Catalogue, 1941, 110, no. 174; Pallucchini, 1960, 181.

## WASHINGTON, National Gallery of Art (Kress Collection)

THE GAME OF THE COOKING-POT                    *Plate 68*

Oil on canvas, 49×61 cm.

*Collection:* Giovannelli, Venice.

In the Gallery's Summary Catalogue listed as *Blindman's Buff.* Datable to *c.* 1744 for its similarity to the paintings at Windsor (Plates 57 and 62), this work and the following one are among the outstanding achievements of Longhi in the 1740s, already in the style of the conversation pieces which suggest the parallel of Longhi's painting with Goldoni's comedies. A later version is in the Salom Collection at Segromigno Monte (Pl. 212).

*Literature:* National Gallery Preliminary Catalogue, 1941, 110, no. 175; Pallucchini, 1960, 181.

## WINDSOR, Royal Collection

BLINDMAN'S BUFF                    *Plate 62*

Oil on canvas, 48×58 cm.

*Collection:* Consul Smith, Venice.

Signed 'Petrus Longhi F. 174...'. A companion to the following painting dated 1744. A preliminary drawing for the stool is in the Museo Correr, no. 540 (Moschini, 1956, fig. 38) (Pl. 63).

*Literature:* Law, 1881, 549; Moschini, 1956, 18; Levey, 1964, 87.

## WINDSOR, Royal Collection

THE GENTLEMAN'S AWAKENING                    *Plate 57*

Oil on canvas, 49×60 cm.

*Collection:* Consul Smith, Venice.

In the 1964 catalogue of the Royal Collection listed as *The Morning Levée*. Signed on the back 'Petrus Longhi 1744'. This is a point of reference for many paintings of the mid 1740s, characterised by the soft graduation of tones of colour and a detailed linear technique. There are five drawings in the Museo Corrette related to this painting, nos 462 recto and verso, 481, 482, 540 recto (Pl. 56-61).

*Literature:* Law, 1881, 551; Moschini, 1956, 18; Levey, 1964, 87.

## WORCESTER (Mass.), Art Museum
### THE VISIT TO THE LIBRARY
*Plate 51*

Oil on canvas, 59×44 cm.

*Collection:* Godfrey Locker-Lampson, London.

A lively interior, probably of the early 1740s for its similarity to the paintings of *The Concert* series (Pl. 37 etc.). This is the period in which Longhi shows traces of French influence, as is shown here by the close resemblance of the composition to Boucher's illustration to *Les Femmes Savantes* of Molière, engraved by Cars in 1734 (Fig. 5). A preliminary study is in the Museo Corrette, no. 470 (Moschini, 1956, fig. 58) (Pl. 50). For one of the ladies Longhi used the same drawing, no. 487 recto (Pl. 43), as for *The Introduction* (Pl. 44) in the Louvre.

*Literature:* Locker-Lampson, 1937, 26; Davis, 1946, 56; Moschini, 1956, 20.

## ZOPPOLA, Castello
### THE DRUNKARDS
*Plate 31*

Oil on canvas, 61×50 cm.

*Collection:* Gambara, Venice, together with the following three works and several others in Venetian galleries.

Rizzi associates these paintings with versions of similar subjects in Ca' Rezzonico, but suggests a slightly later dating, in the 1740s (Cf. Pl. 15-18). Notwithstanding the reservations which must be made about the chronology of Longhi's works, especially in the case of several versions of a subject, this dating should perhaps be put later still. In *The Drunkards* (Pl. 31) we see the old woman of *The Seduction* (Pl. 102) and in *The Polenta* (Pl. 26) the old woman spinning in the *Peasants dancing* (Pl. 90), both works which were certainly not executed before the end of the 1740s. Two drawings for the girl with the barrel and the two drunkards in the background are in the Museo Corrette, nos. 523 and 526. (Pl. 29-30).

*Literature:* Rizzi, 1962, 157; Rizzi, 1966, 104.

## ZOPPOLA, Castello
### A GIRL SPINNING
*Plate 27*

Oil on canvas, 61×50 cm.

*Collection:* Gambara, Venice.

The girl spinning here is the same as in the Ca' Rezzonico painting (Pl. 15). A preliminary drawing for the thoughtful peasant of the *Girl spinning* is in the Museo Corrette, no. 525 (Pl. 28).

*Literature:* Rizzi, 1962, 155; Rizzi, 1966, 100.

## ZOPPOLA, Castello
### THE POLENTA
*Plate 26*

Oil on canvas, 60×50 cm.

*Collection:* Gambara, Venice.

In spite of the similar subject this cannot be considered a version of the Ca' Rezzonico painting (Pl. 18) of several years earlier. The seated peasant girl in the foreground is similar to the *Girl Spinning* (Pl. 19) in Milan.

*Literature:* Rizzi, 1962, 155; Rizzi, 1966, 106.

## ZOPPOLA, Castello
### THE WASHERWOMEN
*Plate 25*

Oil on canvas, 61×50 cm.

*Collection:* Gambara, Venice.

The central figure is similar to the one in the Ca' Rezzonico painting (Pl. 16). A study for the girl with the bucket is in the Museo Corrette, no. 456 (Pl. 24).

*Literature:* Rizzi, 1962, 155; Rizzi, 1966, 102.

## ZURICH, Private collection
### THE SICK LADY
*Plate 138*

Oil on canvas, 55×43 cm.

*Collection:* Feilchenfeld. Exhibited at Zurich in 1955.

Datable to the end of the 1750s by its similarity to *The Embroidery Workroom*, London (Pl. 135). Moschini however attributes it to Longhi's earliest period, c. 1741, together with *The Lady's Toilet* in Chicago (Pl. 137).

*Literature:* Hüttinger, 1955, no. 193; Moschini, 1956, 16.

## WHEREABOUTS UNKNOWN
### A FAMILY SERMON
*Plate 222*

Oil on canvas, 62×50 cm.

Similar to the *Monks, Canons and Friars* in the Pinacoteca Querini Stampalia (Pl. 221), of which some elements are repeated here, the distribution of colour is reminiscent of the best works of the 1750s, such as the *Sacraments* (Pl. 148-54).

*Literature:* Martini, 1964, 108.

### MAGRATH THE GIANT AND THE RHINOCEROS
*Plate 299c*

Oil on canvas, 50.5×64 cm.

Perhaps from the Conti Mapelli Collection, Bergamo.

This unpublished work is a companion to the Furlana (Pl. 299d). Here again Longhi had evidently been commissioned to repeat two earlier works (Pl. 116 and 179). In fact the original inscriptions appear here as a reminder. The painting appears in a good state of preservation, showing the deeper tones of the late period, with vibrant touches of light in the faces and clothes.

### PEASANTS DANCING THE FURLANA
*Plate 91*

Reproduced by Ravà without comment, this is apparently one of the *Furlana* series, this time in a horizontal format, and it includes several figures from the other versions.

*Literature:* Ravà, 1923, 106.

## PEASANTS DANCING THE FURLANA
*Plate 299d*

Oil on canvas, 50.5×62.5 cm.

Perhaps from the collection of the Conti Mapelli, Bergamo.

This unpublished painting, formerly in a Venetian gallery, is a companion to *Magrath the Giant and the Rhinoceros* (Pl. 299c) and provides an example of a variant in which Longhi regroups the figures of the *Furlana* paintings together with the seated peasant girl of the various *Temptation* paintings (Pl. 83 etc.), while the nobleman in the background seems to come from the Brera *Family Concert* (Pl. 117). The brownish prepared ground and the rather heavily charged tonality suggest a date in the late 1760s or 1770s, perhaps close to the paintings of similar 'popular' subjects in the Fornoni Bisacco Collection (Pl. 268 etc.).

## PORTRAIT OF A GENTLEMAN
*Plate 299b*

Oil on canvas, 64×50.5 cm.

Forms a pair with the *Portrait of a Lady* (Pl. 299a), and is also probably mentioned by Martini (1964, 291).

## PORTRAIT OF A GENTLEMAN
*Plate 228*

Probably from the Zen family, Venice, this work is at present apparently in a private collection in the United States. It is one of the wittiest portraits painted by Pietro Longhi. It seems reasonable to propose a dating to the middle of the 1760s by analogy with similar portraits in Ca' Rezzonico and at Udine, of *c.* 1764.

*Literature:* Moschini, 1956, 22; Pallucchini, 1969, 186.

## PORTRAIT OF ADRIANA GIUSTINIAN BARBARIGO
*Plate 286*

Indicated mistakenly by Ravà as in the Brass Collection, this painting remains untraced. On the back of the canvas is an inscription 'Jeronimo Ascanio equiti Justiniano ejus reluctante matre Adriana Barbarigo Matrona omni Historiarum genere eruditissima Petrus Longhi qui celleri eam delineavit pennicillo DDD A 1779'. A version with some alterations is in Ca' Rezzonico (Pl. 287).

*Literature:* Ravà, 1923, 123.

## PORTRAIT OF A LADY
*Plate 299a*

Oil on canvas, 64×50.5 cm.

With the *Portrait of a Gentleman* (Pl. 299b) this is an unpublished example of the very last of Longhi's portraits, executed at a time not far from the *Portrait of a Painter* dated 1781 in Ca' Rezzonico (Pl. 294). The artist draws the faces with a meticulous love of detail, almost with a miniaturist technique, in a spirit which here is bourgeois rather than patrician, close in style to that of his son Alessandro. Probably mentioned by Martini (1964, 291).

## RUSTIC DANCE
*Plate 276*

This painting, probably by Longhi, is datable to the 1770s. The faces of the gentlemen in the background recall *The Advocates* (Pl. 271). A drawing for the girl dancer is in the Museo Correr, no. 564 (Pl. 277).

*Literature:* Ravà, 1923, 82.

## THE SINGING TEST
*Plate 39*

Belonging to the period in which Longhi was painting scenes of the education of a lady, this work belongs between the *Concert* of the Accademia (Pl. 37) and the *Introduction* in the Louvre (Pl. 44). It is of singular elegance, of a time when Longhi was most subject to French influences.

*Literature:* Pilo, 1961, 28.

## THE SINGING TEST
*Plate 198a*

Oil on canvas, 58×49 cm.

*Collections:* Sykes, London; Pakenham, London; as *The Nurse* (Pl. 198). Datable to *c.* 1760.

## THE TICKLE
*Plate 53*

The presence, on the wall in the background, of a painting identical to that in *Milord's Visitor*, New York (Pl. 84) suggests a date earlier than 1749 for this amusing painting. There is an engraving in the same sense, and a preparatory drawing in the Museo Correr, no. 448 (Pl. 58). A later version of the same subject is in the Rubin de Cervin Albrizzi Collection, Venice (Pl. 214).

*Literature:* Ravà, 1923, 29; Moschini, 1956, 20.

# DRAWINGS BY PIETRO LONGHI

**AALEN, Koenig-Fachsenfeld Collection**

SHEPHERD GIRL WITH A FLOWER                    *Plate 417a*

Red and white chalk on brownish grey paper, 273×200 mm.
Study for the *Shepherd Girl*, Museo Civico, Bassano (Pl. 10).

*Literature:* Deusch, 1967, 93.

**BERGAMO, Accademia Carrara**

PRELATE (no. 465)                              *Plate 300*

Black and white chalk on blue-green paper, 195×125 mm.

*Literature:* Ragghianti, 1963, p. 33.

**BERLIN, Kupferstichkabinett**

CARD - PLAYERS (no. 11696)                     *Plate 301*

Black and white chalk, brownish grey paper, 250×385 mm.

GENTLEMAN IN A DOMINO (no. 11718)             *Plate 306*

Black and white chalk on brownish grey paper, 271×391 mm.

GENTLEMAN STANDING AT A TABLE (no. 11643)  *Plate 303*

Black and white chalk, 279×402 mm.

YOUNG MAN ASLEEP (no. 11644)                   *Plate 215*

Black and white chalk, brownish grey paper, 280×388 mm.
Study for *The Sleeper tickled*, Venice (Pl. 214).

MANSERVANT STANDING (no. 11700)

Black and white chalk on brownish grey paper, 313×449 mm.

MASKED LADY (no. 11719)                        *Plate 307*

Black and white chalk on brownish grey paper, 290×374 mm.

OLD PRIEST STANDING (no. 11697)                *Plate 305*

Black and white chalk on brownish grey paper, 292×385 mm.

*Literature:* Byam Shaw, 1933, p. 59.

SEATED LADY, AND A BASKET (no. 11720)          *Plate 302*

Black and white chalk on brownish grey paper, 273×394 mm.

TWO GENTLEMEN IN DOMINOES (no. 11699)    *Plate 169*

Black and white chalk on brownish grey paper, 285×407 mm.
Study for *The Ridotto*, Segromigno Monte (Pl. 168).

**LONDON, Brinsley Ford Collection**

SEATED LADY                                    *Plate 308*

Black and white chalk on light brown paper, 270×360 mm.
Study for *The Sagredo Family*, Venice, (Pl. 120) (?).

*Literature:* Valcanover, 1956, 25.

**LONDON, British Museum**

TWO PEASANTS (1938-3-12-1)                     *Plate 234*

Black and white chalk on light brown paper, 282×388 mm.
Study for *The Master's Arrival*, Venice (Pl. 233).

**LONDON, Private collection**

PRIEST STANDING                                *Plate 309*

Black chalk, 368×165 mm.

*Literature:* Moschini, 1956, fig. 173.

**NEW YORK, Pierpont Morgan Library**

RUSTIC SCENE (no. 1950.10)

Red chalk and wash on white paper, 270×392 mm.

*Literature:* Muraro, 1959, 244; Pignatti, 1965, no. 107.

VENETIAN SENATOR (no. IV, 142)                 *Plate 310*

Black and white chalk on brownish paper, 331×221 mm.

*Literature:* Moschini, 1956, p. 56.

**PARIS, Talleyrand Collection**

PRIEST KNEELING                                *Plate 314*

Black and white chalk on buff paper, 370×280 mm.

*Literature:* Morassi, 1958, no. 73.

**VENICE, Gallerie dell'Accademia**

CHILD, AND MAN STANDING (no. 1682 recto)    *Plate 312*

Black and white chalk, 228×322 mm.

SEATED MAN, AND DRAPERY (no. 1682 verso)   *Plate 313*

Black and white chalk, 228×322 mm.

**VENICE, Museo Correr**

A VOLUME OF DRAWINGS BY LONGHI

The group of drawings by Longhi in the Museo Correr, Venice,
are by far the most important of those that have been preserved,

both because of their large number and because of their intrinsic beauty, and also because of their undoubted authenticity. We are told by Lazari, who published the first list of them in 1859, that the drawings were acquired by Teodoro Correr, the founder of the Museum, directly from Alessandro Longhi, the painter's son. They were perhaps from the first collected together in a volume, and this would seem to be confirmed by the constant measurements of the leaves (c. 290×450 mm.) and the quality of the paper, rather coarse and yellowish, which has become brownish grey with the passage of time. The technique is also constant, black chalk or pencil heightened with white chalk; a few leaves are in red chalk. One feature of the drawings, and the proof that they were made from life, is that they are accompanied by notes on colours and measurements made by the painter, in a round hand with abbreviations which are sometimes difficult to decipher.

There is some doubt as to the number of drawings in the original collection. Lazari lists 140 leaves (in fact 139, with many versos) which he attributes with certainty to Pietro Longhi, evidently on information derived from inventory papers which are now lost. These are the drawings numbered in the inventory from 435 to 574. Then Lazari mentions 'some leaves with drawings in pen and pencil by Alessandro Longhi'; these are probably the drawings inventoried as nos. 575 to 584. Recent research has enabled a further six leaves to be attributed to Pietro and one to those probably by Alessandro, as will be seen in the catalogue which follows.

The present catalogue maintains the distinction made by Lazari, which corresponds substantially with the stylistic characteristics of the respective artists. Among those attributed to Alessandro are the *Portrait of Francesco Morosini*, no. 581 (Plate 430) and *A Poet reciting his Verses*, no. 577 (Plate 278a, p. 95), which recent scholarship attributes to Alessandro rather than to Pietro. The drawing of the *Wineshop at the Sign of the Lion of St Mark's*, no. 584 (Plate 435), appears to bear the date 1790, five years after the death of Pietro, which thus provides another factor for dating (cf. Pignatti, 1964, pp. 47-8, nos. 56 and 57; *Id.*, 1965, p. 210).

*Literature*: Lazari, 1859, 26-8. Other works are cited in the entries of the relevant paintings.

DOCTOR FEELING A PATIENT'S PULSE (no. 435)       *Plate 65*
Black and white chalk on brownish paper, 270×240 mm.
Study for *The Sick Lady*, Venice (Pl. 66).

THE COFFEE-HOUSE (no. 436 recto)       *Plate 316*
Black and white chalk on brownish paper, 281×444 mm.

COFFEE-HOUSE KEEPER, AND CROCKERY (no. 436 verso)
*Plate 317*
Black and white chalk on brownish paper, 267×425 mm.
Study for *The Lady's Country Villa* (lost work).

TWO YOUNG MEN IN DOMINOES; FIGURE SEEN FROM BEHIND (no. 437)       *Plate 45*
Black and white chalk on brownish paper, 293×438 mm.

PAINTER AT AN EASEL (no. 438)       *Plate 195*
Black and white chalk on brownish paper, 284×447 mm.
Study for *The Painter in his Studio*, Stanford (Pl. 193).

MAN IN A DOMINO; STUDY OF DRAPERY (no. 439)
*Plate 46*
Black and white chalk on brownish paper, 290×347 mm.
Study for *The Painter in his Studio*, Venice (Pl. 47).

SEATED GENTLEMAN (no. 440)       *Plate 121*
Black and white chalk on brownish paper, 290×390 mm.
Study for *A Patrician Family*, Venice (Pl. 123).

THE HAIRDRESSER (no. 441 recto)       *Plate 204*
Black and white chalk on brownish paper, 277×435 mm.
Study for *The Hairdresser*, Venice (Pl. 206).

TWO GENTLEMEN IN CLOAKS (no. 441 verso)       *Plate 315*
Black and white chalk on brownish paper, 277×435 mm.

TWO SEATED GENTLEMEN IN DOMINOES (no. 442)
*Plate 318*
Black and white chalk on brownish paper, 292×441 mm.

GUITAR PLAYER (no. 443)       *Plate 127*
Black and white chalk on brownish paper, 280×198 mm.
Study for *The Family Concert*, Venice (Pl. 128).

ACCOUNTANT AT A BENCH; SERVANT WITH A BOWL (no. 444)       *Plate 319*
Black and white chalk on brownish paper, 280×401 mm.

SEATED LADY AT A TABLE (no. 445)       *Plate 185*
Black and white chalk on brownish paper, 318×270 mm.
Study for *In the Estuary Gardens*, Venice (Pl. 186).

TWO FRIARS (no. 446 recto)       *Plate 320*
Black and white chalk on brownish paper, 278×412 mm.

BRACKET; ORNAMENTS; STUDIES OF HANDS (no. 446 verso)       *Plate 321*
Black and white chalk on brownish paper, 278×422 mm.

VIOLIN PLAYER; CAGE (no. 447)       *Plate 52*
Black and white chalk on brownish paper, 288×320 mm.
Study for *The Music Lesson*, San Francisco (Pl. 54).

DRAPERY OF WOMAN'S CLOTHES (no. 448)       *Plate 55*
Black and white chalk on brownish paper, 284×420 mm.
Study for *The Tickle*, whereabouts unknown (Pl. 53).

LADY IN A CRINOLINE; STUDIES OF HAIR (no. 449)
*Plate 136*
Black and white chalk on brownish paper, 288×317 mm.
Study for *The Lady's Toilet*, Chicago (Pl. 137).

THREE STUDIES OF A MAIDSERVANT (no. 450 recto)
*Plate 125*
Black and white chalk on brownish paper, 273×405 mm.
Study for *The Geography Lesson*, Venice (Pl. 126).

SEATED GENTLEMAN, WITH AN EYEGLASS (no. 450 verso)       *Plate 124*
Black and white chalk on brownish paper, 288×430 mm.
Study for *The Geography Lesson*, Venice (Pl. 126).

SEATED NURSE WITH THREE CHILDREN; WOMAN AT A TABLE (no. 451)   *Plate 322*
Black and white chalk on brownish paper, 296×430 mm.

GENTLEMAN OFFERING MONEY; OLD WOMAN (no. 452)   *Plate 101*
Black and white chalk on brownish paper, 295×265 mm.
Study for *The Seduction*, Milan (Pl. 102).

LAWYER AT A TABLE (no. 453)   *Plate 323*
Black and white chalk on brownish paper, 290×385 mm.

LADY AND GENTLEMAN ON A DIVAN (no. 454)   *Plate 324*
Black and white chalk on buff paper, 290×432 mm.

GUITAR PLAYER; FACE AND FEET OF A WOMAN (no. 455)   *Plate 327*
Black and white chalk on brownish paper, 346×270 mm.

MAIDSERVANT WITH TWO PAILS OF WATER (no. 456)   *Plate 24*
Black and white chalk on brownish paper, 415×285 mm.
Study for *The Washerwomen*, Zoppola (Pl. 25).

TWO SEATED WOMEN, MENDING (no. 457 recto)   *Plate 325*
Black and white chalk on grey paper, 280×422 mm.

HEAD OF A PUTTO; HEAD OF A CHILD (no. 457 verso)   *Plate 326*
Black and white chalk on brownish paper, 262×403 mm.

SEATED NOBLEMAN; TWO BOATMEN (no. 458)   *Plate 328*
Black and white chalk on brownish paper, 282×441 mm.

PAINTER SHOWING A PICTURE (no. 459)   *Plate 331*
Black and white chalk on brownish paper, 280×215 mm.

STABLE LAD, YOUNG RIDER AND GROOM WITH HORSE (no. 460)   *Plate 330*
Black and white chalk on brownish paper, 278×416 mm.

FIGURE IN A DOMINO; YOUNG HORSEMAN (no. 461)   *Plate 329*
Black and white chalk on brownish paper, 280×422 mm.

GENTLEMAN IN BED (no. 462 recto)   *Plate 61*
Black and white chalk on brownish paper, 290×445 mm.
Study for *The Gentleman's Awakening*, Windsor (Pl. 57).

WOMAN AT HER HUSBAND'S BEDSIDE (no. 462 verso)   *Plate 56*
Black and white chalk on brownish paper, 271×418 mm.
Study for *The Gentleman's Awakening*, Windsor (Pl. 57).

GENTLEMAN LEANING ON A STOOL (no. 463)   *Plate 122*
Black and white chalk on brownish paper, 218×222 mm.
Study for *A Patrician Family*, Venice (Pl. 123).

LADY AT A TABLE; STUDIES OF FURNISHINGS (no. 464)   *Plate 332*
Black and white chalk on brownish paper, 450×295 mm.

LADY WITH A SKEIN-WINDER (no. 465)   *Plate 471*
Black and white chalk on brownish paper, 280×385 mm.
Study for *The Declaration*, whereabouts unknown (attributed to Pietro Longhi) (Pl. 472).

THREE PEASANTS DRINKING (no. 466)   *Plate 246*
Black and white chalk on brownish paper, 300×405 mm.
Study for *Peasants at an Inn*, Venice (Pl. 244).

TWO SEATED PEASANTS EATING (no. 467)   *Plate 243*
Black and white chalk on brownish paper, 285×429 mm.
Study for *Peasants at an Inn*, Venice (Pl. 244).

A PEASANT (no. 468)   *Plate 247*
Black and white chalk on brownish paper, 420×305 mm.
Study for *Peasants at an Inn*, Venice (Pl. 244).

TWO PEASANTS EATING (no. 469)   *Plate 245*
Black and white chalk on brownish paper, 205×305 mm.
Study for *Peasants at an Inn*, Venice (Pl. 244).

STUDIES OF HANDS AND LEGS; DRAPERY (no. 470)   *Plate 50*
Black and white chalk on brownish paper, 292×435 mm.
Study for *The Visit to the Library*, Worcester (Mass.) (Pl. 51).

TWO MEN WITH BOWLS (no. 471)   *Plate 248*
Black and white chalk on brownish paper, 428×298 mm.
Study for *Peasants at an Inn*, Venice (Pl. 244).

WOMAN SINGING; MAN IN A CLOAK (no. 472)   *Plate 333*
Black and white chalk on brownish paper, 300×389 mm.

LADY IN A CRINOLINE (no. 473)   *Plate 334*
Black and white chalk on brownish paper, 300×275 mm.

TWO LACEMAKERS (no. 474)   *Plate 99*
Black and white chalk on brownish paper, 288×420 mm.
Study for *The Temptation*, Hartford (Conn.) (Pl. 100).

SHOOTING IN THE LAGOON (no. 475)   *Plate 181*
Black and white chalk on buff paper, 292×450 mm.
Study for *Shooting in the Lagoon*, Venice (Pl. 180).

SHOOTING IN THE LAGOON (no. 476)   *Plate 183*
Black and white chalk on brownish paper, 288×448 mm.
Study for *Shooting in the Lagoon*, London (Pl. 182).

SHOOTING IN THE VALLEY (no. 477)   *Plate 240*
Black and white chalk on brownish paper, 300×437 mm.
Study for *Shooting position in a Barrel*, Venice (Pl. 241).

TWO STUDIES OF FIGURES IN A CONFESSIONAL (no. 478 recto)   *Plate 335*
Black and white chalk on brownish paper, 277×396 mm.

TABLE WITH A COVER; WINDOW WITH A CURTAIN (no. 478 verso)   *Plate 336*
Black and white chalk on brownish paper, 300×425 mm.

GIRL PREPARING A SALAD (no. 479)      *Plate 82*
Black and white chalk on brownish paper, 282×300 mm.
Study for *Milord's Salad*, Milan (Pl. 83).

GIRL LEANING ON A STOOL; DRAPERY (no. 480)    *Plate 337*
Black and white chalk on brownish paper, 279×389 mm.

GENTLEMAN IN BED (no. 481)      *Plate 60*
Black and white chalk on brownish paper, 290×435 mm.
Study for *The Gentleman's Awakening*, Windsor (Pl. 57).

GENTLEMAN IN BED, AND A LADY (no. 482)    *Plate 60*
Black and white chalk on brownish paper, 291×369 mm.
Study for *The Gentleman's Awakening*, Windsor (Pl. 57).

NURSE WITH A CHILD; FRAME (no. 483)    *Plate 219*
Black and white chalk on buff paper, 295×442 mm.
Study for *Family Group*, Segromigno Monte (Pl. 221).

SEATED MAN WEARING A DOMINO (no. 484)   *Plate 338*
Black and white chalk on brownish paper, 280×355 mm.

PEASANT GIRL DANCING; OUTLINE OF A LADY (no. 485)
     *Plate 339*
Black and white chalk on grey paper, 268×333 mm.

MAN IN PROFILE; A PEASANT WOMAN (no. 486 recto)
     *Plate 340*
Black and white chalk on brownish paper, 293×445 mm.

HEAD OF AN OLD MAN (no. 486 verso)    *Plate 341*
Black and white chalk on brownish paper, 422×270 mm.

LADY IN A CRINOLINE (no. 487 recto)    *Plate 43*
Black and white chalk on brownish paper, 265×296 mm.
Study for *The Introduction*, Paris (Pl. 44).

OLD MAN SEATED (no. 487 verso)    *Plate 131*
Black and white chalk on brownish paper, 280×296 mm.
Study for *A Meal at Home*, Providence (Rh. I.) (Pl. 132).

TWO CHILDREN, AT A TABLE AND IN A LITTLE CHAIR
(no. 488)      *Plate 217*
Black and white chalk on brownish paper, 280×440 mm.
Study for *The Albrizzi Family*, Venice (Pl. 218).

LADY AND HUNTERS (no. 489)    *Plate 146*
Black and white chalk on brownish paper, 290×395 mm.
Study for *Shooting Hares*, Venice (Pl. 147).

MANSERVANT WITH A TRAY; MAID WITH A TRAY (no.
490)      *Plate 79*
Black and white chalk on brownish grey paper, 270×316 mm.
Study for *The Procuratore pays a Call*, London (Pl. 80).

GENTLEMAN MAKING A BOW (no. 491 recto)   *Plate 189*
Black and white chalk on brownish paper, 278×300 mm.
Study for *The Card-Players*, London (Pl. 190).

STUDY OF A NUDE (no. 491 verso)    *Plate 342*
Black and white chalk on brownish paper, 270×290 mm.

GENTLEMAN WITH TWO CLOAKS; SCALES (no. 492)
     *Plate 110*
Black and white chalk on brownish paper, 278×353 mm.
Study for *The Fortune-Teller*, Venice (Pl. 109).

MEETING OF TWO OLD LADIES (no. 493)   *Plate 344*
Black and white chalk on brownish paper, 275×385 mm.

A FRIAR (no. 494)      *Plate 207*
Black and white chalk on brownish paper, 290×251 mm.
Study for *A Visit from a Friar*, Venice (Pl. 208).

TWO MAIDSERVANTS (no. 495)    *Plate 343*
Black and white chalk on brownish paper, 287×282 mm.

STUDIES OF A GENTLEMAN'S CUTAWAY COAT (no. 496)
     *Plate 345*
Pencil and white chalk on buff paper, 295×425 mm.

MAN SELLING DOUGHNUTS (no. 497)    *Plate 346*
Black and white chalk on brownish paper, 283×229 mm.

TWO GENTLEMEN WEARING DRESSING-GOWNS (no.
498)      *Plate 347*
Black and white chalk on brownish paper, 295×350 mm.

STUDY OF AN ARM HOLDING A JUG; TABLE COVER
(no. 499)      *Plate 348*
Black and white chalk on grey blue paper, 210×332 mm.

YOUNG CLERIC (no. 500 recto)    *Plate 349*
Black and white chalk on buff paper, 272×210 mm.

STUDY OF CLERICAL GARMENTS (no. 500 verso)   *Plate 350*
Black and white chalk on buff paper, 259×195 mm.

SERVANT WITH A TRAY (no. 501)    *Plate 351*
Pencil and white chalk, 195×140 mm.

THREE FIGURES WITH CANDLES (no. 502 recto)   *Plate 352*
Black and white chalk on grey blue paper, 241×356 mm.

STUDIES OF A MAN DRINKING (no. 502 verso)   *Plate 36*
Black and white chalk on blue grey paper, 256×370 mm.
Study for *The Drunkard*, Biella, (Pl. 35).

TWO GENTLEMEN AND A LADY STANDING; A SEATED
GENTLEMAN (no. 503 recto)    *Plate 353*
Black and white chalk on buff paper, 282×422 mm.

SEATED LADY (no. 503 verso)    *Plate 354*
Black and white chalk on buff paper, 403×270 mm.

TWO YOUNG GIRLS (no. 504)    *Plate 69*
Black and white chalk on brownish paper, 264×280 mm.
Study for *A Family Group*, London (Pl. 70).

FRIAR; STUDY OF DRAPERY (no. 505)    *Plate 355*
Black and white chalk on brownish paper, 284×323 mm.

PRIEST AT A WRITING DESK (no. 506) *Plate 356*
Black and white chalk on buff paper, 185×273 mm.

BABY IN A LITTLE CHAIR; TWO HEADS OF BOYS; LADY WITH A FAN (no. 507) *Plate 357*
Black and white chalk on brownish paper, 227×345 mm.

LADY WALKING (no. 508) *Plate 358*
Black and white chalk on brownish paper, 285×420 mm.

MANSERVANT WITH A TRAY (no. 509) *Plate 360*
Black and white chalk on brownish paper, 272×200 mm.

GIRL FEEDING A CANARY (no. 510) *Plate 359*
Black and white chalk on buff paper, 285×338 mm.

SCREEN AND WOODEN CHAIR (no. 511 recto) *Plate 361*
Black and white chalk, on brownish paper, 275×402 mm.

SHEPHERD GIRL (no. 511 verso) *Plate 9*
Black and white chalk on brownish paper, 256×383 mm.
Study for the *Shepherd Girl with a Flower*, Bassano (Pl. 10).

GENTLEMAN AT A WRITING DESK (no. 512 recto) *Plate 362*
Black and white chalk on brownish paper, 276×404 mm.

TWO GENTLEMEN WITH ARMS RAISED (no. 512 verso) *Plate 363*
Black and white chalk on brownish paper, 283×416 mm.

LADY AND SPINET (no. 513 recto) *Plate 364*
Black and white chalk on brownish paper, 281×411 mm.

STUDIES OF THE HEAD AND BUST OF A GENTLEMAN (no. 513 verso) *Plate 365*
Black and white chalk on brownish paper, 268×395 mm.

PRIEST; STUDIES OF DRAPERY (no. 514 recto) *Plate 366*
Black and white chalk on buff paper, 371×238 mm.

SKETCHES OF GIANTS (no. 514 verso) *Plate 4*
Black and white chalk on buff paper, 223×355 mm.
Study for the *Fall of the Giants*, Venice (Plates 3, 5, 6).

SEATED SHEPHERD BOY (no. 515 recto) *Plate 8*
Black and red chalk on brownish paper, 300×424 mm.
Study for the *Shepherd Boy, Seated* Bassano (Pl. 7).

THE TEMPTATIONS OF ST ANTHONY (no. 515 verso) *Plate 367*
Black and white chalk, grey wash on brownish paper, 408×278 mm.

MANSERVANT AT A DOOR; A CHAIR (no. 516 recto) *Plate 368*
Black and white chalk on brownish paper, 265×207 mm.

HANDS AND DRAPERY (no. 516 verso) *Plate 369*
Black and white chalk on brownish paper, 197×255 mm.

FRIAR WITH A TRAY; GENTLEMAN (no. 517 recto) *Plate 370*
Black and white chalk on brownish paper, 271×414 mm.

SEATED MAN (no. 517 verso) *Plate 371*
Black and white chalk on brownish paper, 254×390 mm.

MAIDSERVANT; CHEST OF DRAWERS (no. 518 recto) *Plate 372*
Black and white chalk on brownish paper, 275×422 mm.

CONSOLE, CLOCK AND CURTAIN DRAPERY (no. 518 verso) *Plate 373*
Black and white chalk on brownish paper, 400×255 mm.

GENTLEMAN IN A CLOAK WITH A BOY; MAN IN A CLOAK (no. 519) *Plate 374*
Black and white chalk on brownish paper, 285×360 mm.

PEASANT'S KITCHEN UTENSILS (no. 520) *Plate 375*
Black and white chalk on brownish paper, 278×417 mm.

SLEEPING GIRL; HUNTER (no. 521) *Plate 98*
Black and white chalk on brownish paper, 300×437 mm.
Study for *The Hunter*, Milan (Pl. 97).

MAIDSERVANT WITH A STOOL (no. 522) *Plate 376*
Black and white chalk on brownish paper, 238×270 mm.

PEASANT GIRL BROACHING A CASK OF WINE (no. 523) *Plate 30*
Black and white chalk on buff paper, 438×292 mm.
Study for *The Drunkards*, Zoppola (Pl. 31).

A DWARF WOMAN (no. 524) *Plate 108*
Black and white chalk on brownish paper, 200×281 mm.
Study for *The Tooth-Drawer*, Milan (Pl. 107).

PEASANT SITTING AT A TABLE; DRAPERY (no. 525) *Plate 28*
Black and white chalk on brownish paper, 291×448 mm.
Study for *A Girl spinning*, Zoppola (Pl. 27).

THREE PEASANTS; BOTTLES (no. 526) *Plate 29*
Black and white chalk on brownish paper, 450×290 mm.

SEATED MAN SEWING (no. 527) *Plate 377*
Black and white chalk on brownish paper, 305×231 mm.

CELLARER; YOUTH WITH ONE ARM RAISED (no. 528) *Plate 380*
Black and white chalk on brownish paper, 290×429 mm.

LADY KNEELING (no. 529 recto) *Plate 378*
Black and white chalk on brownish paper, 290×443 mm.

TWO STUDIES OF A WOMAN WITH A HEAD SHAWL (no. 529 verso) *Plate 379*
Black and white chalk on brownish paper, 264×416 mm.

YOUNG MAN ON A HORSE WITH A RIDING MASTER (no. 530) *Plate 381*
Black and white chalk on brownish paper, 290×411 mm.

BOATMAN WITH A BASKET; MANSERVANT WITH A BOX (no. 531) *Plate 382*
Black and white chalk on brownish paper, 286×357 mm.

TWO LADIES; ONE SEATED AND ONE STANDING (no. 532) *Plate 383*
Black and white chalk on brownish paper, 278×426 mm.

NURSE AND CHILD; CHILD STANDING (no. 533) *Plate 385*
Black and white chalk on brownish paper, 283×428 mm.

FEMALE FIGURE; CHAIR AND STOOL (no. 534) *Plate 115*
Black and white chalk on brownish paper, 282×401 mm.
Study for *The Friar's Sermon*, Bergamo (Pl. 114).

CAGE AND PARROT (no. 535) *Plate 384*
Black and white chalk on buff paper, 285×426 mm.

HUNTER SMOKING A PIPE (no. 536) *Plate 237*
Black and white chalk on brownish paper, 298×269 mm.
Study for *The Hunters draw Lots*, Venice (Pl. 238).

THREE STUDIES OF A CUTAWAY COAT (no. 537) *Plate 386*
Black and white chalk on brownish paper, 278×402 mm.

PRIEST IN AN ARMCHAIR (no. 538) *Plate 223*
Black and white chalk on brownish paper, 265×245 mm.
Study for *The Schoolboy's Punishment*, Genoa (Pl. 224).

NURSE WITH A CHILD ON HER ARM (no. 539) *Plate 205*
Black and white chalk on brownish paper, 300×223 mm.
Study for *The Hairdresser*, Venice (Pl. 207).

GENTLEMAN IN BED, AND A LADY (no. 540 recto) *Plate 59*
Black and white chalk on brownish paper, 292×432 mm.
Study for *The Gentleman's Awakening*, Windsor (Pl. 59).

THREE STUDIES OF STOOLS (no. 540 verso) *Plate 63*
Black and white chalk on brownish paper, 278×408 mm.
Study for *Blind Man's Buff*, Windsor (Pl. 62).

GENTLEMAN WITH A CLOAK (no. 541 recto) *Plate 387*
Black and white chalk on brownish paper, 275×425 mm.

FEMALE DRAPERY; TWO HANDS HOLDING A CUP (no. 541 verso) *Plate 388*
Black and white chalk on brownish paper, 260×402 mm.

DANCING MASTER; STUDIES OF HANDS (no. 542) *Plate 40*
Black and white chalk on brownish paper, 287×445 mm.
Study for *The Dancing Lesson*, Venice (Pl. 41).

BED (no. 543 - 542 verso) *Plate 389*
Black and white chalk on brownish paper, 271×425 mm.

LADY AT A SPINET (no. 544 recto) *Plate 391*
Black and white chalk on brownish paper, 264×425 mm.

BENCH WITH A CLOAK (no. 544 verso) *Plate 392*
Black and white chalk on brownish paper, 290×450 mm.

GENTLEMAN WITH A CLOAK (no. 545) *Plate 81*
Black and white chalk on brownish paper, 289×193 mm.
Study for *Milord's Salad*, Milan (Pl. 83).

MAIDSERVANT ATTENDING AN INVALID (no. 546) *Plate 390*
Black and white chalk on brownish paper, 284×351 mm.

LADY STANDING, AND STUDIES OF HAIR (no. 547 recto) *Plate 393*
Black and white chalk on brownish paper, 264×393 mm.

STUDY OF DRAPERY AND A PAINTING (no. 547 verso) *Plate 77*
Black and white chalk on brownish paper, 280×412 mm.
Study for *A Lady receives Visitors*, New York (Pl. 76).

SERVANT WITH A TRAY (no. 548) *Plate 394*
Black and white chalk on brownish paper, 301×160 mm.

SAVOYARD JUGGLER WITH A MARMOSET (no. 549) *Plate 395*
Black and white chalk on brownish paper, 231×268 mm.

TWO PEASANTS STANDING WITH A WHEELBARROW (no. 550) *Plate 396*
Black and white chalk on brownish paper, 290×443 mm.

SPINET PLAYER (no. 551 recto) *Plate 397*
Black and white chalk on brownish paper, 430×284 mm.

SEATED MAN (no. 551 verso) *Plate 398*
Black and white chalk on brownish paper, 270×410 mm.

LADY IN A CRINOLINE; MAID WITH A TRAY (no. 552) *Plate 399*
Black and white chalk on brownish paper, 286×414 mm.

LADY WITH A BOOK; ARTIST WITH A PENCIL (no. 553) *Plate 188*
Black and white chalk on brownish paper, 277×410 mm.
Study for *Coffee-Time*, London (Pl. 187).

MANSERVANT WEARING A CAP (no. 554 recto) *Plate 400*
Black and white chalk on brownish paper, 270×409 mm.

TABLE WITH A READING STAND (no. 554 verso) *Plate 401*
Black and white chalk on brownish paper, 256×388 mm.

GENTLEMAN IN A DOMINO (no. 555 recto) *Plate 202*
Black and white chalk on brownish paper, 275×352 mm.
Study for *A Visit from a Domino*, Venice (Pl. 203).

SKETCH FOR AN ASSUMPTION OF THE VIRGIN (?) (no. 555 verso) *Plate 402*
Black and white chalk on brownish paper, 342×251 mm.

GENTLEMAN; SERVANT WITH A TRAY (no. 556) *Plate 403*
Black and white chalk on brownish paper, 288×388 mm.

PEASANT WITH A MANDOLINE (no. 557) *Plate 14*
Black and white chalk on brownish paper, 409×277 mm.
Study for *A Girl Spinning*, Venice (Pl. 15).

SEATED PEASANT WOMAN; HEAD OF A PEASANT (no. 558)                                    *Plate 404*

Black and white chalk on brownish paper, 280×418 mm.

CARD-PLAYER (no. 559)                                   *Plate 273*

Black and white chalk on brownish parer, 275×270 mm.
Study for *The Interrupted Game of Cards*, Bergamo (Pl. 272).

TWO MAIDSERVANTS; A CHAIR WITH CLOTHES (no. 560)                                                *Plate 405*

Black and white chalk on brownish paper, 280×402 mm.

LADY RISING (no. 561)                                  *Plate 476*

Black and white chalk on buff paper, 281×352 mm.
Study for *The Lady's Awakening*, Segromigno Monte, attributed to Pietro Longhi (Pl. 473).

DRAPING OF A SKIRT (no. 562)                           *Plate 477*

Black and white chalk on buff paper, 274×272 mm.
Study for *The Lady's Awakening*, Segromigno Monte, attributed to Pietro Longhi (Pl. 473).

SEATED GENTLEMAN READING (no. 563)                     *Plate 475*

Black and white chalk on buff paper, 276×384 mm.
Study for *The Lady's Awakening*, Segromigno Monte, attributed to Pietro Longhi (Pl. 473).

GIRL DANCING (no. 564 recto)                           *Plate 277*

Black and white chalk on brownish paper, 257×408 mm.
Study for the *Rustic Dance*, whereabouts unknown (Pl. 276).

FIGURE OF A MAN STANDING (no. 564 verso)     *Plate 406*

Black and white chalk on brownish paper, 391×240 mm.

STUDY OF HANDS HOLDING A PRAYERBOOK AND A CLOSED FAN; CLASPED HANDS (no. 565 recto)     *Plate 155*

Black and white chalk on brownish paper, 281×415 mm.
Study for *Confession*, Florence (Pl. 156).

PEASANT DRINKING (no. 565 verso)                       *Plate 407*

Black and white chalk on brownish paper, 260×395 mm.

MANSERVANT OFFERING A CHAIR TO A LADY (no. 566)
                                                       *Plate 408*

Black and white chalk on brownish paper, 280×365 mm.

FEMALE FIGURES; CURTAIN (no. 567)                      *Plate 409*

Black and white chalk on brownish paper, 238×398 mm.

COOKING-POT SUSPENDED ON A CHAIN (no. 568) *Plate 411*

Black and white chalk on brownish paper, 281×313 mm.

EMBROIDERESSES (no. 569)                               *Plate 134*

Black, red and white chalk on buff paper, 228×376 mm.
Study for *The Embroidery Workroom*, London (Pl. 135).

LADY AND GENTLEMAN IN DOMINOES; LADY WALKING (no. 570)                                          *Plate 410*

Black and white chalk on brownish paper, 276×420 mm.

GIRL SPINNING (no. 571)                                *Plate 249*

Black and white chalk on brownish paper, 289×283 mm.
Study for *A Girl spinning*, Boston (Mass.) (Pl. 251).

OLD WOMAN READING; GENTLEMAN (no. 572)    *Plate 470*

Black and white chalk on brownish paper, 261×409 mm.
Study for *The Declaration*, whereabouts unknown, (Pl. 469), attributed to Pietro Longhi.

GENTLEMAN LEANING ON A CHAIR (no. 573)    *Plate 412*

Black and white chalk on brownish paper, 278×390 mm.

TWO STUDIES OF A SENATOR (no. 574)                     *Plate 140*

Black and white chalk on brownish paper, 268×384 mm.
Study for *The Doge Pietro Grimani giving Audience*, Venice (Pl. 139).

**VENICE, Museo Correr**

*OTHER DRAWINGS*

TURKEY AND TWO DUCKS (no. 905)                         *Plate 413*

Black chalk on brownish paper, 176×110 mm.

PEASANT (no. 6058)                                     *Plate 111*

Black chalk on brownish paper, 290×176 mm.
Study for *The Fortune-Teller*, Venice (Pl. 109).

SEATED YOUNG MAN APPLYING A SEAL (no. 6059)
                                                       *Plate 414*

Black and white chalk on brownish paper, 252×147 mm.

GENTLEMAN SMOKING IN AN ARMCHAIR (no. 6060)
                                                       *Plate 415*

Black and white chalk on brownish paper, 242×172 mm.

SEATED GENTLEMAN (no. 6061)                            *Plate 416*

Black and white chalk on brownish paper, 234×185 mm.

SEATED GENTLEMAN; STUDY OF A LEFT HAND (no. 6062)                                               *Plate 417*

Black and white chalk on brownish paper, 303×199 mm.

# DRAWINGS OF UNCERTAIN ATTRIBUTION

**ANN ARBOR (Mich.), University of Michigan**
TWO FIGURES                                    *Plate 418*
French in style, in the manner of Pater.

**CAMBRIDGE (Mass.), Fogg Art Museum**
FIGURE OF AN ABBÉ (no. 1932.318)              *Plate 419*
Pencil and white chalk on blue grey paper, 292×216 mm.
Probably by Alessandro Longhi, as suggested by Mongan and
Sachs; perhaps a study for *The Pisani Family* (Pl. 481).
*Literature:* Mongan and Sachs, 1946, no. 326.

**MILAN, Alessandro Orsi Collection**
STUDIES OF DRAPERY                             *Plate 420*
Red chalk on grey paper, 445×320 mm.
The line is too delicate for this to be attributed with conviction
to Longhi; perhaps by Piazzetta. The technique is also unusual.
*Literature:* Griseri, 1966, 188.

**OXFORD, Ashmolean Museum**
THREE FIGURES OF GENTLEMEN (no. 1022)         *Plate 421*
Pencil and white chalk on buff paper, 213×255 mm.
Too flowing and detailed to be by Longhi; more probably by
Panini.
*Literature:* Parker, 1956, II, no. 1022.

**TURIN, Private collection**
PORTRAIT OF A HUNTER
Black chalk, 180×145 mm.
Unlike Longhi's usual manner, French in taste.
*Literature:* Griseri, 1966, 188.

**TURIN, Private collection**
STUDIES FOR A HARPIST
Black chalk, pen and wash on blue paper, 320×240 mm.
Too plastic for Longhi: more probably by Trevisani.
*Literature:* Griseri, 1966, 188.

**VENICE, Museo Correr**
TWO FIGURES IN ANCIENT DRESS (no. 575 recto)   *Plate 422*
Pencil and brown wash on buff paper, 435×280 mm.
*Literature:* Lazari, 1859, 26-8 (as for all drawings in the Museo
Correr to no. 574).

STUDY OF A FOREARM AND OF A FEMALE HEAD (no.
575 verso)                                     *Plate 423*
Pencil on brownish paper, 260×417 mm.

MALE NUDE (no. 576 recto)                       *Plate 424*
Black and white chalk on brownish paper, 432×286 mm.

FEMALE HEAD INCLINED TO THE RIGHT (no. 576 verso)
                                               *Plate 425*
Black and white chalk on brownish paper, 407×265 mm.

A POET RECITING HIS VERSES (no. 577)            *Fig. 28*
Pencil, pen and brown ink and brown wash, 345×417 mm.
Published by Byam Shaw and always considered to be by Ales-
sandro. According to Watson, a sketch for the painting at Port
Sunlight which the present author attributes to Pietro Longhi
(Pl. 278).
*Literature:* Byam Shaw, 1933, 60; Watson, 1964, 17; Pignatti, 1965,
210.

STUDY OF TWO FEMALE HEADS (no. 578 recto)      *Plate 426*
Black and white chalk on brownish paper, 278×435 mm.

HEAD OF A YOUNG WOMAN; ARM RAISED (no. 578 verso)
                                               *Plate 427*
Black and white chalk on brownish paper, 412×262 mm.

A CLERIC WEARING A CAP (no. 579)                *Plate 428*
Black and white chalk on brownish paper, 420×297 mm.

DOGE WITH HIS RIGHT ARM RAISED (no. 580)        *Plate 429*
Black and white chalk on brownish paper, 373×273 mm.

PORTRAIT OF FRANCESCO MOROSINI (no. 581)    *Plate 430*
Black and white chalk on grey paper, 269×205 mm.
*Literature:* Pignatti, 1964, no. 17.

PORTRAIT OF AN OLD MAN IN A FUR HAT (no. 582)
*Plate 431*
Pencil and red chalk on brownish paper, 303×205 mm.

PORTRAIT OF A BALDING OLD WOMAN (no. 583 recto)
*Plate 432*
Black and white chalk on brownish paper, 241×183 mm.

HEAD OF A YOUNG MAN (no. 583 verso)    *Plate 433*
Black and white chalk on brownish paper, 241×183 mm.

THE WINE SHOP AT THE SIGN OF THE LION OF ST MARK (no. 584)    *Plate 435*
Black and white chalk on buff paper, 275×422 mm.
It appears to be dated 1790 top left.
*Literature:* Pignatti, 1964, no. 58.

HEAD OF A YOUNG WOMAN (no. 1633)    *Plate 434*
Black and white chalk on brownish paper, 275×200 mm.

**VIENNA, Albertina**
PORTRAIT OF A GENTLEMAN (no. 394)    *Plate 436*
Black and white chalk on light brown paper, 294×194 mm.
Probably by Alessandro Longhi, as the Catalogue to the collection suggests.
*Literature:* Stix, 1926, no. 394.

# PAINTINGS OF UNCERTAIN ATTRIBUTION

**AMIENS, Musée de Picardie**

PORTRAIT OF A SENATOR                    *Plate 486*

Oil on canvas, 41×26 cm.

*Collection:* Lavallard (1890).

On the back is an inscription identifying the portrait as of 'Sebastian Foscar(ini?), knight and procuratore'. A Sebastian Foscarini dei Carmini, born in 1717, was Ambassador to Spain and Vienna, and was still alive in 1767. There is no evidence to support the attribution, which is dubious. In spite of the difference in size, the work has however some affinity with the portrait at Udine (Pl. 230) of 1764. This work was exhibited as by Longhi in the *De Tiepolo à Goya* Exhibition at Bordeaux, 1956, no. 27.

*Literature: Donation des frères Lavallard*, 1899.

**AMSTERDAM, Rijksmuseum**

THE RIDOTTO                              *Plate 485*

Oil on canvas, 85×108.5 cm.

From the von Rath bequest, this painting is attributed to Pietro Longhi in the Museum catalogue. Moschini attributes it to the Master of the Ridotto, who is given this title as the author of four large canvases in Ca' Rezzonico. It is the work of an imitator of Longhi who elongates the figures in a particular way, and uses a bright, full-bodied palette in a manner between that of Carlevaris and that of Fontebasso.

*Literature: Rijksmuseum Catalogue*, 1953 (no. 1481-B1) Moschini, 1956, 54; Pallucchini, 1960, 190.

**BADEN-SALEM, Collection of the Grand Dukes of Bavaria**

THE CONVENT PARLOUR                      *Plate 455*

Attributed to Longhi by Ravà, this work is companion to *The Ridotto* (Pl. 454) and may perhaps be attributed to De Gobbis.

*Literature:* Ravà, 1909, 41.

**BADEN-SALEM, Collection of the Grand Dukes of Bavaria**

THE RIDOTTO                              *Plate 454*

Attributed to Longhi by Ravà, it is companion to *The Convent Parlour* (Pl. 455) in the same collection. Of doubtful authenticity, in many respects it suggests comparison with works attributed to De Gobbis.

*Literature:* Ravà, 1909, 41.

**BASLE, Kunstmuseum**

FIGURE

Attributed to Longhi by Brosch, it is now considered to be the work of P.L. Ghezzi.

*Literature:* Brosch, 1929, 373.

**BELLUNO, Museo Civico**

THE DOGE'S '*BALOTIN*'                   *Plate 484*

Oil on canvas, 131×72.5 cm.

Attributed to Pietro Longhi, on its presentation to the Museum by Giampiccoli, and accepted as his by Fogolari and Fiocco, the painting was attributed instead to Alessandro Longhi by Pevsner, and following him by all modern critics. Recently Valcanover, while supervising restoration work, has discovered that it is part of a larger work and that round the portrait of the '*Balotin*' are traces of other figures which completed the painting. The '*Balotin*' was a boy responsible for drawing lots to decide voters in the preliminaries to the election of a doge. Evidently this was a far larger painting, with life-size figures of adults, and the boy was only a small part of it. The original work was identified by Valcanover as the second large canvas painted for the Pisani family by Alessandro Longhi, who mentions it in his *Vita* of 1761. The so-called '*Balotin*' was identified as the young Ermolao II Pisani, and the date of the painting, on the basis of the probable ages of the persons portrayed, was fixed as the last months of 1758, together with that of another painting now in the collection of the Bentivogli heirs at Venice (Pl. 481-3). Any possibility of attributing this work to Pietro Longhi must therefore by eliminated.

*Literature:* Fogolari, 1910, 285; Fiocco, 1929, 527; Pevsner, 1929, 78; Moschini, 1932, 112; Pallucchini, 1946, 194; Valcanover, 1961, 227.

**Formerly BENNEBROECK, Von Pannwitz Collection**

THE PALMIST

Attributed to Pietro Longhi by Van Marle, this painting is apparently at present in the United States. According to Arslan it may be a work by Longhi.

*Literature:* Van Marle, 1935, 403; Arslan, 1943, 63.

**BERGAMO, Accademia Carrara**

YOUNG GIRL WITH A FAN

Oil on canvas, 65×49 cm.

Attributed to Pietro Longhi by Ravà, it is now correctly attributed in the Gallery to Ceruti (Fig. 14).

## BERGAMO, Accademia Carrara
GAMES AT THE VILLA                                          Plate 479

Oil on canvas, 70×90 cm.

*Collection:* Baglioni.

Attributed to Pietro Longhi by Berenson, it is listed as such by the Gallery. It cannot be accepted without reservation as a work by Longhi's hand and is more probably by a follower of the painter.

*Literature:* Berenson, 1911, 112.

## BOSTON (Mass.), Museum of Fine Arts (no. 40.722)
PORTRAIT OF A GENTLEMAN

Oil on canvas, 66×54 cm.

Attributed to Pietro Longhi by Brosch, and listed as an attribution in the Museum. Obviously a work by Alessandro Longhi of *c.* 1780, in the style of the *Portrait of Gian Maria Sasso* in the Museo Correr (reproduced in Pignatti, 1960, 147).

*Literature:* Brosch, 1929, 357.

## BOSTON (Mass.), Museum of Fine Arts (no. 17.588)
PORTRAIT OF A YOUNG MAN

Oil on canvas, 99×82 cm.

*Collection:* Ross.

Attributed to Pietro Longhi by Brosch. Listed as 'Attributed to Pietro Longhi' by the Museum. Some affinity with Ghislandi.

*Literature:* Brosch, 1929, 357.

## BOSTON (Mass.), Museum of Fine Arts (no. 17.589)
PORTRAIT OF A MAN

Oil on canvas, 65 ×48 cm.

Attributed to Pietro Longhi by Brosch. Listed as 'Attributed to Pietro Longhi' by the Museum. It is not a Venetian work.

*Literature:* Brosch, 1929, 357.

## BUDAPEST, Szépmüvészti Múzeum
PORTRAIT OF GOLDONI

Oil on canvas, 93.5×73.5 cm.

*Collection:* De Nemes.

Attributed to Pietro Longhi by Brosch. It is now considered by the Museum to be probably the work of Gaetano Preda (information kindly supplied by Dr. Fenyo).

*Literature:* Brosch, 1929, 357.

## CAMBRIDGE (Mass.), Fogg Art Museum
PORTRAIT OF A NOBLEMAN                                      Plate 485

Oil on canvas, 44.5×35.5 cm.

*Collections:* Prince Massimo, Rome; Winthrop, Boston.

Attributed to Pietro Longhi by the Museum. As has already been shown, this is a work of Bartolomeo Nazzari; confirmation of this is afforded by comparison with the Egerton portrait in Ca' Rezzonico, which was formerly attributed to Pietro Longhi but is now seen to be a small version of the fullsize painting signed by Nazzari in Tatton Park, Cheshire, and datable in consequence to 1730-40, as the dress of the sitter suggests.

*Literature:* Moschini, 1960, fig. 69; Pallucchini, 1960, 186; Pignatti, 1960, 257.

## CASTAGNOLA, Thyssen Collection
THE PERFUME-SELLER

Oil on canvas, 43×36 cm.

Attributed to Pietro Longhi in the Catalogue of the collection, it is a version, with a few variations, of the painting in Ca' Rezzonico, of doubtful authenticity.

*Literature:* Heinemann, 1958, 61.

## DRESDEN, Gemäldegalerie (no. 595)
PORTRAIT OF A LADY

Oil on canvas, 68×58 cm.

Attributed to Pietro Longhi by Brosch, and subsequently to 'an eighteenth-century painter' by Posse (Catalogue, 1929, 231). Unrelated to Longhi.

*Literature:* Brosch, 1929, 357.

## DUBLIN, National Gallery of Ireland
PORTRAIT OF CHRISTOPHER NUGENT

Oil on canvas, 73×58 cm.

Attributed to Pietro Longhi by Brosch and exhibited as such in the Gallery, but more in the manner of Nazzari. Nugent was a General in the service of the Venetian Republic.

## FERRARA, Marchese Stefano Paulucci Collection
PORTRAIT OF A LADY

Oil on canvas, 40×31 cm.

Perhaps the painting attributed to Pietro Longhi by Ravà. It appears to be an almost identical version of the painting now in a private collection in Milan.

*Literature:* Ravà, 1923, 122.

## FLORENCE, Donzelli Collection
ORIENTAL CHILD

Oil on canvas, 75×55 cm.

Attributed to Longhi by Riccoboni, but there are no grounds for such an attribution.

*Literature:* Riccoboni, 1947, 453.

## FLORENCE, Venturi Collection
PORTRAIT OF A VIOLINIST

Oil on canvas, 148×74 cm.

Attributed to Pietro Longhi by Morandotti on the evidence of an inscription 'Pietro Longhi 1764' which, however, does not resolve all doubts about the authenticity of this work.

*Literature:* Morandotti, 1941, 57.

**FLORENCE, Private collection**

SELF-PORTRAIT (?) WITH A PUPIL

Attributed to Pietro Longhi by Martini. If the eldery instructor is to be identified as Pietro Longhi this does not guarantee that this is a self-portrait, and the work seems rather to belong to the early stages of Alessandro's career.

*Literature:* Martini, 1964, 263.

**FRANKFURT, Städelsches Kunstinstitut**

PORTRAIT OF MARCHESA CONCINA

Oil on canvas, 75×58 cm.

Attributed to Pietro Longhi by Brosch, confirmed by Arslan, it is exhibited as such in the Gallery. Unrelated to Longhi.

*Literature:* Brosch, 1929, 357; Arslan, 1943, 63.

**FRANKFURT, Städelsches Kunstinstitut**

THE QUACK

Oil on canvas, 59×72 cm.

Attributed to Pietro Longhi by Brosch, but by Fiocco to Alessandro. The Gallery attributes it to Pietro, but it is the work of a follower, close in style to the Master of the Ridotto.

*Literature:* Brosch, 1929, 373; Fiocco, 1929, fig. 87b.

**GENOA, Private collection**

PORTRAIT OF A BOY

Oil on canvas, 69×90 cm.

Attributed to Pietro Longhi by Arslan, it seems to be the work of a Lombard painter.

*Literature:* Arslan, 1946, 59.

**GENOA, Private collection**

PORTRAIT OF A YOUNG MAN

Oil on canvas, 69×90 cm.

Attributed to Pietro Longhi by Arslan, it seems the work of a Lombard painter.

*Literature:* Arslan, 1946, 59.

**Formerly HAMBURG, Scholz-Forni Collection**

A CONCERT

Attributed to Pietro Longhi by Goering but rejected by Arslan. Close in manner to the Master of the Ridotto.

*Literature:* Goering, 1940, 119; Arslan, 1943, 63.

**HARTFORD (Conn.), Wadsworth Atheneum Museum of Art**

PORTRAIT OF THE SINGER SCALZI                          *Plate 441*

Oil on canvas, 47×35.6 cm.

*Collections:* Meus, Paris; Arnold Seligman, New York.

Formerly considered to be by Longhi, together with a companion work now in the Feltrinelli collection, Milan (Pl. 443), it was later attributed by Voss to Flipart and is exhibited as such in the Museum. According to the researches of Professor W.J. Coe of the University of California, Scalzi is dressed for the part of Arbace in the opera *Artaserse* by Vinci, which was performed in Rome in 1730. Flipart was in Rome before going on to Venice in *c.* 1737 (information kindly supplied by C.C. Cunningham). The attribution to the French painter is therefore a plausible one, and in that case the work belongs to the years in which Flipart moved to Venice and came into contact with Longhi.

*Literature:* Blunt, 1957, 153.

**KANSAS CITY (Mo.), W. Rockhill Nelson Gallery of Art**

THE LADY'S AWAKENING                          *Plate 478*

Oil on canvas, 70×58 cm.

*Collection:* Agnew, London.

Attributed to Pietro Longhi in the Gallery catalogue. It is probably derived from the engraving made by Flipart from a painting by Longhi *c.* 1740. The arrangement of light areas in the composition is reminiscent of the group of paintings by the Master of the Reflections. There are other versions of the subject at Segromigno Monte, Milan and London. The drawings in the Museo Correr, nos. 561-3, show that the engraving was made in reverse.

*Literature:* W. *Rockhill Nelson Gallery of Art Catalogue,* 1959, 75.

**INNSBRUCK, Ferdinandeum (no. 529)**

PORTRAIT OF CONTE MIGAZZI

Oil on canvas, 85×68 cm.

Attributed to Pietro Longhi by Riccoboni, but closer to the style of Lampi. Conte Cristoforo Migazzi was born in Trent in 1714 and became bishop. in 1757. Here he is shown as a youth but already in canonicals.

*Literature:* Riccoboni, 1959, fig. 10.

**Formerly LONDON, Cavendish Bentinck collection**

THE COFFEE-HOUSE

Oil on canvas, 69×54 cm.

Attributed to Pietro Longhi by Berenson. Sold at Sotheby's, 3.7.1963 (lot 4). Painted with lively brushwork, almost like Guardi, this work has affinities with the group of paintings by the Master of the Reflections.

*Literature:* Berenson, 1897, 106; Graves, 1921, II, no. 577.

**Formerly LONDON, Cavendish Bentinck Collection**

THE PAINTER IN HIS STUDIO

Oil on canvas, 69×54 cm.

Companion to the above.

*Literature:* Berenson, 1897, 106; Graves, 1921, II, no. 578.

**LONDON, Earl of Harewood Collection**

THE CONVENT PARLOUR

Oil on canvas, 28×42 cm.

*Collection:* Clarincarde.

Attributed to Pietro Longhi in the collection. Companion to the following, it is not by Longhi.

*Literature:* Borenius, 1934, 19.

**LONDON, Earl of Harewood Collection**

THE PEDLAR

Oil on canvas, 38×26 cm.

*Collection:* Clarincarde.

Attributed to Longhi in the collection. It is not by Longhi.

*Literature:* Borenius, 1936, 19.

**LONDON, Earl of Harewood Collection**

THE RIDOTTO

Oil on canvas, 28×42 cm.

*Collection:* Clarincarde.

Attributed to Pietro Longhi in the collection. At present in Harewood House, Yorkshire, it is not by Longhi.

*Literature:* Borenius, 1936, 19.

**MILAN, Aldo Crespi Collection**

THE DECLARATION

Oil on canvas, 72×55 cm.

*Collection:* Giovannelli, Venice.

Attributed to Pietro Longhi in the collection. It appears to be a version of Flipart's print in the same sense as the painting of the same title to which it is related (Pl. 469). Perhaps the work of the Master of the Reflections.

*Literature:* Rosa, 1956, no. 40.

**MILAN, Aldo Crespi Collection**

THE HAIRPIECE

Oil on canvas, 53×38 cm.

*Collection:* Giovannelli, Venice.

Attributed to Pietro Longhi by Ravà, but probably not entirely his work.

*Literature:* Ravà, 1923, 9; Rosa, 1956, no. 42.

**MILAN, Aldo Crespi Collection**

THE LADY'S AWAKENING

Oil on canvas, 57.5×48 cm.

Attributed to Pietro Longhi in the collection, but probably not by him.

*Literature:* Rosa, 1956, no. 43.

**MILAN, Aldo Crespi Collection**

THE MILLINER

Oil on canvas, 72×50 cm.

*Collection:* Giovannelli, Venice.

Attributed to Pietro Longhi by Ravà. A rather lifeless version of the painting in the Fogg Art Museum (Pl. 250).

*Literature:* Ravà, 1923, 102; Rosa, 1956, no. 41.

**MILAN, Aldo Crespi Collection**

PORTRAIT OF JOHANN MOSER DE FILSEK

Oil on canvas, 44×32.

*Collection:* Giovannelli, Venice.

Attributed to Pietro Longhi in the collection. It reproduces a part of the portrait in Ca' Rezzonico, perhaps at the request of De Filsek (Pl. 142). The heavy linear technique does not appear to be the work of Longhi.

*Literature:* Morazzini, 1931, pl. LXIX; Rosa, 1956, no. 44.

**MILAN, Aldo Crespi Collection**

PORTRAIT OF A YOUNG MAN WITH A DOG

Oil on canvas, 58×50 cm.

*Collection:* Giovannelli, Venice.

Attributed to Pietro Longhi in the exhibition *Il Ritratto Italiano*, and is probably the work listed by Berenson. It does not appear to be by Longhi.

*Literature:* Berenson, 1911, 112; *Il Ritratto Italiano*, 1927, Pl. XVIII; Rosa, 1956, no. 39.

**Formerly MILAN, Crespi-Morbio Collection**

CARLO GOLDONI IN HIS STUDY                    *Plate 447*

Attributed to Longhi by Gamba, but its resemblance to the signed painting in the Museo Civico, Udine, suggests that it is the work of Gramiccia.

*Literature:* Gamba, 1923, 535.

**MILAN, Luisa Feltrinelli Doria Collection**

PORTRAIT OF ROSA PASQUALI                    *Plate 443*

Oil on canvas, 53×49 cm.

*Collection:* Drey, London.

An unpublished painting, believed to be by Longhi but later recognised as the companion to the portrait of Scalzi at Hartford (Pl. 441) and thus attributed to Flipart. According to the information kindly supplied by Morassi, the painting portrays Rosa Pasquali, nicknamed 'la Bavarese', a virtuoso singer in the service of the Elector of Bavaria. In 1737 Rosa Pasquali sang in the melodrama *Rosbale*, by Porpora, at the theatre of S. Giovanni Grisostomo, in which the part of Sirbace was sung by Scalzi (Blunt, 1956, 153), (cf. plate 441).

**MILAN, Treccani Collection**

THE GAME OF CARDS                    *Plate 467*

Attributed to Pietro Longhi by Modigliani. Companion to *The Spinet* (Pl. 466). There is a similar version in Ca' Rezzonico (reproduced in Pignatti, 1960, 217). Attributable to the follower of Longhi, close in manner to Flipart, who is known as the Master of the Reflections for his individual technique.

*Literature:* Morassi, 1931, 1034.

**MILAN, Treccani Collection**

THE SPINET                    *Plate 466*

Oil on canvas, 59×49 cm.

Attributed to Pietro Longhi by Modigliani, a companion to *The Game of Cards* and probably by the Master of the Reflections.

*Literature:* Morassi, 1931, 1034.

**Formerly MILAN, Venier Collection**
PORTRAIT OF A NUN
Oil on canvas, 46×39 cm.
Attributed to Pietro Longhi by Coletti, but not by him.
*Literature:* Coletti, 1957, pl. 52.

**MILAN, Private collection**
A LITTLE PEASANT GIRL
Oil on canvas, 90×60 cm.
Attributed to Pietro Longhi by Arslan, it is closer in style to Nogari and Magiotto.
*Literature:* Arslan, 1946, 59.

**MILAN, Private collection**
A JEWISH WEDDING                             *Plate 468*
Oil on canvas, 87×63 cm.
*Collection:* Barozzi, Venice.
Attributed to Pietro Longhi by Fiocco, who sees French influence. Perhaps, like the Treccani canvases, the work of the Master of the Reflections.
*Literature:* Fiocco, 1956, 206.

**MILAN, Private collection**
A PAINTER IN HIS STUDIO
Oil on canvas, 92×115 cm.
Attributed to Pietro Longhi by Arslan, but suggested as possibly the work of Flipart by Pallucchini.
*Literature:* Arslan, 1946, 60; Pallucchini, 1960, 190.

**MILAN, Private collection**
PORTRAIT OF A BOY
Oil on canvas, 92×73 cm.
Attributed to Pietro Longhi by Riccoboni, but closer to the style of Amigoni.
*Literature:* Riccoboni, 1947, 52.

**MILAN, Private collection**
PORTRAIT OF LUCREZIA LUPO FANTINI
Attributed to Pietro Longhi by Riccoboni, but it does not seem to be his work.
*Literature:* Riccoboni, 1959, 205.

**MILAN, Private collection**
PORTRAIT OF FRANCESCA MARIA PICCARDI
Oil on canvas, 76×67 cm.
Attributed to Pietro Longhi by Riccoboni, but it does not appear to be his work.
*Literature:* Riccoboni, 1959, 205.

**MILAN, Private collection**
PORTRAIT OF A YOUNG GIRL
Oil on canvas, 44.5×34.5 cm.

Attributed to Pietro Longhi in *L'Arte*, 1941, but not by him.
*Literature:* *L'Arte*, 1941, I, Pl. XXII.

**MODENA, Pinacoteca Estense**
PORTRAIT OF A CLERK
Oil on canvas, 126×89 cm.
Attributed to Pietro Longhi by Berenson, but to Traversi by Pallucchini.
*Literature:* Berenson, 1911, 112; Pallucchini, 1945, 236.

**MOSCOW, Pushkin Museum**
THE MEETING OF THE PROCURATORE AND HIS WIFE
Attributed to Pietro Longhi by the Museum, it is a version of the painting in New York (Pl. 78).

**NEW YORK, Walter P. Chrysler collection**
PORTRAIT OF SENATORE PISANI
Oil on canvas, 150×125 cm.
*Collection:* Liechtenstein.
Attributed to Pietro Longhi in the exhibition *Il Ritratto Italiano*, 1911, but to Alessandro by Ravà. It is however closer in style to the work by Pasquetti in Ca' Rezzonico (cf. Pignatti, 1960, 277).
*Literature:* Ravà, 1923, 10; *Il Ritratto Italiano*, 1927, pl. XVII.

**NEW YORK, P. Drey Collection**
PORTRAIT OF A GENTLEMAN
Oil on canvas, 94×76 cm.
*Collections:* Mill and Reinhard, New York.
Attributed to Pietro Longhi by Richardson. Probably by Uberti.
*Literature:* Richardson, 1952, 44; Morassi, 1953, 55.

**OXFORD, Ashmolean Museum (no. 279)**
A PROCURATORE RECEIVING A PETITION
Oil on canvas, 59×46 cm.
Attributed with reservations to Pietro Longhi by the Museum, it is work of a follower close in style to the Master of the Ridotto.
*Literature:* *Ashmolean Annual Report*, 1911, 26; Parker, 1961, 88.

**PADUA, Museo Civico**
PEASANTS DANCING THE FURLANA
Oil on canvas, 61×49 cm.
*Collections:* Cipollato Federici, Padua.
Attributed to Pietro Longhi by Moschetti, but probably a copy of the painting in Ca' Rezzonico (Pl. 92).

**PADUA, Museo Civico**
PORTRAIT OF ALESSANDRO PETRETTINI
Oil on canvas, 95×77 cm.
*Collection:* Pasquale Petrettini, Padua.
Attributed to Pietro Longhi by Moschetti, but not by him.
*Literature:* Moschetti, 1938, 208.

**PADUA, Museo Civico**

PORTRAIT OF MARIA PETRETTINI

Oil on canvas, 95×77 cm.

*Collection:* Pasquale Petrettini, Padua.

Attributed to Pietro Longhi by Moschetti, but not by him.

*Literature:* Moschetti, 1938, 208.

**PADUA, Museo Civico**

PORTRAIT OF A NOBLE LADY OF THE PETRETTINI FAMILY

Oil on canvas, 94×77 cm.

*Collection:* Pasquale Petrettini, Padua.

Attributed to Pietro Longhi by Moschetti, but not by him.

*Literature:* Moschetti, 1938, 208.

**PADUA, Museo Civico**

THE WASHERWOMEN

Oil on canvas, 61×49 cm.

*Collection:* Cipollato Federici, Padua.

Attributed to Pietro Longhi by Moschetti and shown as such. It is a workshop version of the painting in Ca' Rezzonico (Pl. 16).

*Literature:* Moschetti, 1938, 467; Grossato, 1957, no. 205.

**PARIS, Jean Cailleux Collection**

PORTRAIT OF A PAINTER                          *Plate 442*

Oil on canvas, 75.5×57.5 cm.

An unpublished painting, which Cailleux judges to be 'Italian in taste but French in execution' and attributes to Flipart, dating it to *c.* 1740. It is thus a work of the painter's last years in Paris or soon after his arrival in Venice to work in the studio of Wagner, where he came into contact with Longhi.

**PHILADELPHIA (Pa.), Pennsylvania Museum of Art**

THE SINGING LESSON                             *Plate 450*

Oil on canvas, 53×72 cm.

*Collection:* Wilstach.

Attributed to Pietro Longhi and accepted as such by Moschini, who dates to *c.* 1741, like the Petworth version (Pl. 280). A careful examination, however, suggests that it is a copy of the 1790s, executed in a manner which resembles that of De Gobbis.

*Literature: Wilstach Collection Catalogue*, 1922, no. 187; Moschini, 1956, 20.

**Formerly ROME, Palazzo Doria**

THE CONVENT PARLOUR                            *Plate 464*

Attributed to Pietro Longhi by Ravà with the imprecise location 'Palazzo Doria'; but it is closer in style to the Master of the Ridotto, like the two following canvases, with which it forms a series.

*Literature:* Ravà, 1923, 74.

**Formerly ROME, Palazzo Doria**

THE MASKED BALL                                *Plate 465*

Forms a series with *The Convent Parlour* and *The Ridotto*.

*Literature:* Ravà, 1923, 75.

**Formerly ROME, Palazzo Doria**

THE RIDOTTO                                    *Plate 463*

Forms a series with *The Masked Ball* and *The Convent Parlour*.

*Literature:* Ravà, 1923, 75.

**ROTTERDAM, Boymans Museum (no. 1463)**

PORTRAIT OF A PRIEST

Oil on canvas, 62.2×51.2 cm.

*Collection:* Swetchin, The Hague.

Attributed to Pietro Longhi in the Museum, but is more probably the work of Amigoni.

*Literature:* Schmidt-Degener, 1918, 8.

**ROUEN, Musée des Beaux-Arts**

FIGURES

Two paintings attributed to Pietro Longhi by Brosch, which are now considered to be by Traversi (information supplied by Mlle. Popovitch).

*Literature:* Brosch, 1929, 373.

**ROVIGO, Accademia dei Concordi**

PORTRAIT OF ROMUALDO SASSO

Oil on canvas, 129×95 cm.

Formerly attributed to Pietro Longhi in the Guide to the Gallery, it is unrelated to the painter's style.

*Literature:* Guida, 1931, 25.

**SALZBURG, Schloss Neuhaus, Topic Collection**

THE CONCERT                                    *Plate 439*

Oil on canvas, 88×73 cm.

Unpublished painting, auctioned at Sotheby's, 1961 no. 144. This a companion to *The Hairdresser* (Pl. 437), and was formerly attributed to Pietro Longhi but is probably by Flipart, by whom there is an engraving of the same picture in the same sense (Pl. 440). It is a work of considerable interest which may lead to further attributions to this artist in his 'Longhi period', when his style is characterised by an easy elegance of composition and a rather cold palette in a variety of tones with flickering effects of light.

**SALZBURG, Schloss Neuhaus, Topic Collection**

THE HAIRDRESSER                                *Plate 437*

Oil on canvas, 88×73 cm.

An unpublished painting, like the preceding canvas, auctioned at Sotheby's in 1961, no. 745. As for *The Concert* an engraving in the same sense by Flipart has been identified (Pl. 438). This shows in the background a painting by Amigoni, who was Flipart's teacher (Pallucchini, 1960, 190).

**SAN DIEGO (Cal.). Fine Arts Gallery**

THE CONVENT PARLOUR                    *Plate 457*

Oil on canvas, 89×114 cm.

An unpublished version of the well-known subject which may belong to the group of paintings attributed to De Gobbis. Together with its companion (Pl. 456) it was sold at Sotheby's from the collection of Dr. Olaf Sundin on 15.5.1929, nos. 28-9. Prof Zeri kindly informs me that the painting is now in San Diego.

**SAN DIEGO (Cal.). Fine Arts Gallery**

THE RIDOTTO                            *Plate 456*

Oil on canvas, 89×114 cm.

Companion work to the above.

**SEGROMIGNO MONTE, Heirs to the Salom Collection**

THE COFFEE-HOUSE                       *Plate 452*

Oil on canvas, 76×60 cm.

Attributed to Pietro Longhi by Ravà, but stylistically close to De Gobbis.

*Literature:* Ravà, 1923, 52.

**SEGROMIGNO MONTE, Heirs to the Salom Collection**

THE LADY'S AWAKENING                   *Plate 473*

Oil on canvas, 70×54 cm.

Attributed to Pietro Longhi by Ravà but considered by Arslan to be the work of an imitator, it appears to be a companion to *The Declaration* (Pl. 469), which is probably the work of the Master of the Reflections. It is however in the same sense as Flipart's print (Pl. 474) and in reverse to the drawings for the lady and the gentleman in the Museo Correr, nos. 561-563.

*Literature:* Ravà, 1923, 6; Arslan, 1943, 60.

**SEGROMIGNO MONTE, Heirs to the Salom Collection**

THE MUSIC LESSON                       *Plate 451*

Oil on canvas, 76×60 cm.

Attributed to Pietro Longhi by Ravà. A similar version is in the Casa di Goldoni, Venice. Clearly not by Longhi and perhaps attributable to De Gobbis.

*Literature:* Ravà, 1923, 30.

**SEGROMIGNO MONTE, Heirs to the Salom Collection**

THE RHINOCEROS                         *Plate 480*

Oil on canvas, 76×60 cm.

Attributed to Pietro Longhi by Ravà and confirmed by Bassi, but considered by Moschini and Pallucchini to be the work of a follower of the artist. Fiocco attributes it to Alessandro with another version, which he reproduces, in a private collection in Venice (1929, pl. 87), which however seems more probably the work of Gramiccia. This is certainly a painting of considerable merit, not readily to be rejected as an attribution to Pietro Longhi.

*Literature:* Ravà, 1923, 57; Fiocco, 1929, 67; Bassi, 1950, 34; Moschini, 1956, 54; Pallucchini, 1960, 190.

**SEGROMIGNO MONTE, Heirs to the Salom Collection**

THE RIDOTTO                            *Plate 453*

Oil on canvas, 76×50 cm.

Attributed to Pietro Longhi by Ravà, but more probably by De Gobbis.

*Literature:* Ravà, 1923, 68.

**STOCKHOLM, University**

PEASANTS

Attributed to Pietro Longhi by Brosch, but it is certainly the work of a French painter.

*Literature:* Brosch, 1929, 357.

**VENICE, Ca' d'Oro**

THE GEOGRAPHY LESSON                   *Plate 446*

Attributed to Pietro Longhi by Gamba. Its similarity to *Goldoni in his Study* (Pl. 447), formerly in Milan, suggests that it may be by Gramiccia.

*Literature:* Gamba, 1916, 333.

**VENICE, Ca' Rezzonico (no. 365)**

A BANQUET IN CASA NANI

Oil on canvas, 130×96 cm.

*Collection:* Teodoro Correr, Venice.

Attributed to Pietro Longhi by Lorenzetti, this painting records the banquet given in honour of the Elector of Cologne in 1755. It is the work of a follower of Longhi, whose delicate brushwork is similar to that in *Games at the Villa* (Pl. 479) at Bergamo.

*Literature:* Lorenzetti, 1936, 46; Pignatti, 1960, 221.

**VENICE, Ca' Rezzonico (no. 141)**

THE DECLARATION

Oil on canvas, 72×55 cm.

*Collection:* Teodoro Correr, Venice.

Attributed to Pietro Longhi by Ravà. Companion to *The Game of Cards* in the same gallery, to be attributed to the Master of the Reflections. There is another version in the A. Crespi Collection, Milan. It is a copy of the engraving made by Flipart of a painting by Longhi datable to before 1750, perhaps a version of the painting whose whereabouts are unknown, in horizontal format, for which there are drawings in the Museo Correr, nos. 465 and 572 (Ravà, 1923, 37).

*Literature:* Lazari, 1859, 29; Lorenzetti, 1951, 10; Pignatti, 1960, 216.

**VENICE, Ca' Rezzonico (no. 845)**

A FAMILY GATHERING                     *Plate 445*

Oil on canvas, 54×72 cm.

*Collection:* Manfredini.

Attributed to Pietro Longhi by Lorenzetti and Valcanover. It should however probably be attributed to Gramiccia, whose grey-brown tones and characteristic construction of features by short, abrupt strokes are shown here.

*Literature:* Lorenzetti, 1951, 70; Valcanover, 1956, 25; Pignatti, 1960, 223.

**VENICE, Ca' Rezzonico (no. 316)**
FOUR VENETIAN SCENES - THE RIDOTTO     *Plate 459*
Oil on canvas, 96×131 cm.
*Collection:* Tironi, Venice.

It forms a series with the following three paintings, of the same provenance, and attributed to Pietro Longhi by Ravà. It is only superficially similar to a Longhi painting and is characterised by a particular manner, an elongated line and dense colour with shifting effects of light which suggest rather Diziani or Fontebasso and Carlevaris. It belongs to a group of paintings classified as by the Master of the Ridotto. The paintings on the wall are, according to Pallucchini, copies of works by Sebastiano Ricci, which suggests a dating not much later than 1750. Many variants of this and the following paintings are to be found in private collections.

*Literature:* Ravà, 1923, 71; Pignatti, 1960, 219.

**VENICE, Ca' Rezzonico (no. 315)**
FOUR VENETIAN SCENES - THE CONVENT PARLOUR
     *Plate 460*
Oil on canvas, 96×131 cm.
Forms a series with the preceding and following paintings.
*Literature:* Ravà, 1923, 721; Pignatti, 1960, 219.

**VENICE, Ca' Rezzonico (no. 317)**
FOUR VENETIAN SCENES - THE EMBROIDERY WORK-ROOM     *Plate 461*
Oil on canvas, 96×116 cm.
Forms a series with the preceding and following paintings.
*Literature:* Pignatti, 1960, 219.

**VENICE, Ca' Rezzonico (no. 318)**
FOUR VENETIAN SCENES - A RUSTICAL MEAL     *Plate 462*
Oil on canvas, 96×131 cm.
Forms a series with the preceding paintings.
*Literature:* Pignatti, 1960, 219.

**VENICE, Ca' Rezzonico (no. 2250)**
PORTRAIT OF SAMUEL EGERTON
Oil on paper, 52×42 cm.

Attributed to Pietro Longhi by Lorenzetti, but it was recently identified as by Bartolomeo Nazzari on the basis of the discovery of a similar full-length portrait, signed and dated 1732, now at Tatton Park, Cheshire.

*Literature:* Lorenzetti, 1936, 58; Pignatti, 1960, 257.

**VENICE, Ca' Rezzonico (no. 140)**
THE GAME OF CARDS
Oil on canvas, 72×55 cm.
*Collection:* Teodoro Correr, Venice.

Attributed to Pietro Longhi by Ravà. There is an identical version in the Treccani Collection, Milan. It should be attributed to the follower of Longhi known as the Master of the Reflections for his lively treatment of light.

*Literature:* Lazari, 1859, 29; Ravà, 1923, 36; Lorenzetti, 1951, 10; Pignatti, 1960, 216.

**VENICE, Ca' Rezzonico (no. 909)**
PORTRAIT OF A GENTLEMAN ON HORSEBACK     *Plate 448*
Oil on canvas, 43×34 cm.
*Collection:* Sagredo, Venice.

Attributed to Pietro Longhi by Lorenzetti. Datable to towards the end of the century by comparison with the *Portrait of a Painter* (Pl. 294) by Pietro Longhi, and by the costume. The attribution to Longhi does not appear tenable, and the manner suggests that of Gramiccia.

*Literature:* Lorenzetti, 1936, 58; Pignatti, 1960, 190.

**VENICE, Ca' Rezzonico (no. 339)**
PORTRAIT OF CARLO GOLDONI
Oil on canvas, 126×105 cm.
*Collection:* Cicogna, Venice.

Attributed to Pietro Longhi by Berenson but later generally recognised as by Alessandro. It is not impossible that the portrait was begun by Pietro, who may have painted the face, and finished by Alessandro.

*Literature:* Berenson, 1894, 104; Fiocco, 1929, 37; Moschini, 1932, 112; Pallucchini, 1951-52, II, 93; Pignatti, 1960, 156.

**VENICE, Ca' Rezzonico**
THE TOOTH-DRAWER     *Plate 449*
Oil on canvas, 49×60 cm.
*Collection:* Teodoro Correr, Venice.

Attributed to Pietro Longhi by Lorenzetti, it is a copy of the painting in the Brera (Pl. 107) datable to *c.* 1746, but differs from it, as has already been observed, in the treatment of colour. Here the pigment is smooth and glossy with cold tones, and the figures seem to droop rather heavily. Comparison with the paintings by De Gobbis formerly at Palazzo Stucky (reproduced in Pallucchini, 1960, fig. 492) may suggest a new attribution for this and other canvases of modest achievement attributed to Longhi.

*Literature:* Lorenzetti, 1936, 55; Pignatti, 1960, 25.

**VENICE, Church of San Pantalon**
ST ANDREW AND ST PETER     *Plate 482*
Oil on canvas, 190×180 cm. approx.

First mentioned by Gianantonio Moschini, these two paintings on a pendentive of the third chapel on the left in San Pantalon have been traditionally attributed to Pietro Longhi and dated to *c.* 1780, the year in which his son Alessandro signed and dated the two pendentives opposite. Although it is known that Pietro's activities in the life school of the Academy continued late into his life, this attribution cannot be accepted without a very close examination, which at present is not possible.

*Literature:* Moschini, 1815, II, 250; Moschini, 1932, 127; Moschini, 1956, 40.

## VENICE, Heirs to the Bentivoglio d'Aragona Collection
THE PISANI FAMILY                    *Plates 481 and 483*
Oil on canvas, 255×341 cm.

Attributed to Pietro Longhi in the *Settecento Italiano* exhibition, Venice, it was later attributed to Alessandro. A recent restoration has revealed the signature 'Alessandro Longhi' on the book on the right of the painting, and two other signatures 'Longhi' in other parts of the painting. Pallucchini suggested that Pietro had collaborated in the work, being responsible for the lady and the children; a hypothesis which according to Valcanover has now been invalidated as a result of the restoration of the so-called *Doge's 'Balotin'* at Belluno (Pl. 484), Ermolao II Pisani, which is the only extant part of it certainly painted by Alessandro *c.* 1758. In the light of recent discoveries it is difficult to justify the suggestion of a collaboration, and the two large paintings must be due entirely to Alessandro, as he himself states in his *Vita*, written in 1761.

*Literature: Il Settecento Italiano*, 1929, 82; Pallucchini, 1951-52, II, 75; Pallucchini, 1960, 187; Valcanover, 1961, 229.

## VENICE, Brass Collection
PORTRAIT OF A GENTLEMAN
Oil on canvas, 99×74 cm.

Attributed to Pietro Longhi by Ravà, probably by Lampi.
*Literature:* Ravà, 1923, 121.

## Formerly VENICE, Brass Collection
PORTRAIT OF A GENTLEMAN
Oil on canvas, 202×113 cm.

Attributed to Pietro Longhi by Morandotti, to Alessandro by Pallucchini, which is more probable.
*Literature:* Morandotti, 1941, 56; Pallucchini, 1960, 217.

## Formerly VENICE, Brass Collection
PORTRAIT OF A LADY
Oil on canvas, 74×63 cm.

Attributed to Pietro Longhi by Ravà, but not by him.
*Literature:* Ravà, 1923, 120.

## Formerly VENICE, Brass Collection
PORTRAIT OF M.V. MENEGHEL
Oil on canvas, 119×80 cm.

Attributed with reservations to Pietro Longhi by Moschini, but not by him.
*Literature:* Moschini, 1932, 146; Morandotti, 1941, 55.

## Formerly VENICE, Brass Collection
PORTRAIT OF A WOMAN
Oil on canvas, 77×59 cm.
Attributed to Pietro Longhi by Morandotti. Possibly by Nogari.
*Literature:* Morandotti, 1941, 54.

## Formerly VENICE, Morosini Gatterbug Collection
THE LADY WITH A RED GLOVE
Attributed to Pietro Longhi by Ravà, but not by him.
*Literature:* Ravà, 1923, 117.

## Formerly VENICE, Naya Collection
PORTRAIT OF A CARDINAL
Attributed to Pietro Longhi by Riccoboni, but seems related to the sketches by Alessandro now in the Orsi collection, Milan.
*Literature:* Riccoboni, 1959, 202.

## VENICE, Private collection
A BOY OF THE VALLEY
Attributed to Pietro Longhi by Riccoboni, but does not appear to be by him.
*Literature:* Riccoboni, 1959, 200.

## VENICE, Private collection
YOUNG WOMAN WITH A MASK
Oil on canvas, 53×43 cm.
Attributed to Pietro Longhi by Riccoboni, but does not appear to be by him.
*Literature:* Riccoboni, 1959, 202.

## Formerly VENICE, Private collection
PORTRAIT OF A YOUNG GIRL
Exhibited as by Pietro Longhi in the *Settecento Italiano* exhibition, Venice, and listed as such in the Brass collection. Confirmed with some reservations by Arslan, it is perhaps by Zuccarelli.
*Literature: Settecento Italiano*, 1929, 39; Arslan, 1946, 59.

## VENICE, Private collection
PORTRAIT OF A LADY
Oil on canvas, 114×89 cm.
Attributed to Pietro Longhi by Riccoboni, but it does not appear to be by him.
*Literature:* Riccoboni, 1959, 202.

## Formerly VENICE, Private collection
PORTRAIT OF A NOBLEMAN WITH A WHIP
Oil on canvas, 47×29 cm.
Attributed to Pietro Longhi by Riccoboni, but it does not appear to be by him.
*Literature:* Riccoboni, 1959, 202.

**VENICE, Toniolo Collection**

PORTRAIT OF G.B. TONIOLO

Attributed to Pietro Longhi by Riccoboni, but it does not appear to be by him.

*Literature:* Riccoboni, 1959, 206.

**VENICE, Toniolo Collection**

PORTRAIT OF ELISABETTA TONIOLO NANI

Attributed to Pietro Longhi by Riccoboni, but it does not appear to be by him.

*Literature:* Riccoboni, 1959, 206.

**Formerly VENICE, O.V. Collection**

PORTRAIT OF A YOUNG WOMAN WITH A ROSE

Attributed to Pietro Longhi by Riccoboni, appears rather to be by Alessandro. By Pietro Longhi according to Martini.

*Literature:* Riccoboni, 1959, 205; Martini, 1964, 291.

**VENICE, Gallerie dell'Accademia (no. 5581)**

PORTRAIT OF POPE CLEMENT XIII

Oil on canvas, 99×74 cm.

Attributed to Pietro Longhi by Riccoboni, who incorrectly locates it in Ca' Rezzonico. Arslan excludes the possibility of the attribution.

*Literature:* Arslan, 1943, 63; Riccoboni, 1959, 202.

**VENICE, Gallerie dell'Accademia (no. 808)**

PORTRAIT OF A GENTLEMAN

Oil on canvas, 81×62 cm.

Initialled 'P.L.' and attributed to Pietro Longhi by Marconi, it has none of the characteristics of the artist.

*Literature:* Marconi, 1949, 60.

**VENICE, Galleria Frezzati**

BOY WITH A FLUTE

Oil on canvas, 68×57.5 cm.

Published by Fiocco, together with the next painting, as by Gamberini, but then attributed to Pietro Longhi by Arslan. It looks more typical of the style of Nogari.

*Literature:* Fiocco, 1943, IX; Arslan, 1946, 59.

**VENICE, Galleria Frezzati**

GIRL WITH A CAGE

Oil on canvas, 68×57.5 cm.

Companion to the preceding work.

*Literature:* Fiocco, 1943, IX; Arslan, 1946, 59.

**VENICE, Pinacoteca Querini Stampalia (no. 26.277)**

PORTRAIT OF CATERINA CONTARINI QUERINI

Oil on canvas, 55×45 cm.

Attributed to Pietro Longhi in the *Itinerario* of the Gallery but probably, as Moschini claims, the work of Alessandro during the period of the *Pisani Family* paintings (Pl. 481 and 483).

*Literature:* Moschini, 1932, 146; *Itinerario*, 1946, 25.

**VENICE, Pinacoteca Querini Stampalia (no. 13)**

PORTRAIT OF THE PROVVEDITORE ANDREA QUERINI

Oil on canvas, 210×130 cm.

Attributed to Pietro Longhi in the *Itinerario* of the Gallery, but probably by Castelli.

*Literature:* *Itinerario*, 1946, 30; Pignatti, 1950, 218.

**ZOPPOLA, Castello**

PORTRAIT OF A PROCURATORE

Rizzi locates this painting as at Zoppola, and attributes it to Pietro Longhi.

*Literature:* Rizzi, 1966, 108.

**WHEREABOUTS UNKNOWN**

BISON AND LYNX

Attributed to Pietro Longhi by Ravà, the canvas bears an inscription 'Painting of the bison and the lynx brought to Venice during Carnival, 1770 M.V.'. Certainly the work of a follower.

*Literature:* Ravà, 1923, 63; Moschini, 1956, 64; Pallucchini, 1960, 185.

THE DECLARATION                                    *Plate 469*

Attributed to Pietro Longhi by Ravà, it is at least a copy of an original, perhaps by the hand of the Master of the Reflections, to judge by the rendering in the engravings. Reproductions are known of the work in prints by Flipart, in reverse, as well as by Hayd, in the same sense of the painting. Both bear the inscrption 'Pietro Longhi pinxit'. The drawings, in the same sense, of the lady spinning and the gentleman with the old woman, in the Museo Correr, nos. 465 and 571 (Moschini, 1956, fig. 48, 50) confirm the existence of the original painting. It must have been executed before 1750, since it was engraved by Flipart, who left Venice in that year.

*Literature:* Ravà, 1923, 37.

THE MASKS

Attributed to Pietro Longhi by Ravà, who wrongly located it in the Museo Correr, confusing it with a similar painting in a vertical format now in the Casa di Goldoni, Venice. It shows no trace of the artist's style.

*Literature:* Ravà, 1923, 30.

PAINTER AND MODEL

Oil on canvas, 62×62 cm.

Attributed to Pietro Longhi in *L'Arte* but shows no trace of the artist's style.

*Literature:* *L'Arte*, 1941, XVI.

## PORTRAIT OF THE GREAT CAPTAIN

Oil on canvas, 182×116 cm.

Attributed to Piero Longhi by Fiocco, but it does not appear to be by him.

*Literature:* Fiocco, 1943, 72.

## PORTRAIT OF A KNIGHT OF MALTA

*Plate 486a*

Miniature on ivory, 6.7×4.7 cm.

An unpublished work which bears on the cuff of the right sleeve the inscription 'P. Longhi f.'. From the collection of the Barons Sordeaux aux Villains, Levico (Trento), who amassed a large collection in the last century. This miniature is listed in the inventory dated 2 May 1874, no. 696, as 'gouache on ivory signed P. Longhi, purchased for 400 florins'. This is the only known example of a miniature attributed to Longhi, so that at present the authenticity of this work, of singular delicacy of line and limpidity of colour, must depend upon the entry in the register, which there is no reason to suspect. The signature appears consistent with the painting around it and seems to have been executed at the same time as the embroidery of the cuff.

## PORTRAIT OF A GENTLEMAN

Attributed to Pietro Longhi by Riccoboni, but it does not appear to be by him.

*Literature:* Riccoboni, 1947, fig. 169.

## PORTRAIT OF A YOUNG MAN WITH A BIRD

Oil on canvas, 96×71 cm.

Attributed to Pietro Longhi by Fiocco, but it does not appear to be by him.

*Literature:* Fiocco, 1943, 71.

## PORTRAIT OF MARGARITA HANCHIN

An inscription says 'True portrait of Margarita Hanchin, 18 years and 9 months old, born in Ansbach, 7 feet tall, who came to Venice, in December 1772, and of Francesco Poggi, the man with one leg'. Attributed to Longhi by Ravà. The work of a follower.

*Literature:* Ravà, 1923, 63; Moschini, 1956, 64.

# LOST WORKS

**BONN**

**Rheinisches Landesmuseum:** a work mentioned by Brosch in *Thieme-Becker A.L.*, Leipzig, 1919. It is not in the Museum.

**CAMBRIDGE (Mass.)**

**Norton Collection:** *Portrait of a Senator.* Mentioned by Berenson, 1911, p. 112. It is apparently not at present in the Fogg Museum.

**DRESDEN**

*Masquerade.* Sent by Longhi in 1749, mentioned in a letter from Longhi to Remondini, of 13.5.1749 (see Document 6).

**FLORENCE**

**Loeser Collection:** *Scene at a Mill.* Mentioned by Berenson, 1911, p. 112.

**LONDON**

**Cavendish Bentinck Collection:** *A Visit to Nuns.* Mentioned by Berenson, 1911, p. 112. Exhibited at Burlington Fine Arts Club, 1911, no. 5 (Graves, 1921, vol. II).

**Mond Collection:** *The Game of Cards.* Mentioned by Berenson, 1911, p. 112.

**Victor Perowne Collection:** *The Ridotto* and *The Convent Parlour.* Mentioned by Borenius, 1936.

**Richter Collection:** *The Game of Cards* and *The Lady's Toilet.* Mentioned by Berenson, 1911, p. 112.

**VENICE**

**Sta. Maria delle Grazie:** *St John the Baptist* and two other small paintings. Mentioned by Zanetti, 1733, p. 469.

**Scuola di San Pasquale Baylon:** *The Miracle of the Loaves and Fishes, The Canaanite's Daughter, The Centurion.* Mentioned by Zanetti, 1733, p. 237.

**Cecilia Emo Morosini della Sbarra Collection:** *The Coffee-House.* Mentioned in the letter from Pietro Longhi to G.B. Remondini, of 12 January 1753 (see Document 11).

**Resident Murray Collection:** *Portrait of John Murray and his Family.* Mentioned in Joseph Smith's sale, London, 17.5.1776, Lot 81.

**Consul Smith Collection:** *A Peasant drinking and a Girl sleeping* and *A Girl spinning.* Mentioned in the list of paintings bought by George III in 1762 (Levey, 1964, p. 87).

**Whereabouts unknown:** *The Holy Family.* Mentioned by Goldoni as in the process of being etched by Pitteri in the Dedication of *Il Frappatore* (*Commedie*, ed. Paperini, Florence, 1755, p. 301).

**VERONA**

**Oratory of San Biagio:** *Joseph's Blessing* and *The Coronation of the Virgin.* Mentioned by Valcanover, 1958, p. 684.

## WORKS RECORDED IN PRINTS

*The Coffee-House.* Engraved by Wagner 'Petrus Longhi ven. Pinxit'. The original was in Florence in 1752, in the house of Cecilia Emo Morosini (see above) (Pl. 490).

*The Singing Lesson.* Engraved by F. Bartolozzi; 'Pietro Longhi pin.' (Plate 491).

*The Lady's Toilet.* Engraved by Gutwein; 'Petrus Longhi pin.' (Plate 493).

*The Lady's Country Villa.* Engraved by Faldoni; 'Pietro Longhi pin.'. The scene is the Coffee-House at Mira. It is probably the print mentioned by Longhi in his letter to Remondini of 7 December 1748 (see Document 5). Drawing no. 436 in the Museo Correr contains studies for the background (Moschini, 1956, p. 60) (Plate 488).

*The Juggler.* Engraved by Alessandro Longhi. The painter's name is missing, but the subject and the atmosphere are close to Pietro Longhi's paintings, like *Borgogna's Show* (Pl. 489).

*Antonio Diedo Eques...* 'Petrus Longhi delin. Christophorus Dell'Acqua excud.' (Plate 492).

*Petrus Longhi Pictor Venetus.* Engraved by Cattini, datable to *c.* 1740-50. It perhaps records a lost self-portrait (Fig. 2, p. 50). *Petrus Longhi Pictor.* Etched by Alessandro Longhi, included in the *Compendio* of 1761. It perhaps records a lost self-portrait (Fig. 1, p. 49).

*Petrus Longhi Venetus.* Anonymous engraving, dated 1766. It perhaps records a lost self-portrait (Fig. 3, p. 50).

127

# BIBLIOGRAPHY

1733 (A.M. ZANETTI), *Descrizione di tutte le pubbliche pitture della città di Venezia...*, Venice, 1733 (1732).

1740 G.B. ALBRIZZI, *Forestiere illuminato intorno le cose più rare, e curiose, antiche e moderne della città di Venezia*, Venice, 1740.

1750 C. GOLDONI, *Al Signor Pietro Longhi Veneziano celebre pittore, sonetto...*, Venice, 1750.

1753 P.A. ORLANDI and P. GUARIENTI, *Abecedario Pittorico*, Venice, 1753.

1755 G. GOLDONI, *Le Commedie del Dottore Carlo Goldoni...*, vol. X, Florence, 1755.

1756 *Brevi notizie della Santa Casa di Maria Vergine madre di Dio in Loreto e dell'altare... eretta nella chiesa Parrocchiale e Colleggiata di S. Pantaleone...*, Venice, 1756.

1758 C.N. COCHIN, *Voyage d'Italie*, Paris, 1758.

1760 G. GOZZI, in 'Gazzetta Veneta', n. 55, del 13-VIII-1760.

1761 G. GOZZI, *Mio Signore*, in 'L'Osservatore Veneto', n. IV, 14-II-1761, pp. 28-29.

1762 A. LONGHI, *Compendio delle Vite dei pittori veneziani istorici più rinomati del presente secolo...*, Venice, 1762 (1761).

1764 *Catalogo dei studenti della nuova Accademia di disegno eretta da S.E. Almorò Pisani*, Venice, n.d.

1770 G. GRADENIGO, *Poesie in lode del celebre ritrattista veneziano il Signor Alessandro Longhi*, Venice, 1770.

1771 A.M. ZANETTI, *Della pittura veneziana...*, Venice, 1771.

1793 *Le pitture sculture ed architetture della città di Rovigo*, Rovigo, 1793.

1795 P. BRANDOLESE, *Pitture sculture ed architetture ed altre cose notabili di Padova*, Padua, 1795.
L. LANZI, *Storia pittorica dell'Italia*, Bassano, 1795.

1806 G.A. MOSCHINI, *Stato delle Belle Arti di Venezia nel secolo XVIII*, in 'Della Letteratura Veneziana del secolo XVIII', vol. III, Venice, 1806.

1815 G.A. MOSCHINI, *Guida per la città di Venezia...*, Venice, 1815.

1817 G.A. MOSCHINI, *Guida per la città di Padova...*, Venice, 1817.

1818 S. TICOZZI, *Dizionario dei pittori...*, vol. I, Milan, 1818.

1819 G.A. MOSCHINI, *Itinéraire de la ville de Venise*, Venice, 1819.

1822 G. BOTTARI and S. TICOZZI, *Raccolta di lettere sulla pittura, scultura ed architettura...*, vol. IV, Milan, 1822.

1837 F. ZANOTTO, *Storia della pittura veneziana*, Venice, 1837.

1839 K.G. NAGLER, *Neues Allgemeines Künstlerlexikon*, vol. VIII, Munich, 1839.

1840 F. DE BONI, *Biografia degli artisti*, Venice, 1840.

1842 E.A. CICOGNA, *Delle inscrizioni veneziane*, vol. V, Venice, 1842.

1848 A. SIREN, *Dictionnaire des peintres*, Paris, 1848.

1854 (P.J. MARIETTE), *Abecedario de P.J. Mariette...*, vol. III, Paris, 1854-56.

1856 P. SELVATICO, *Storia estetico-critica delle arti del disegno*, vol. II, Venice, 1856.

F. ZANOTTO, *Nuovissima guida di Venezia*, Venice, 1856.

1859 V. LAZARI, *Notizie delle opere d'Arte e d'Antichità della raccolta Correr*, Venice, 1859.

1862 V. LAZARI, *Elogio di Pietro Longhi pittore veneziano*, in 'Atti dell'Imp. R. Accademia di Belle Arti in Venezia dell'anno 1861', Venice, 1862.

1865 *Galleria Giulio Pompei*, Verona, 1865.

1868 C. BLANC, *Histoire des peintres de toutes les écoles — Ecole vénitienne*, Paris.

1878 C. YRIARTE, *Venise*, Paris, 1878.

1880 I. LERMOLIEFF (Giovanni Morelli), *Die Werke der italienischen Meister in den Galerien von München, Dresden und Berlin*, Leipzig, 1880.

P.G. MOLMENTI, *La Storia di Venezia nella vita privata*, Turin, 1880.

1881 LAW, *An historical Catalogue...*, Hampton Court, 1881.

1886 F.C. MARTIN, *The Lancret of the Lagoon*, in 'Art Journal', 1886.

1890 J. ADDINGTON SYMONDS, *Pietro Longhi*, in 'The Memoirs of Count Carlo Gozzi', vol. II, London, 1890.

G. NICOLETTI, *Lista di nomi di artisti tolta dai libri di tanse o luminarie della fraglia dei pittori*. Catalogue IV, in 'Ateneo Veneto', 1890.

1891 E. MASI, *Carlo Goldoni e Pietro Longhi*, in 'Studi sulla storia del teatro italiano nel secolo XVIII', Florence, 1891.

V. MALAMANI, *Il Settecento a Venezia*, Turin-Rome, 1891-92.

1893 A.C. DELL'ACQUA, *La Venezia del Canaletto e la Venezia del Longhi*, in 'Ateneo Veneto', 1893, pp. 153-187.

1894 B. BERENSON, *Venetian Painters of the Renaissance*, New York-London, 1894 (2nd ed. 1897).

E. DE GONCOURT and J. DE GONCOURT, *L'Italie d'hier, notes de voyage 1855-1856*, Paris, 1894.

1899 *Donation des Frères Lavallard*, Amiens, 1899.

1902 G. FRIZZONI, *L'Esposizione artistica della città di Baden-Baden*, in 'L'Arte', 1902, pp. 340-346.

1904 G.A. SIMONSON, *Francesco Guardi*, London, 1904.

1905 U. MONNERET DE VILLARD, *Note su Pietro Longhi*, in 'Emporium', March 1905, pp. 200-211.

1906 A. DE VESME, *Le Peintre-Graveur italien*, Milan, 1906.

F. MALAGUZZI VALERI, *I disegni della R. Pinacoteca di Brera*, Milan, 1906.

G.A. SIMONSON, *Guardi and Longhi*, in 'The Burlington Magazine', 1906, p. 53.

1907 G. FRIZZONI, *L'Accademia Carrara*, Bergamo, 1907.

G.A. SIMONSON, *La mascherata al Ridotto di Venezia di Francesco Guardi*, in 'L'Arte', 1907, pp. 241-146.

1908 P. MOLMENTI, *La storia di Venezia nella vita privata...*, 4th ed. Bergamo, 1908.

P. MOLMENTI, *Di Pietro Longhi e di alcuni suoi quadri*, in 'Emporium', January 1908, pp. 31-38.

P. MONNIER, *Venise au XVIIIe siècle*, Paris, 1908.

1909 P. MOLMENTI, *Il palazzo Grassi a Venezia e un affresco attribuito al Tiepolo*, in 'Emporium', 1909, pp. 177-188.

H. POSSE, *Die Gemäldegalerie des Kaiser-Friedrich Museums*, Berlin, 1909.

A. RAVÀ, *Pietro Longhi*, Bergamo, 1909.

A. RAVÀ, *Guardi e Longhi*, in 'L'Arte', 1909, p. 456.

G.A. SIMONSON, *Guardi e Longhi*, in 'L'Arte', 1909, p. 379.

1910 R. BRATTI, *Ritratti di Pietro e di Alessandro Longhi*, in 'Arte Nostra', 1910.

G. FOGOLARI, *Dipinti del Museo Civico di Belluno*, in 'Boll. d'Arte', 1910, pp. 285-292.

1911 *Ashmolean Museum Annual Report*, 1911, p. 16.

B. BERENSON, *The Venetian Painters of the Renaissance*, New York-London, 1911.

T. BORENIUS, *L'Esposizione di pittura veneta del XVIII secolo al Burlington Fine Arts Club di Londra*, in 'Rassegna d'Arte', 1911, pp. 150-152.

A. GRAF, *L'anglomania e l'influsso inglese nel secolo XVIII*, Turin, 1911.

M. MARANGONI, *La mostra del ritratto italiano a Firenze*, in 'Vita d'Arte', 1911, pp. 15-12.

*Mostra del Ritratto italiano*, Florence, 1911.

A. RAVA, *Contributo alla biografia di Pietro Longhi*, in 'Rassegna Contemporanea', IV, Rome, 1911.

Z. VON TAKACS, *Die Neuerwerbungen des Museums für Bildende Kunst in Budapest*, in 'Der Cicerone', 1911, pp. 857-882.

N. TARCHIANI, *La mostra del ritratto italiano...*, in 'Rassegna d'Arte', May 1911, pp. 77-92.

1912    O. SIREN, *Beskr. Fort. Stockholms Hogskolas...*, Stockholm, 1912.

1913    *Collection Comm. M. Guggenheim - Catalogue of the auction sale held in Venice, 30 September 1913.*

G. FOGOLARI, *L'Accademia veneziana di Pittura e Scultura nel Settecento*, in 'L'Arte', 1913, pp. 241-272 e 364-394.

1914    F. MALAGUZZI VALERI, *Ignoti dipinti veneti del Settecento a Milano*, in 'Rassegna d'Arte', 1914, pp. 1-14.

P. MOLMENTI, *Epistolari veneziani del secolo XVIII*, Milan, 1914.

*New Acquisitions of pictures*, in 'Bulletin of the Metropolitan Museum', IX, New York, 1914.

1916    C. GAMBA, *La Ca' d'Oro e la collezione Franchetti*, in 'Bollettino d'Arte', 1916, pp. 322-334.

1917    *Sale Catalogue of the E. Volpi collection*, New York, 1917.

1918    F. SCHMIDT-DEGENER, *Museum Boymans Annual Report*, 1918, p. 10.

1920    C.H. COLLINS-BAKER, *Petworth House Catalogue*, 1920.

T. FRIMMEL, *Studien und Skizzen zur Gemäldekunde*, Berlin, V, 1920.

M. MARANGONI, *Giuseppe Maria Crespi detto lo Spagnuolo*, in 'Dedalo', I, 1920-21, pp. 575-647.

1921    A. GRAVES, *Art Sales*, London, 1921.

1922    *Mostra della pittura italiana del Sei e Settecento a Palazzo Pitti*, Rome-Milan-Florence, 1922.

O. RONCHI, *Guida storico-artistica di Padova e dintorni*, Padua, 1922.

*Wilstach collection Catalogue*, Philadelphia, 1922.

A. RAVÀ, *Marco Pitteri incisore veneziano*, Florence.

1923    M.A. PERATE, *La peinture en Italie au XVIII siècle*, in 'Michel, Histoire de l'Art', VII, Paris, 1923.

A. RAVÀ, *Pietro Longhi*, Florence, 1923.

C. GAMBA, *La raccolta Crespi-Morbio*, in 'Dedalo', 1923-24, pp. 535-554.

1924    G.A. MOSCHINI, *Dell'incisione in Venezia*, Venice, 1924.

U. OJETTI, L. DAMI and N. TARCHIANI, *La pittura italiana del Seicento e Settecento alla Mostra di Palazzo Pitti*, Rome, 1924.

G. FOGOLARI, *In tabarro e bauta*, in 'Strenna dell'Illustrazione Italiana', 1924-25, pp. 1-24.

1925    E. DACIER, *La gravure de genre et de moeurs*, Paris-Brussels, 1925.

M. NUGENT, *Alla mostra della pittura italiana del '600 e '700*, I, San Casciano, 1925.

PINACOTECA QUERINI STAMPALIA, *Catalogo*, Venice, 1925.

G. FIOCCO, *Il Ridotto e il Parlatorio del Museo Correr*, in 'Dedalo', 1925-26, pp. 538-546.

E. MODIGLIANI, *Settecento veneziano nelle raccolte private milanesi*, in 'Strenna dell'Illustrazione Italiana', 1925-26, p. 33.

1926    M. NICOLLE, *Pietro Longhi*, in 'La Renaissance de l'art français', April, 1926.

A. STIX and L. FRÖLICH BUM, *Beschreibender Katalog der Handzeichnungen in der graph. Smlg. Albertina. Die Zeichnungen der Venezianischen Schule*, Vienna, 1926.

1927    V. BLOCH, *La pittura italiana a Berlino*, in 'Vita Artistica', August-September, 1927, pp. 174-180.

G. FIOCCO, *Michelangelo Morlaiter*, in 'Bollettino d'Arte', October, 1927, pp. 219-231.

*Italienische Malerei des 17. und 18. Jahrhunderts*, Berlin, 1927.

R. LONGHI, *Di Gaspare Traversi*, in 'Vita Artistica', August-September, 1927, pp. 145-167.

*Il Ritratto Italiano dal Caravaggio al Tiepolo*, Bergamo, 1927.

G. LORENZETTI, *Venezia e il suo estuario*, Venice-Milan.

1928   A. CALABI, *Francesco Bartolozzi*, in 'Bollettino d'Arte', September, 1928, pp. 103-121.

G. DAMERINI, *I pittori veneziani del '700*, Bologna, 1928.

V. MOSCHINI, *Mostra di disegni del Settecento veneziano alle RR. Gallerie di Venezia*, in 'Bollettino d'Arte', March, 1928, pp. 465-472.

*Museum Ferdinandeum, Katalog der Gemäldesammlung*, Innsburck, 1928.

N. PEVSNER and O. GRAUTOFF, *Barockmalerei in den romanischen Ländern*, Wildpark-Potsdam, 1928.

L. RÉAU, *La gravure d'illustration*, Paris-Brussels, 1928.

1929   L. BROSCH, *Pietro Longhi*, in 'Thieme-Becker Allgemeines Lexikon der Bildenden Künstler', vol. XXIII, Leipzig, 1929, pp. 357-358.

M. BRUNETTI, *Disegni del '700*, in 'Le Tre Venezie', July, 1929, pp. 59-64.

G. DAMERINI, *La vita avventurosa di Caterina Dolfin Tron*, Milan, 1929.

G. FIOCCO, *La pittura veneziana del Seicento e Settecento*, Verona, 1929.

G. FIOCCO, *La pittura veneziana alla Mostra del Settecento*, in 'Rivista di Venezia', 1929, pp. 497-581.

G. FOGOLARI, *Valori della pittura veneziana settecentesca*, in 'Le Tre Venezie', July, 1929, pp. 15-21.

V. MOSCHINI, *Catalogo delle opere d'arte della Ca' d'oro*, Venice, 1929.

G. ORTOLANI, *Voci e visioni del Settecento veneziano*, Bologna, 1929.

N. PEVSNER, *Die Rokoko-Ausstellung in Venedig*, in 'Zeitschrift für Bildende Kunst', October, 1929.

T. SENSI, *L'abbigliamento femminile nel '700*, in 'Le Tre Venezie', July, 1929, pp. 65-68.

*Il Settecento Italiano*, Venice, 1929.

V. MOSCHINI, *I disegni del '700 alla Mostra di Venezia*, in 'Dedalo', 1929-30, pp. 301-370.

1930   G. DELOGU, *Pittori veneti minori del Settecento*, Venice, 1930.

*Sammlung Schloss Rohoncz*, Munich, 1930.

1931   *Guida della Pinacoteca dei Concordi di Rovigo*, Rovigo, 1931.

A. MORASSI, *La raccolta Treccani*, in 'Dedalo', July, 1931, pp. 1012-1037.

G. MORAZZONI, *La moda a Venezia nel secolo XVIII*, Milan, 1931.

V. MOSCHINI, *La pittura italiana del Settecento*, Florence, 1931.

L. VENTURI, *Pitture italiane in America*, Milan, 1931.

1932   G. FOGOLARI, *Pittura del Settecento Italiano*, in 'Strenna dell'Illustrazione Italiana', 1932.

V. MOSCHINI, *Per lo studio di Alessandro Longhi*, in 'L'Arte', 1932, pp. 110-147.

V. MOSCHINI, *Un ritratto inedito di Alessandro Longhi*, in 'Dedalo', 1932, pp. 772-780.

1933   J. BYAM SHAW, *Some Venetian Draughtsmen of the Eighteenth Century*, in 'Old Master Drawings', March, 1933, pp. 47-63.

1934   G. LORENZETTI and L. PLANISCIG, *La collezione dei Conti Donà delle Rose a Venezia*, Venice, 1934.

V. MOSCHINI, *Pietro Longhi*, in 'Enciclopedia Italiana', vol. XXI, Rome, 1934.

P.L. PASSARELLA, *Il 'salvataggio' di quindici quadri di Pietro Longhi*, in 'Le Tre Venezie', 1934, pp. 686-690.

*Quindici quadri di Pietro Longhi assicurati alla Querini-Stampalia*, in 'Rivista di Venezia', November, 1934, pp. 487-497.

1935   G. FIOCCO, *Giacomo Ceruti a Padova*, in 'Bollettino d'Arte', September, 1935, pp. 139-115.

R. VAN MARLE, *La pittura all'esposizione di arte antica italiana di Amsterdam*, in 'Bollettino d'Arte', March, 1935, pp. 389-408.

E. MODIGLIANI, *Catalogo della R. Pinacoteca di Brera*, Milan, 1935.

L.E. ROWE, *A painting by Longhi*, in 'Bulletin of the Rhode Island School of Design', XXIII, 4 October 1935, pp. 64-66.

W. ARSLAN, *Studi sulla pittura del primo '700 veneziano*, in 'La Critica d'Arte', 1935-36, pp. 184-187; 238-250.

1936   T. BORENIUS, *Catalogue of the pictures and drawings at Harewood House*, Oxford, 1936.

132

J. BYAM SHAW, *Pietro Longhi. A man playing a lute...*, in 'Old Master Drawings', March 1936, pp. 64-65.

H. COMSTOCK, *Panels by Pietro Longhi from the Giovanelli collection*, in 'The Connoisseur', vol. 97, 1936.

M. GOERING, *Italienische Malerei des 17. und 18. Jahrhunderts*, Berlin, 1936.

G. LORENZETTI, *Ca' Rezzonico*, Venice, 1936.

R. PALLUCCHINI, *Precisazioni alla R. Galleria Estense*, in 'Bollettino d'Arte', June 1936, pp. 533-549.

M.D. SLOANE, *A Genre Scene by Longhi*, in 'The Bulletin of the Metropolitan Museum of Art', New York, March 1936, pp. 51-52.

S. SITWELL, *Conversation Pieces*, London, 1936.

1937 CHICAGO ART INSTITUTE, *Catalogue of the Worcester collection*, Chicago, 1937.

G. LOCKER LAMPSON, *A few Italian paintings collected by G. Locker Lampson*, London, 1937.

1938 G. LORENZETTI, *Ca' Rezzonico*, Venice, 1938.

A. MOSCHETTI, *Il Museo Civico di Padova*, Padua, 1938.

A. PETRUCCI, *Il volto segreto dell'incisione italiana del Settecento*, in 'Bollettino d'Arte', June 1938, pp. 541-558.

1939 G. DAMERINI, *Settecento Veneziano*, Milan, 1939.

M. GOERING, *Eine Tanzszene von Giuseppe Maria Crespi*, in 'Pantheon', 1939, pp. 1-2.

1940 G. FIOCCO, *Pitture del Settecento italiano in Portogallo*, Rome, 1940.

M. GOERING, *Die Sammlung Scholz-Forni*, in 'Pantheon', 1940, pp. 116-122.

*The Toledo Museum of Art. Four centuries of Venetian painting*, Toledo, 1940.

H.B. WEHLE, *The Metropolitan Museum of Art. A Catalogue of Italian, Spanish and Byzantine Paintings*, New York, 1940.

1941 *Collezioni private*, in 'L'Arte', 1941, III, tav. XVI.

HÔTEL DROUOT, *Vente 20 Nevembre*, Paris, 1941.

*Mercato antiquario*, in 'L'Arte', 1941, I, tav. XXXV.

A. MORANDOTTI, *Mostra della pittura veneziana del Settecento*, Rome, 1941.

A. MORASSI, *Domenico Tiepolo*, in 'Emporium', June, 1941, pp. 265-282.

NATIONAL GALLERY OF ART, *Preliminary Catalogue of Paintings and Sculptures*, Washington, 1941.

1942 G. BRIGANTI, *Nota alla Mostra del Settecento veneziano a Palazzo Massimo*, in 'Le Tre Venezie', March 1941, pp. 105-108.

P.G. GALIZZI, *Le chiese di San Pellegrino*, Bergamo, 1942.

P.G. GALIZZI, *La parrocchiale di S. Pellegrino dalle origini ai restauri del 1941*, in 'Bergomum', April, 1942.

L. LIVAN, *Notizie d'arte tratte dai Notatori e dagli Annali del N.H. Pietro Gradenigo*, Venice, 1942.

G. LORENZETTI, *La pittura italiana del Settecento*, Novara, 1942.

E. MODIGLIANI, *La collezione di Luigi Albertini*, Rome, 1942.

1943 E. ARSLAN, *Di Alessandro e Pietro Longhi*, in 'Emporium', 1943, 8, pp. 51-63.

G. FIOCCO, *Pittura barocca veneziana*, Padua, 1943.

R. PALLUCCHINI, *I disegni di F. Guardi al Museo Correr*, Venice, 1943.

1945 R. GALLO, *I Pisani ed i palazzi di S. Stefano e di Strà*, Venice, 1945.

R. PALLUCCHINI, *Cinque secoli di pittura veneta*, Venice, 1945.

R. PALLUCCHINI, *I dipinti della Galleria Estense di Modena*, Rome, 1945.

1946 E. ARSLAN, *Inediti di Pietro e Alessandro Longhi*, in 'Emporium', 1946, 2, pp. 59-65.

A.F. BLUNT, *Catalogue of the Exhibition of the King's Pictures*, London, 1946.

M. DAVIS, *Two Eighteenth-Century paintings*, in 'Worcester Museum Annual', V, 1946, pp. 56-62.

GALLERIA QUERINI STAMPALIA, *Itinerario delle sale di esposizione*, Venice, 1946.

R. LONGHI, *Viatico per cinque secoli di pittura veneziana*, Florence, 1946.

A. MONGAN and P. SACHS, *Drawings in the Fogg Museum of Art*, Cambridge, Mass. 1946.

R. PALLUCCHINI, *I capolavori dei Musei veneti*, Venice, 1946.

1947 O. Benesch, *Venetian drawings of the Eighteenth Century in America*, New York, 1947.

G. Delogu, *Disegni veneziani del Settecento*, Milan-Zürich, 1947.

F. Hartt, *Settecento Fantasy and Comedy*, in 'Smith College Museum of Art Bulletin', 1947, pp. 22-30.

R. Pallucchini, *Trésors de l'Art Vénitien*, Milan-Brussels, 1947.

R. Pallucchini, *La mostra delle collezioni private in Venezia*, in 'Arte Veneta', 1947, pp. 149-150.

R. Pallucchini, *Veneti al Fogg Museum*, in 'Arte Veneta', 1947, pp. 237-238.

T. Pignatti, *Per l'iconografia di Francesco Guardi*, in 'Arte Veneta', 1947, p. 294.

*Quattrocento pitture inedite*, Venice, 1947.

A. Riccoboni, *Pittura veneta*, Venice, 1947.

1948 F. Arcangeli and C. Gnudi, *Mostra celebrativa di Giuseppe M. Crespi*, Bologna, 1948.

A. Blunt, *Dipinti veneziani del XVII e XVIII secolo nelle Collezioni Reali d'Inghilterra*, in 'Arte Veneta', 1948, pp. 127-130.

*A Gallery of XVIII Century Venetian Paintings. A Special exhibition*, Louisville, 1948.

*Kunstschätze der Lombardei*, Zürich, 1948.

R. Pallucchini, *Disegni veneziani del Settecento in America*, in 'Arte Veneta', 1948, pp. 157-158.

R. Pallucchini, *Settecentisti veneti in mostra a Louisville*, in 'Arte Veneta', 1948, pp. 172-173.

R. Pallucchini, *Veneti alle mostre svizzere*, in 'Arte Veneta', 1948, pp. 166-170.

1949 G. Arnolds, *Zeichnungen des Kupferstichkabinetts in Berlin. Italienische Zeichnungen*, Berlin, 1949.

R. Bassi Rathgeb, *Ceruti, Longhi e Ceresa in tre dipinti sconosciuti dell'eredità Suardo*, in 'Rivista di Bergamo', March-April, 1949.

H.D. Gronau, *Pitture veneziane in Inghilterra*, in 'Arte Veneta', 1949, pp. 182-183.

S. Marconi, *Le Gallerie dell'Accademia di Venezia*, Venice, 1949.

R. Pallucchini, *Studi sui disegni veneti*, in 'Arte Veneta', 1949, pp. 172-173.

1950 E. Bassi, *L'Accademia di Belle Arti di Venezia nel suo bicentenario*, Venice, 1950.

V. Golzio, *Il Seicento e il Settecento*, Turin, 1950.

R.B.K. McLanathan, *Dipinti veneziani acquistati negli ultimi anni dal Museo di Belle Arti di Boston*, in 'Arte Veneta', 1950, pp. 162-163.

R. Pallucchini, *La mostra del Bicentenario dell'Accademia veneziana di Belle Arti. Il Settecento*, in 'Arte Veneta', 1950, pp. 170-171.

M. Petrocchi, *Il tramonto della Repubblica di Venezia...*, in 'Miscellanea di Studi e Memorie della Deputazione di Storia Patria', vol. VII, Venice, 1950.

T. Pignatti, *I ritratti settecenteschi della Querini Stampalia*, in 'Bollettino d'Arte', 1950, pp. 216-218.

1951 J. Byam Shaw, *Venetian Art at Whitechapel*, in 'The Burlington Magazine', February 1951, pp. 61-62.

M. Brunetti, *Un eccezionale collegio peritale: Piazzetta, Tiepolo, Longhi*, in 'Arte Veneta', 1951, pp. 158-160.

*Catalogus von de tentoongestelle Schilderijen Pastels en Aquarellen*, Amsterdam, 1951.

N. di Carpegna, *Longhi*, in 'Enciclopedia Cattolica', vol. VII, Rome, 1951, pp. 1513-1514.

N. Von Holst, *La pittura veneziana tra il Reno e la Neva*, in 'Arte Veneta', 1951, pp. 131-140.

R. Longhi, *Dialogo fra il Caravaggio e il Tiepolo*, in 'Paragone', nov. 1951, pp. 57-64.

G. Lorenzetti, *Ca' Rezzonico*, Venice, 1951.

*La Moda in cinque secoli di pittura*, Turin, 1951.

A. Morassi, *Pitture veneziane del Settecento in una mostra a Londra*, in 'Emporium', 1951, pp. 215-226.

R. Pallucchini, *La pittura veneziana del Settecento*, II, Bologna, 1951.

R. Pallucchini, *La mostra della moda a Torino*, in 'Arte Veneta', 1951, p. 220.

R. Pallucchini, *La pittura veneziana del Settecento alla Whitechapel Gallery di Londra*, in 'Arte Veneta', 1951, pp. 209-214.

*Rijksmuseum Amsterdam Catalogues...*, Amsterdam, 1951.

*Rococo returns to San Diego*, in 'Art News', March 1951.

F. Valcanover, *Postilla su Pietro Longhi 'pittore di storia'*, in 'Arte Veneta', 1951, pp. 169-170.

*Venise*, special issue of 'L'Amour de l'Art', Paris, 1951.

F.J.B. Watson, *Eighteenth-Century Venice*, London, 1951.

1952   C. Baroni and G.A. Dell'Acqua, *Tesori d'Arte in Lombardia*, Milan, 1952.

R. Bassi-Rathgeb, *Ricordi longheschi nel bergamasco*, in 'Gazzetta di Bergamo', April 1952, p. 26.

*Educazione e svaghi di un giovan signore*, in 'Le Vie d'Italia', February 1952, pp. 217-224.

F. Fosca, *De Watteau à Tiepolo*, Geneva, 1952.

E.P. Richardson, *Venice 1700-1800*, Detroit, 1952.

R. Salvini, *Catalogo degli Uffizi*, Florence, 1952.

L. Venturi and R. Skira Venturi, *La peinture italienne*, vol. III, Geneva, 1952.

1953   M. Dazzi, *Alessandro Longhi. Ritratto di Daniele IV Dolfin*, in 'Arte Veneta', 1953, pp. 178-181.

*Drawings by old masters: Royal Academy of Arts Diploma Gallery*, London, 1953.

G. Fiocco, *Segnalazioni per Giacomo Ceruti*, in 'Emporium', 1953, pp. 51-55.

*Loan Exhibition of thirty-nine Masterpieces of Venetian Painting...*, London, 1953.

R. Longhi, *Pittura e Teatro nel Settecento italiano*, in: R. Bacchelli and R. Longhi, *Teatro e Immagini del Settecento italiano*, Turin, 1953.

R. Longhi, R. Cipriani and G. Testori, *I pittori della realtà in Lombardia*, Milan, 1953.

G. Mariacher, *Per il nuovo allestimento del Museo Correr...*, in 'Arte Veneta', 1953, pp. 205-209.

G. Mazzotti, *Le Ville Venete*, 2nd ed., Treviso, 1953.

A. Morassi, *Una mostra del Settecento veneziano a Detroit*, in 'Arte Veneta', 1953, pp. 49-62.

M. Muraro, *Mostra di disegni del Sei e Settecento*, Florence, 1953.

M. Muraro, *Nuova Guida di Venezia e delle sue isole*, Florence, 1953.

A. Ottino della Chiesa, *Brera*, Novara, 1953.

R. Pallucchini, *Cinque secoli di pittura veneta a Sciaffusa...*, in 'Arte Veneta', 1953, pp. 194-199.

R. Pallucchini, *Introduction à la peinture vénitienne du XVIIIe siècle*, in 'Les Arts Plastiques', Brussels, October-December 1953.

P. Poirier, *La peinture vénitienne*, Paris, 1953.

M. Pittaluga, *Acquafortisti veneziani del Settecento*, Florence.

1954   E. Arslan, *Cinque disegni veneti*, in 'Arte Veneta', 1954, p. 289.

D. Beltrami, *Storia della popolazione di Venezia...*, Padua, 1954.

G.L. Bertolini, *La Lezione o l'Audizione di geografia*, in 'Ateneo Veneto', 1954, pp. 9-12.

*European Masters of the Eighteenth Century. Winter Exhibition 1954-55*, London, 1954.

*Inaugural Exhibition*, Fort Worth Art Center, Fort Worth, 1954.

G. Ronci, *Da Caravaggio a Tiepolo*, Rome, 1954.

G. Testori, *Il Ghislandi, il Ceruti e i Veneti*, in 'Paragone', 1954, n. 57, pp. 16-33.

F. Valcanover, *Mostra di pittura del Settecento nel bellunese*, Venice, 1954.

F. Valcanover, *Un nuovo ritratto di Alessandro Longhi*, in 'Archivio Storico di Belluno Feltre e Cadore', April-September 1954, pp. 33-36.

M. Valsecchi, *La pittura veneziana*, Milan, 1954.

1955   *Dipinti inediti di Pietro Longhi*, in 'Arte Figurativa Antica e Moderna', July-August, 1955, p. 32.

R. Edwards, *Early Conversation Pictures from the Middles Ages to about 1730*, London, 1955.

G. Fiocco, *Cento antichi disegni veneziani*, Venice, 1955.

G. Fiocco, *La mostra di Fra Galgario a Bergamo e l'Accademia Carrara*, in 'Arte Veneta', 1955, p. 269.

E. Hüttinger, *Unbekannte Schönheit...*, Zürich, 1955.

E. Hüttinger, *Schönheit des 18. Jahrhunderts*, Zürich, 1955.

R. Levi-Pisetzky, *La couleur dans l'habillement italien*, in 'Actes du premier Congrès International d'histoire du costume', Venice, 1955.

A. Morassi, *Una mostra del Settecento a Zurigo*, in 'Arte Veneta', 1955, pp. 275-278.

*Mostra del Settecento veneziano*, Milan, 1955.

A. Ottino della Chiesa, *Accademia Carrara*, Bergamo, 1955.

R. Pallucchini, *Il Settecento veneziano a Milano*, in 'Arte Veneta', 1955, pp. 264-268.

L. Pelandi, *L'arte e gli artisti*, in 'La Rivista di Bergamo', July-August, 1955.

F. Valcanover, *Gallerie dell'Accademia di Venezia*, Novara, 1955.

F. Watson, *Venetian paintings at the Royal Academy 1954-55*, in 'Arte Veneta', 1955, pp. 253-264.

1956 M. Berengo, *La società veneta alla fine del Settecento*, Florence, 1956.

N. Dazzi, *Il Fiore della lirica veneziana*, Venice, 1956.

G. Fiocco, *Una pittura di Pietro Longhi*, in 'Arte Veneta', 1956, pp. 206-7.

M. Levey, *The Eighteenth-Century Italian Schools*, National Gallery, London, 1956.

V. Moschini, *Pietro Longhi*, Milan, 1956.

K.T. Parker, *Catalogue of the collection of Drawings in the Ashmolean Museum*, Oxford, 1956.

G. Rosa, *La collezione Crespi*, Milan, 1956.

C. Someda de Marco, *Il Museo Civico... di Udine*, Udine, 1956.

F. Valcanover, *Affreschi sconosciuti di Pietro Longhi*, in 'Paragone', 1956, n. 73, pp. 21-26.

F. Valcanover, *Due ritratti di Pietro Longhi*, in 'Venezia e l'Europa', 1956, p. 362.

1957 A. Blunt and E. Croft Murray, *Venetian Drawings of the XVII and XVIII centuries...*, London, 1957.

L. Coletti-T. Spini, *Collezione Ottaviano Venier*, Bergamo, 1957.

C. Donzelli, *I pittori Veneti del Settecento*, Florence, 1957.

L. Grossato, *Il Museo Civico di Padova. Dipinti e sculture dal XIV al XIX secolo*, Venice, 1957.

1958 A. Chastel, *L'Arte italiana*, Florence, 1958.

G. De Logu, *Pittura veneziana dal XIV al XVIII secolo*, Bergamo, 1958.

R.J. Heinemann, *Sammlung Schloss Rohoncz*, Lugano, 1958.

A. Morassi, *Dessins Vénitiens du dix-huitième siècle de la Collection du Duc de Talleyrand*, Milan, 1958.

V. Moschini, *Un altro Pietro Longhi*, in 'Arte Veneta', 1958, p. 222.

F. Valcanover, *Pietro Longhi*, in 'Enciclopedia Universale dell'Arte', Venice-Rome, 1958, VIII, col. 683-688.

1959 *Handbook of the collections in the William Rockhill Nelson Gallery of Art*, Kansas City, 1959.

M. Levey, *Painting in XVIII-Century Venice*, London, 1959.

M. Muraro, *Figure di Francesco Guardi*, in 'Emporium', 1959, pp. 243-252.

A. Riccoboni, *Ritratti e figure di Pietro Longhi*, in 'Emporium', 1959, pp. 199-206.

M. Valsecchi, *Un tesoro di famiglia a Villa Reale*, in 'L'Illustrazione Italiana', January, 1959, pp. 73-98.

1960 R. Pallucchini, *La pittura veneziana del Settecento*, Venice-Rome, 1960.

T. Pignatti, *Il Museo Correr di Venezia. Dipinti del XVII e XVIII secolo*, Venice, 1960.

1961 K.T. Parker, *Catalogue of Paintings in the Ashmolean Museum*, Oxford, 1961.

T. Pignatti, *Il Settecento*, in 'Pittura in Europa', vol. IV, Milan, 1961.

T. Pignatti, *Seconda mostra di dipinti restaurati del Sei e Settecento al Museo Correr*, in 'Bollettino dei Musei Civici Veneziani', 1961, I, pp. 13-27.

G.M. Pilo, *Longhi allievo del Balestra*, in 'Arte Figurativa', January-February, 1961, pp. 29-34.

F. Valcanover, *New light on Alessandro Longhi's 'Balotin del doxe'*, in 'The Connoisseur', 1961, pp. 227-229.

1962 F. Antal, *Hogarth and his place in European Art*, London, 1962.

G. Nicodemi, *Il dono di Carlo Grassi al Comune di Milano*, Milan, 1962.

A. Rizzi, *Quattro Pietro Longhi e un Tiepolo*, in 'Emporium', 1962, 10, pp. 155-164.

1963 *Arricchimenti nelle collezioni private*, in 'Acropoli', 1963, pp. 237-257.

*La Collezione Conte Paolo Gerli di Villa Gaeta*, in 'Acropoli', 1963, pp. 314-325.

*Collezioni private a Milano e in Italia*, in 'Acropoli', 1963, pp. 56-79.

F. Haskell, *Patrons and Painters*, London, 1963.

NATIONAL GALLERY OF IRELAND, *Concise Catalogue of Oil Pictures*, Dublin, 1963.

C.L. RAGGHIANTI, *Antichi disegni e stampe dell' Accademia Carrara di Bergamo*, Bergamo, 1963.

1964   M. LEVEY, *The Later Italian Pictures in the Royal Collection*, London, 1964.

E. MARTINI, *La pittura veneziana del Settecento*, Venice, 1964.

L. MENEGAZZI, *Il Museo Civico di Treviso. Dipinti e sculture dal XII al XIX secolo*, Venice, 1964.

*Pietro Longhi*, in 'The Burlington Magazine', November 1964, p. XLVII.

T. PIGNATTI, *Disegni Veneti del Settecento nel Museo Correr di Venezia*, Venice, 1964.

F. VALCANOVER, *Longhi*, Milan, 1964.

F. WATSON, *An unfamiliar conversation piece by Alessandro Longhi*, in 'Bollettino dei Musei Civici Veneziani', 1964, IV, pp. 17-20.

1965   P.R. CIARDI, *La raccolta Cagnola. Dipinti e sculture*, Pisa, 1965.

T. PIGNATTI, *I Disegni Veneziani del Settecento*, Rome, 1965.

T. PIGNATTI, *La fraglia dei pittori di Venezia*, in 'Bollettino dei Musei Civici Veneziani', 1965, n. 3, pp. 16-39.

1966   A. GRISERI, *Inediti per il disegno veneto del '600 e '700*, in 'Arte Veneta', 1966, pp. 177-189.

F. HASKELL, *Mecenati e Pittori*, Florence, 1966.

A. RIZZI, *Mostra della pittura veneta del Settecento in Friuli*, Udine, 1966.

1967   J. CAILLEUX, *Les Guardi et Pietro Longhi*, in 'Problemi Guardeschi', Venezia, 1967, pp. 51-54.

W. DEUSCH, *Unbekannte Handzeichnungen Alter Meister, Sammlung Freiherr von Koenig-Fachsenfeld*, Stuttgart, 1967.

L. MALLÈ and G. TESTORI, *Giacomo Ceruti...*, Turin, 1967.

*Pietro Longhi*, in 'The Burlington Magazine', May 1967, p. XXXIII.

A. RIZZI, *Carlevarijs...*, Venice, 1967.

1968   T. PIGNATTI, *Les Dessins de Pietro Longhi*, in 'L'Oeil' Oct. 1968, pp. 14-23.

F. VALCANOVER, *Il «Catalogo ragionato» delle opere di Pietro Longhi*, in 'Arte Veneta', 1968, pp. 229-231.

PAINTINGS AND DRAWINGS BY PIETRO LONGHI

1. ST. PELLEGRINO CONDEMNED TO DEATH. S. Pellegrino, Parish Church.

2. THE ADORATION OF THE MAGI. Venice, Scuola di S. Giovanni Evangelista.

3. THE FALL OF THE GIANTS. Venice, Ca' Sagredo.

4. SKETCHES FOR THE GIANTS. Venice, Museo Correr (no. 514 verso).

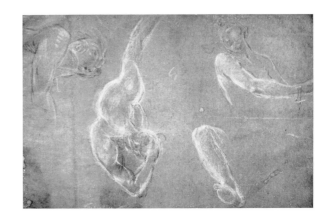

5. THE FALL OF THE GIANTS. Venice, Ca' Sagredo.

6. THE FALL OF THE GIANTS. Venice, Ca' Sagredo.

7. SEATED SHEPHERD BOY. Bassano, Museo Civico.

8. SEATED SHEPHERD BOY. Venice, Museo Correr (no. 515 recto).

9. SHEPHERD GIRL. Venice, Museo Correr (no. 511 verso).

10. SHEPHERD GIRL WITH A FLOWER. Bassano,
Museo Civico.

11. SHEPHERD BOY STANDING. Bassano, Museo Civico.

12. SHEPHERD GIRL WITH A COCK. Bassano, Museo Civico.

13. SHEPHERD BOY STANDING. Rovigo, Seminario Vescovile.

14. PEASANT WITH A MANDOLINE. Venice, Museo Correr (no. 557).

15. A GIRL SPINNING. Venice, Ca' Rezzonico.

16. THE WASHERWOMEN. Venice, Ca' Rezzonico.

17. THE MERRY COUPLE. Venice, Ca' Rezzonico.

18. THE POLENTA. Venice, Ca' Rezzonico.

19. A GIRL SPINNING. Milan, Private Collection.

20. PEASANTS DANCING. Ferrara, Paulucci Collection.

21. PEASANT GIRL AND MUSICIAN. Ferrara, Paulucci Collection.

22. PEASANT GIRL AND MAN DRINKING. Ferrara, Paulucci Collection.

23. THE DRINKERS. Milan, Galleria d'Arte Moderna.

24. MAIDSERVANT WITH TWO PAILS OF WATER. Venice, Museo Correr (no. 456).

25. THE WASHERWOMEN. Zoppola, Castello.

26. THE POLENTA. Zoppola, Castello.

27. A GIRL SPINNING. Zoppola, Castello.

28. PEASANT SITTING AT A TABLE. Venice, Museo Correr (no. 525).

29. THREE PEASANTS. Venice, Museo Correr (no. 526).

30. PEASANT GIRL BROACHING A CASK OF WINE. Venice, Museo Correr (no. 523).

31. THE DRUNKARDS. Zoppola, Castello.

32. A GIRL SPINNING. Venice, Querini Stampalia.

33. GIRLS SPINNING. Venice, Querini Stampalia.

34. SLEEPING PEASANT GIRL. Venice, Querini Stampalia.

35. THE DRUNKARD. Biella, Private Collection.

36. STUDIES OF A MAN DRINKING. Venice, Museo Correr (no. 502 verso).

37. THE CONCERT. Venice, Accademia.

38. THE TAILOR. Venice, Accademia.

39. THE SINGING TEST. Whereabouts unknown.

40. THE DANCING-MASTER;
STUDIES OF HANDS. Venice,
Museo Correr (no. 542).

41. THE DANCING LESSON. Venice, Accademia.

42. THE TOILET. Venice, Accademia.

43. LADY IN A CRINOLINE. Venice,
Museo Correr (no. 487 recto).

44. THE INTRODUCTION. Paris, Louvre.

45. TWO YOUNG MEN IN DOMINOES. Venice, Museo Correr (no. 437).

46. MAN IN A DOMINO. Venice, Museo Correr (no. 439).

47. THE PAINTER IN HIS STUDIO. Venice, Ca' Rezzonico.

48. THE PAINTER IN HIS STUDIO. Dublin, National Gallery of Ireland.

49. THE PAINTER IN HIS STUDIO. Formerly Keir, Stirling Collection.

50. STUDIES OF HANDS AND LEGS. Venice, Museo Correr (no. 470).

51. THE VISIT TO THE LIBRARY. Worcester (Mass.), Art Museum.

52. VIOLIN-PLAYER. Venice, Museo Correr (no. 447).

53. THE TICKLE. Whereabouts unknown.

54. THE MUSIC LESSON. San Francisco, California Palace of the Legion of Honor.

55. DRAPERY AND OTHER STUDIES. Venice, Museo Correr (no. 448).

56. WOMAN AT HER HUSBAND'S BEDSIDE. Venice, Museo Correr (no. 462 verso).

57. THE GENTLEMAN'S AWAKENING. Windsor Castle, Royal Collection.

58. GENTLEMAN IN BED, AND A LADY. Venice, Museo Correr (no. 482).

59. GENTLEMAN IN BED, AND A LADY. Venice, Museo Correr (no. 540 recto).

60. GENTLEMAN IN BED. Venice, Museo Correr (no. 481).

61. GENTLEMAN IN BED. Venice, Museo Correr (no. 462 recto).

62. BLINDMAN'S BUFF. Windsor Castle, Royal Collection.

63. THREE STUDIES OF STOOLS. Venice, Museo Correr
(no. 540 verso).

64. THE WET-NURSE. Venice, Ca' Rezzonico.

65. DOCTOR FEELING A PATIENT'S PULSE.
Venice, Museo Correr (no. 435).

66. THE SICK LADY. Venice, Ca' Rezzonico.

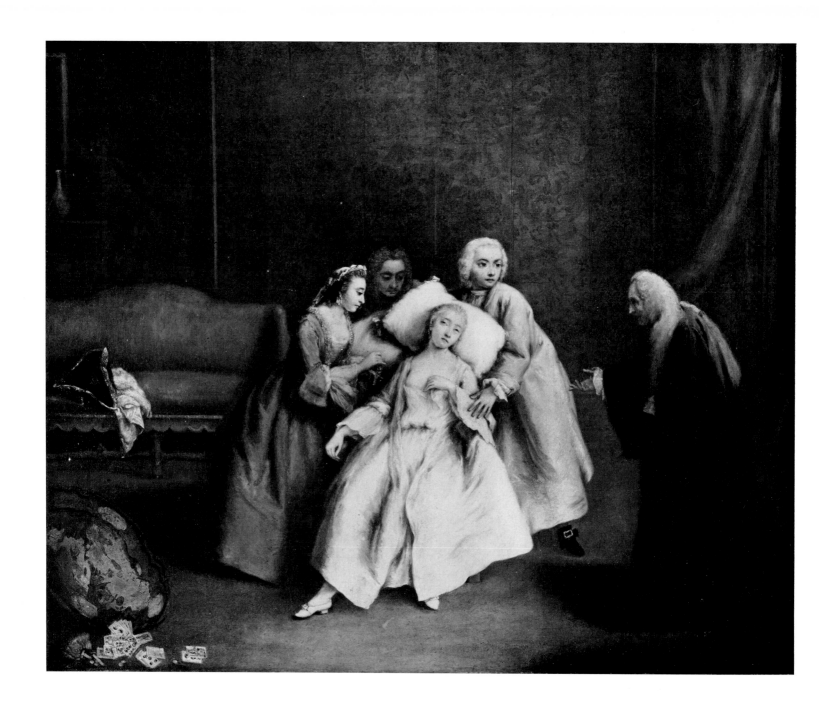

67. THE FAINT. Washington, National Gallery of Art (Samuel H. Kress Collection).

68. BLINDMAN'S BUFF. Washington, National Gallery of Art (Samuel H. Kress Collection).

69. TWO YOUNG GIRLS. Venice, Museo Correr (no. 504).

70. A FAMILY GROUP. London, National Gallery.

71. THE VIRGIN AND CHILD, WITH SAINTS AND ANGELS. Venice, Church of S. Pantalon.

72. THE MADONNA OF LORETO. Venice, Church of S. Pantalon.

73. A FEMALE MARTYR. Venice, Church of S. Pantalon.

74. APPARITION OF THE VIRGIN. Venice, Church of S. Pantalon.

75. THE VIRGIN AND CHILD, WITH FEMALE SAINTS. Venice, Church of S. Pantalon.

76. A LADY RECEIVES VISITORS. New York, Metropolitan Museum of Art.

77. STUDY OF DRAPERY AND OF A PAINTING.
Venice, Museo Correr (no. 547 verso).

78. THE MEETING OF THE PROCURATORE AND HIS WIFE. New York, Metropolitan Museum of Art.

79. A SERVANT WITH A TRAY; A MAID WITH A TRAY. Venice, Museo Correr (no. 490).

80. THE PROCURATORE PAYS A CALL. London, National Gallery.

81. GENTLEMAN WITH A CAPE. Venice, Museo Correr (no. 545).

82. GIRL PREPARING SALAD. Venice, Museo Correr (no. 479).

83. MILORD'S SALAD. Milan, A. Crespi Collection.

84. MILORD'S VISITOR. New York, Metropolitan Museum of Art.

85. THE INDISCREET GENTLEMAN. Formerly Florence, Riccio Collection.

86. WOMAN SELLING DOUGHNUTS. Milan, Galleria d'Arte Moderna.

87. MAN SELLING DOUGHNUTS. Formerly Munich, H. Vollert Collection.

88. WOMAN SELLING DOUGHNUTS. Venice, Ca' Rezzonico.

89. MAN SELLING SALAD. Longleat, Collection of the Marquis of Bath.

90. PEASANTS DANCING. Chicago, Art Institute (Worcester Collection).

91. PEASANTS DANCING THE FURLANA. Whereabouts unknown.

92. PEASANTS DANCING THE FURLANA. Venice, Ca' Rezzonico.

93. PEASANTS DANCING THE FURLANA. Northampton (Mass.), Smith College Museum of Art.

94. PEASANTS DANCING THE FURLANA. Venice, Querini Stampalia.

95. THE FORTUNE-TELLER. Venice, Ca' Rezzonico.

96. THE NEEDLEWORK SCHOOL. Venice, Ca' Rezzonico.

100. THE TEMPTATION. Hartford (Conn.), Wadsworth Atheneum.

101. GENTLEMAN OFFERING MONEY; OLD WOMAN. Venice, Museo Correr (no. 452).

102. THE SEDUCTION. Milan, A. Crespi Collection.

103. THE MILLINER. New York, Metropolitan Museum of Art.

104. THE DANCING-GIRL. Milan, A. Crespi Collection.

105. THE MILLINER. London, Brinsley Ford Collection.

106. THE DANCING-GIRL. London, Private Collection.

107. THE TOOTH-DRAWER. Milan, Galleria di Brera.

108. A DWARF. Venice, Museo Correr (no. 524).

109. THE FORTUNE-TELLER. Venice, Accademia.

110. GENTLEMAN WITH A CLOAK. Venice, Museo Correr (no. 492).

111. PEASANT. Venice, Museo Correr (no. 6058).

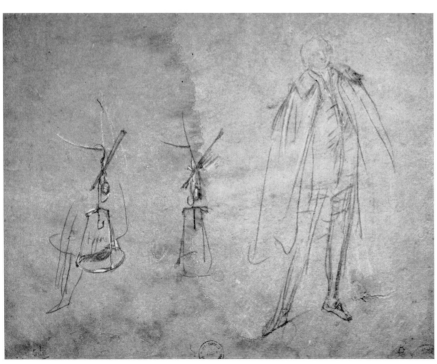

112. THE APOTHECARY. Venice, Accademia.

113. THE BETROTHAL. Milan, Gerli Collection.

114. THE FRIAR'S SERMON. Bergamo, Private Collection.

115. FEMALE FIGURE; CHAIR AND STOOL.
Venice, Museo Correr (no. 534).

116. THE RHINOCEROS. Venice, Ca' Rezzonico.

117. THE CONCERT. Milan, Galleria di Brera.

118. THE RHINOCEROS. London, National Gallery.

119. THE MOOR'S LETTER. Venice, Ca' Rezzonico.

120. THE SAGREDO FAMILY. Venice, Querini Stampalia.

121. SEATED GENTLEMAN. Venice, Museo Correr (no. 440).

122. GENTLEMAN LEANING ON A STOOL.
Venice, Museo Correr (no. 463).

123. A PATRICIAN FAMILY, Venice, Ca' Rezzonico.

124. SEATED GENTLEMAN. Venice, Museo Correr (no. 450 verso).

125. THREE STUDIES OF A MAIDSERVANT. Venice, Museo Correr (no. 450 recto).

126. THE GEOGRAPHY LESSON. Venice, Querini Stampalia.

127. A GUITAR-PLAYER. Venice, Museo Correr (no. 443).

128. THE FAMILY CONCERT. Venice, Ca' Rezzonico.

129. THE GEOGRAPHY LESSON. Padua, Museo Civico.

130. PORTRAIT OF A LADY. Milan, Private collection.

131. OLD MAN SEATED. Venice, Museo Correr (no. 487 verso).

132. A MEAL AT HOME. Providence (R. I.), Rhode Island School of Design.

133. THE SPINET. Milan, Heirs of Senatore M. Crespi.

134. EMBROIDRESSES. Venice, Museo Correr (no. 569).

135. THE EMBROIDERY WORKROOM. London, National Gallery.

136. LADY IN A CRINOLINE. Venice, Museo Correr (no. 449).

137. THE LADY'S TOILET. Chicago, Art Institute (Flora Erskine Miles Fund).

138. THE SICK LADY. Zurich, Private Collection.

139. THE DOGE PIETRO GRIMANI GIVING AUDIENCE.
Venice, Museo Correr.

140. TWO STUDIES OF A SENATOR. Venice, Museo Correr
(no. 574).

141. PORTRAIT OF THE DOGE PIETRO GRIMANI. Bergamo, Private Collection.

142. PORTRAIT OF WILLIAM GRAHAM, 2ND DUKE OF MONTROSE.
Venice, Ca' Rezzonico.

143. BOYS RIDING. Florence, Museo Stibbert.

144. THE RIDE. Venice, Ca' Rezzonico.

145. PORTRAIT OF EUGENE OF SAVOY. Venice,
Ca' Rezzonico.

146. LADY AND HUNTERS. Venice, Museo Correr (no. 489).

147. SHOOTING HARES. Venice, Querini Stampalia.

148. BAPTISM. Venice, Querini Stampalia.

149. CONFIRMATION. Venice, Querini Stampalia.

150. COMMUNION. Venice, Querini Stampalia.

151. MATRIMONY. Venice, Querini Stampalia.

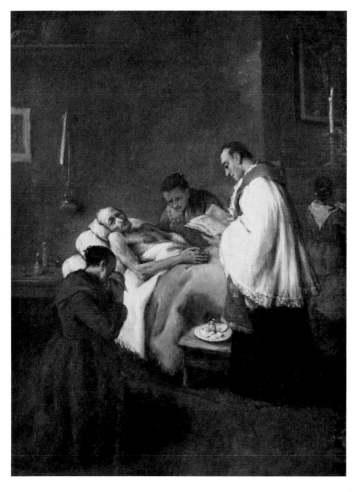

152. EXTREME UNCTION. Venice, Querini Stampalia.

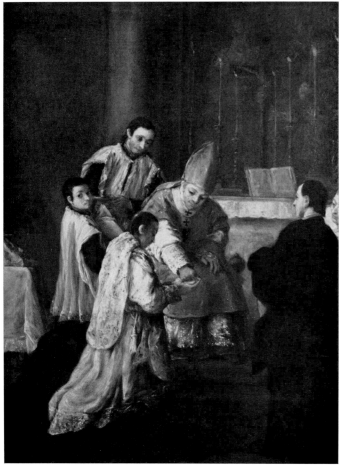

153. HOLY ORDERS. Venice, Querini Stampalia.

154. CONFESSION. Venice, Querini Stampalia.

155. STUDY OF HANDS. Venice, Museo Correr
(no. 565 recto).

156. CONFESSION. Florence, Uffizi.

157. CONFESSION. Rome, Senatore Albertini Collection.

158. A MIRACLE OF ST LAWRENCE. Brescia, Suore Ancelle della Carità.

159. THE FRIAR'S SERMON. Milan, Private Collection.

160. THE QUACK. Venice, Ca' Rezzonico.

161. THE QUACK. Segromigno Monte, Heirs to the Salom Collection.

162. THE QUACK. London, Private Collection.

163. THE COSMORAMA. Segromigno Monte, Heirs to the Salom Collection.

164. THE PERFUME-SELLER. Venice, Ca' Rezzonico.

165. THE COSMORAMA. Venice, Querini Stampalia.

166. THE FORTUNE-TELLER. London, National Gallery.

167. THE RECEPTION IN THE COURTYARD. St. Louis, City Art Museum.

168. THE RIDOTTO. Segromigno Monte, Heirs to the Salom Collection.

169. TWO GENTLEMEN IN DOMINOES. Berlin, Kupferstichkabinett.

170. THE RIDOTTO. Venice, Querini Stampalia.

171. THE RIDOTTO. Venice, Querini Stampalia.

172. THE RIDOTTO. Bergamo, Accademia Carrara.

173. MEETING OF DOMINOES. Venice, Ca' Rezzonico.

174. THE CARD-PLAYERS. Milan, Galleria d'Arte Moderna.

175. PORTRAIT OF POPE CLEMENT XIII REZZONICO.
Venice, Ca' Rezzonico.

176. THE ALCHEMISTS. Venice, Ca' Rezzonico.

177. PORTRAIT OF A GENTLEMAN. Bergamo, Private Collection.

178. PORTRAIT OF A LADY. Formerly New York, Newhouse Gallery.

179. PORTRAIT OF MAGRATH THE GIANT. Venice, Ca' Rezzonico.

180. SHOOTING IN THE LAGOON. Venice, Querini Stampalia.

181. SHOOTING IN THE LAGOON. Venice, Museo Correr
(no. 475).

182. SHOOTING IN THE LAGOON. London, O'Nians Gallery.

183. SHOOTING IN THE LAGOON. Venice, Museo Correr (no. 476).

184. THE TOOTH-DRAWER. Formerly Venice, Heirs to the Ravà Collection.

185. SEATED LADY. Venice, Museo Correr (no. 445).

186. IN THE ESTUARY GARDENS. Venice, Ca' Rezzonico.

187. COFFEE TIME. London, Hallsborough Gallery.

188. LADY WITH A BOOK; ARTIST WITH A PENCIL. Venice, Museo Correr (no. 553).

189. GENTLEMAN MAKING A BOW. Venice, Museo Correr (no. 491 recto).

190. THE CARD-PLAYERS. London, Hallsborough Gallery.

191. FAMILY CONVERSATION. London, Hallsborough Gallery.

192. THE SPINET RECITAL. London, Hallsborough Gallery.

193. CONVERSATION. Stanford, Cal., Stanford University Museum.

194. THE PAINTER IN HIS STUDIO. Stanford, Cal., Stanford University Museum.

195. PAINTER AT THE EASEL. Venice, Museo Correr (no. 438).

196. COFFEE TIME. Formerly Padua, Miari Collection.

197. THE MANDOLINE RECITAL. Formerly Venice, Papadopoli Collection.

198. THE NURSE. London, Private Collection.

198a. THE SINGING TEST. Whereabouts unknown.

199. FAMILY GROUP. Venice, Barnabò Collection.

200. THE VISIT FROM A LADY. Milan, A. Crespi Collection.

201. THE LADY READS ALOUD. Milan, A. Crespi Collection.

202. GENTLEMAN IN A DOMINO. Venice, Museo Correr
(no. 555 recto).

203. THE VISIT FROM A DOMINO. Venice, Ca' Rezzonico.

204. THE HAIRDRESSER. Venice, Museo Correr (no. 441 recto).

205. NURSE WITH A CHILD ON HER ARM. Venice, Museo Correr (no. 539).

206. THE HAIRDRESSER. Venice, Ca' Rezzonico.

207. A FRIAR. Venice, Museo Correr (no. 494).

208. THE VISIT FROM A FRIAR. Venice, Ca' Rezzonico.

209. THE LADY AT THE DRESSMAKER'S. Venice, Ca' Rezzonico.

210. THE TOILET. Venice, Ca' Rezzonico.

211. THE FAINT. Segromigno Monte, Heirs to the Salom Collection.

212. BLINDMAN'S BUFF. Segromigno Monte, Heirs to the Salom Collection.

213. THE LADY'S HAIR IS DRESSED. Venice, Ca' Rezzonico.

214. THE SLEEPER TICKLED. Venice, Barone Rubin de Cervin
Albrizzi Collection.

215. YOUNG MAN ASLEEP. Berlin, Kupferstichkabinett.

216. FAMILY GROUP. Verona, Museo di Castelvecchio.

217. TWO CHILDREN, AT A TABLE AND IN A LITTLE CHAIR.
Venice, Museo Correr (no. 488).

218. THE ALBRIZZI FAMILY. Venice, Barone Rubin de Cervin Albrizzi Collection.

219. NURSE WITH A CHILD. Venice, Museo Correr (no. 483).

220. FAMILY GROUP. Segromigno Monte, Heirs to the Salom Collection.

221. MONKS, CANONS AND FRIARS OF VENICE. Venice, Querini Stampalia.

222. A FAMILY SERMON. Whereabouts unknown.

223. PRIEST IN AN ARMCHAIR. Venice, Museo Correr (no. 538).

224. THE SCHOOLBOY'S PUNISHMENT. Genoa, Trucchi Collection.

225. THE TEMPTATION OF ST ANTHONY. Venice, Querini Stampalia.

226. THE PHILOSOPHER PYTHAGORAS. Venice, Accademia.

227. PORTRAIT OF FRANCESCO GUARDI. Venice, Ca' Rezzonico.

228. PORTRAIT OF A GENTLEMAN. Whereabouts unknown.

229. PORTRAIT OF A VIOLINIST. New York, R. Manning Collection.

230. THE PROCURATORE LUDOVICO MANIN. Udine, Museo Civico.

231. PORTRAIT OF THE DOGE'S STEWARD. Genoa, Trucchi Collection.

232. PORTRAIT OF A POLISH GENTLEMAN. Venice, Brass Collection.

233. THE MASTER'S ARRIVAL. Venice, Querini Stampalia.

234. TWO PEASANTS. London, British Museum.

235. PREPARING THE GUNS. Venice, Querini Stampalia.

236. UNLOADING THE HUNTER'S EQUIPMENT. Venice, Querini Stampalia.

237. HUNTER SMOKING A PIPE. Venice, Museo Correr (no. 536).

238. THE HUNTERS DRAW LOTS. Venice, Querini Stampalia.

239. DEPARTURE OF THE HUNTERS. Venice, Querini Stampalia.

240. SHOOTING IN THE VALLEY. Venice, Museo Correr (no. 477).

241. SHOOTING POSITION IN A BARREL. Venice, Querini Stampalia.

242. COUNTING THE BAG. Venice, Querini Stampalia.

243. TWO SEATED PEASANTS EATING. Venice,
Museo Correr (no. 467).

244. PEASANTS AT AN INN. Venice, Querini Stampalia.

245. TWO PEASANTS EATING. Venice, Museo Correr (no. 469).

246. THREE PEASANTS DRINKING. Venice, Museo Correr (no. 466).

247. A PEASANT. Venice, Museo Correr (no. 468).

248. TWO MEN WITH BOWLS. Venice, Museo Correr (no. 471).

249. A GIRL SPINNING. Venice, Museo Correr (no. 571).

250. THE MILLINER. Cambridge (Mass.), Fogg Art Museum.

251. A GIRL SPINNING. Boston (Mass.), Museum of Fine Arts.

252. THE LION SHOW. Venice, Querini Stampalia.

253. BORGOGNA'S SHOW. Segromigno Monte, Heirs to the Salom Collection.

254. THE QUACK. London, Private Collection.

255. THE ELEPHANT. Segromigno Monte, Heirs to the Salom Collection.

256. PORTRAIT OF MATILDE QUERINI DA PONTE. Algiers, Musée National.

257. PORTRAIT OF STEFANO QUERINI. Paris, J. Cailleux Collection.

258. PORTRAIT OF MARINA QUERINI BENZON. Formerly Venice, E. Charmet-Padoan Collection.

259. PORTRAIT OF A GENTLEMAN IN GREEN. Milan, A. Orsi Collection.

260. PORTRAIT OF A GENTLEMAN. Treviso, Museo Civico.

261. PORTRAIT OF BENEDETTO GANASSONI. Venice, Ca' Rezzonico.

262. THE VISIT TO THE CONVENT. Venice, Ca' Rezzonico.

263. THE VISIT TO THE INVALID. Venice, Ca' Rezzonico.

264. PEASANTS PLAYING CARDS. Ferrara, Paulucci Collection.

265. A GIRL SPINNING. Venice, Fornoni Bisacco Collection.

266. THE POLENTA. Venice, Fornoni Bisacco Collection.

267. THE QUACK. Venice, Fornoni Bisacco Collection.

268. PEASANTS DANCING THE
FURLANA. Venice, Fornoni
Bisacco Collection.

269. THE ALCHEMISTS. Gazzada, Villa Cagnola.

270. CONFESSION. Bergamo, Baronessa Guffanti Scotti Collection.

271. THE ADVOCATES. Padua, Private Collection.

272. THE INTERRUPTED GAME OF CARDS. Bergamo, Private Collection.

273. CARD-PLAYER. Venice, Museo Correr (no. 559).

274. COFFEE TIME. Florence, Private Collection.

275. ORIENTAL SCENE. Formerly Venice, Brass Collection.

276. RUSTIC DANCE. Whereabouts unknown.

277. GIRL DANCING. Venice, Museo Correr (no. 564 recto).

278. A POET RECITING HIS VERSES. Port Sunlight, Lady Lever Art Gallery.

279. THE MORNING CUP OF CHOCOLATE. Venice, Ca' Rezzonico.

280. THE SINGING LESSON. Petworth, Petworth House, J. Wyndham Collection.

281. THE BAGLIONI FAMILY. San Bartolomeo di Crema, Stramezzi Collection.

282. THREE MERRY FELLOWS. Rome, Morandotti Collection.

283. THE VISIT TO GRANDMAMA. Venice, Curtis Collection.

284. KISSING HANDS. Providence (R. I.), Rhode Island School of Design.

285. THE VISIT TO GRANDMAMA. Bergamo, Accademia Carrara.

286. PORTRAIT OF ADRIANA GIUSTINIAN BARBARIGO. Whereabouts unknown.

287. PORTRAIT OF ADRIANA GIUSTINIAN BARBARIGO. Venice, Ca' Rezzonico.

288. THE DANCER BINETTI. Milan, Heirs of Senatore M. Crespi.

289. THE QUINTET. Turin, Private Collection.

290. LITERARY GENTLEMEN IN A LIBRARY. Formerly Paris, D'Atri Collection.

291. THE USURERS. Formerly Venice, N. Barozzi Collection.

292. THE TUTOR TO THE GRIMANI FAMILY. Milan, Orsi Collection.

293. THE MICHIEL FAMILY. Venice, Querini Stampalia.

294. PORTRAIT OF A PAINTER. Venice, Ca' Rezzonico.

295. PORTRAIT OF A WRITER. Milan, Orsi Collection.

296. PORTRAIT OF A PRELATE. Milan, Orsi Collection.

297. A YOUNG GIRL EMBROIDERING. Bologna, Morandi Collection.

298. PORTRAIT OF A PAINTER. Milan, Orsi Collection.

299. PORTRAIT OF PIERO RINALDI. Venice, Ca' Rezzonico.

299a. PORTRAIT OF A LADY. Whereabouts unknown.

299b. PORTRAIT OF A GENTLEMAN. Whereabouts unknown.

299c. MAGRATH THE GIANT, AND THE RHINOCEROS. Whereabouts unknown.

299d. PEASANTS DANCING THE FURLANA. Whereabouts unknown.

300. A PRELATE. Bergamo, Accademia Carrara.

301. CARD-PLAYERS. Berlin, Kupferstichkabinett.

302. SEATED LADY, AND A BASKET. Berlin, Kupferstichkabinett.

303. GENTLEMAN STANDING AT A TABLE. Berlin, Kupferstichkabinett.

304. MANSERVANT STANDING. Berlin, Kupferstichkabinett.

305. OLD PRIEST STANDING. Berlin, Kupferstichkabinett.

306. GENTLEMAN IN A DOMINO. Berlin, Kupferstichkabinett.

307. MASKED LADY. Berlin, Kupferstichkabinett.

308. SEATED LADY. London, Brinsley Ford Collection.

309. PRIEST STANDING. London, Private
Collection.

310. VENETIAN SENATOR. New York, Pierpont
Morgan Library.

311. RUSTIC SCENE. New York, Pierpont Morgan Library.

312. CHILD, AND MAN STANDING. Venice, Accademia.

313. SEATED MAN, AND DRAPERY. Venice, Accademia.

314. PRIEST KNEELING. Paris, Talleyrand
Collection.

315. TWO GENTLEMEN IN CLOAKS. Venice, Museo Correr (no. 441 verso).

316. THE COFFEE-HOUSE. Venice, Museo Correr (no. 436 recto).

317. COFFEE-HOUSE KEEPER, AND CROCKERY. Venice, Museo Correr
(no. 436 verso).

318. TWO SEATED GENTLEMEN IN DOMINOES. Venice, Museo Correr (no. 442).

319. ACCOUNTANT AT A BENCH; SERVANT WITH A BOWL. Venice, Museo Correr (no. 444).

320. TWO FRIARS. Venice, Museo Correr (no. 446 recto).

321. BRACKET, ORNAMENTS, STUDIES OF HANDS. Venice, Museo Correr (no. 446 verso).

322. SEATED NURSE WITH THREE CHILDREN; WOMAN AT A TABLE. Venice, Museo Correr (no. 451).

323. LAWYER AT A TABLE. Venice, Museo Correr (no. 453).

324. LADY AND GENTLEMAN ON A DIVAN. Venice, Museo Correr (no. 454).

325. TWO SEATED WOMEN, MENDING. Venice, Museo Correr
(no. 457 recto).

326. HEAD OF A PUTTO; HEAD OF A CHILD. Venice, Museo Correr
(no. 457 verso).

327. GUITAR-PLAYER; FACE AND FEET OF A
WOMAN. Venice, Museo Correr (no. 455).

328. SEATED NOBLEMAN; TWO BOATMEN. Venice, Museo Correr (no. 458).

329. FIGURE IN A DOMINO; YOUNG HORSEMAN. Venice, Museo Correr
(no. 461).

330. STABLE LAD, YOUNG RIDER AND GROOM WITH A HORSE. Venice,
Museo Correr (no. 460).

331. PAINTER SHOWING A PICTURE.
Venice, Museo Correr (no. 459).

332. LADY AT A TABLE; STUDIES OF FURNISHINGS. Venice, Museo Correr
(no. 464).

333. WOMAN SINGING; MAN IN A CLOAK. Venice, Museo Correr (no. 472).

334. LADY IN A CRINOLINE. Venice, Museo Correr (no. 473).

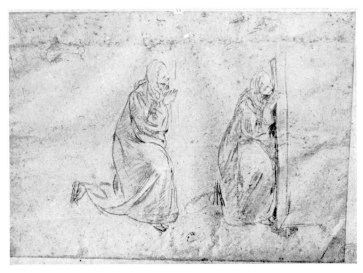

335. TWO STUDIES OF FIGURES IN A CONFESSIONAL. Venice, Museo Correr (no. 478 recto).

336. TABLE WITH A COVER; WINDOW WITH A CURTAIN. Venice, Museo Correr (no. 478 verso).

337. GIRL LEANING ON A STOOL; DRAPERY. Venice, Museo Correr (no. 480).

338. SEATED MAN WEARING A DOMINO. Venice, Museo Correr (no. 484).

339. PEASANT GIRL DANCING; SKETCH OF A LADY. Venice, Museo Correr (no. 485).

340. MAN IN PROFILE; A PEASANT WOMAN. Venice, Museo
Correr (no. 486 recto).

341. HEAD OF AN OLD MAN. Venice, Museo
Correr (no. 486 verso).

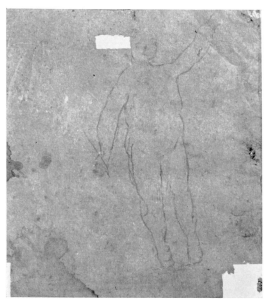

342. STUDY OF A NUDE. Venice, Museo Correr
     (NO. 491 verso).

343. TWO MAIDSERVANTS. Venice, Museo Correr (no. 495).

344. MEETING OF TWO LADIES. Venice, Museo Correr (no. 493).

345. STUDIES OF A GENTLEMAN'S CUTAWAY COAT. Venice, Museo Correr (no. 496).

346. MAN SELLING DOUGHNUTS. Venice, Museo Correr (no. 497).

347. TWO GENTLEMEN WEARING DRESSING-GOWNS. Venice, Museo Correr (no. 498).

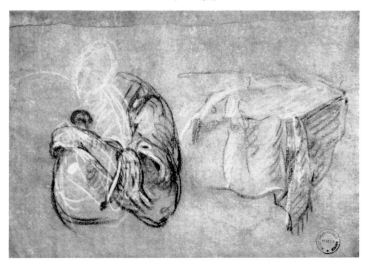

348. STUDY OF AN ARM HOLDING A JUG; TABLE COVER. Venice, Museo Correr (no. 499).

349. YOUNG CLERIC. Venice, Museo Correr (no. 500 recto).

350. STUDY OF CLERICAL GARMENTS. Venice, Museo Correr (no. 500 verso).

351. SERVANT WITH A TRAY. Venice,
Museo Correr (no. 501).

352. THREE FIGURES WITH CANDLES. Venice, Museo Correr
(no. 502 recto).

353. TWO GENTLEMEN AND A LADY STANDING; A SEATED GENTLEMAN.
Venice, Museo Correr (no. 503 recto).

354. SEATED LADY. Venice, Museo Correr (no. 503 verso).

355. FRIAR; STUDY OF DRAPERY. Venice, Museo Correr
(no. 505).

356. PRIEST AT A WRITING DESK. Venice, Museo Correr (no. 506).

357. BABY IN A LITTLE CHAIR; TWO HEADS OF A BOY; LADY WITH A FAN. Venice, Museo Correr (no. 507).

358. LADY WALKING. Venice, Museo Correr (no. 508)

359. GIRL FEEDING A CANARY. Venice, Museo Correr (no. 510).

360. MANSERVANT WITH A TRAY. Venice,
Museo Correr (no. 509).

361. SCREEN AND WOODEN CHAIR. Venice, Museo Correr (no. 511 recto).

362. GENTLEMAN AT A WRITING DESK. Venice, Museo Correr
(no. 512 recto).

363. TWO GENTLEMEN WITH ARMS RAISED. Venice, Museo Correr
(no. 512 verso).

364. LADY AND SPINET. Venice, Museo Correr (no. 513 recto).

365. STUDIES OF THE HEAD AND BUST OF A GENTLEMAN. Venice, Museo
Correr (no. 513 verso).

366. PRIEST; STUDIES OF DRAPERY.
Venice, Museo Correr (no. 514 recto).

367. THE TEMPTATIONS OF ST. ANTHONY.
Venice, Museo Correr (no. 515 verso).

368. MANSERVANT AT A DOOR; A CHAIR. Venice, Museo Correr (no. 516 recto).

369. HANDS AND DRAPERY. Venice, Museo Correr (no. 516 verso).

370. FRIAR WITH A TRAY; GENTLEMAN. Venice, Museo Correr
(no. 517 recto).

371. SEATED MAN. Venice, Museo Correr (no. 517 verso).

372. MAIDSERVANT; CHEST OF DRAWERS. Venice, Museo Correr
(no. 518 recto).

373. CONSOLE, CLOCK AND CURTAIN DRAPERY.
Venice, Museo Correr (no. 518 verso).

374. GENTLEMAN IN A CLOAK WITH A BOY; MAN IN A CLOAK.
Venice, Museo Correr (no. 519).

375. PEASANT; KITCHEN UTENSILS. Venice, Museo Correr (no. 520).

376. MAIDSERVANT WITH A STOOL. Venice, Museo Correr (no. 522).

377. SEATED MAN SEWING. Venice, Museo Correr (no. 527).

378. LADY KNEELING. Venice, Museo Correr (no. 529 recto).

379. TWO STUDIES OF A WOMAN WITH A HEAD SHAWL. Venice, Museo Correr (no. 529 verso).

380. CELLARER; YOUTH WITH ONE ARM RAISED. Venice, Museo Correr (no. 528).

381. YOUNG MAN ON A HORSE WITH A RIDING-MASTER. Venice, Museo Correr (no. 530).

382. BOATMAN WITH A BASKET; MANSERVANT WITH A BOX. Venice, Museo Correr (no. 531).

383. TWO LADIES, ONE SEATED AND ONE STANDING. Venice, Museo Correr (no. 532).

384. CAGE AND PARROT. Venice, Museo Correr (no. 535).

385. NURSE AND CHILD; CHILD STANDING. Venice, Museo Correr (no. 533).

386. THREE STUDIES OF A CUTAWAY COAT. Venice, Museo Correr (no. 537).

387. GENTLEMAN WITH A CLOAK. Venice, Museo Correr (no. 541 recto).

388. FEMALE DRAPERY; TWO HANDS HOLDING A CUP. Venice, Museo Correr (no. 541 verso).

389. A BED. Venice, Museo Correr (no. 543).

390. MAIDSERVANT ATTENDING AN INVALID. Venice, Museo Correr (no. 546).

391. LADY AT A SPINET. Venice, Museo Correr (no. 544 recto).

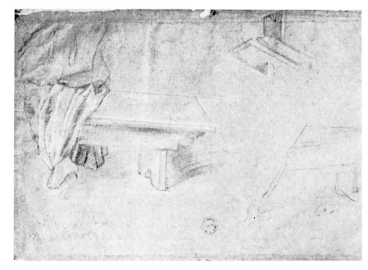

392. BENCH WITH A CLOAK. Venice, Museo Correr (no. 544 verso).

393. LADY STANDING, AND OTHER STUDIES. Venice, Museo Correr (no. 547 recto).

394. SERVANT WITH A TRAY. Venice, Museo Correr (no. 548).

395. SAVOYARD JUGGLER WITH A MARMOSET. Venice, Museo Correr (no. 549).

396. TWO PEASANTS STANDING WITH A WHEELBARROW. Venice, Museo Correr (no. 550).

397. SPINET-PLAYER. Venice, Museo Correr (no. 551 recto).

398. SEATED MAN. Venice, Museo Correr (no. 551 verso).

399. LADY IN A CRINOLINE; MAID WITH A TRAY. Venice, Museo Correr (no. 552).

400. MANSERVANT WEARING A CAP. Venice, Museo Correr
(no. 554 recto).

401. TABLE WITH A READING STAND. Venice, Museo Correr
(no. 554 verso).

409. STUDIES OF DRAPERY. Venice, Museo Correr (no. 567).

408. MANSERVANT OFFERING A CHAIR TO A LADY. Venice, Museo Correr (no. 566).

410. LADY AND GENTLEMAN IN DOMINOES; LADY WALKING. Venice, Museo Correr (no. 570).

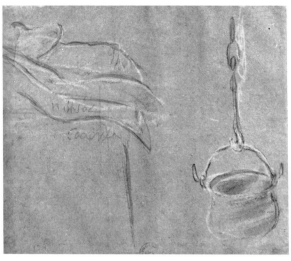

411. COOKING-POT SUSPENDED ON A CHAIN. Venice, Museo
Correr (no. 568).

412. GENTLEMAN LEANING ON A CHAIR. Venice, Museo Correr
(no. 573).

413. TURKEY AND TWO DUCKS.
Venice, Museo Correr (no. 905).

414. SEATED YOUNG MAN APPLYING A
SEAL. Venice, Museo Correr
(no. 6059).

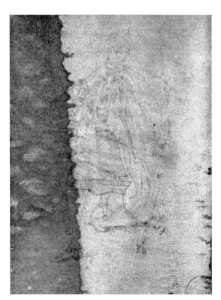

415. GENTLEMAN SMOKING, SEATED IN AN
ARMCHAIR. Venice, Museo Correr
(no. 6060).

416. SEATED GENTLEMAN. Venice, Museo
Correr (no. 6061).

417. SEATED GETLEMAN; STUDY OF A
LEFT HAND. Venice, Museo Correr
(no. 6062).

417a. SHEPHERD GIRL WITH A FLOWER.
Aalen, Koenig-Fachsenfeld
Collection.

# DRAWINGS OF UNCERTAIN ATTRIBUTION

418. FRENCH, EIGHTEENTH CENTURY: *Two figures*. Ann Arbor,
University of Michigan.

419. A. LONGHI (?): *Figure of an abbé*.
Cambridge (Mass.), Fogg Art
Museum

420. VENETIAN, EIGHTEENTH CENTURY:
*Studies of drapery*. Milan, Orsi
Collection.

421. PANINI (?): *Three figures of gentlemen*. Oxford, Ashmolean Museum.

422. A. LONGHI (?): *Two figures in
antique dress*. Venice, Museo
Correr (no. 575 recto).

423. A. LONGHI (?): *Study of a forearm and of a female head*. Venice,
Museo Correr (no. 575 verso).

424. A. LONGHI (?): *Male nude.*
Venice, Museo Correr
(no. 576 recto).

425. A. LONGHI (?): *Female head.*
Venice, Museo Correr
(no. 576 verso).

426. A. LONGHI (?): *Studies of two female heads.* Venice, Museo Correr
(no. 578 recto).

427. A. LONGHI (?): *Head of a young woman;
raised arm.* Venice, Museo Correr
(no. 578 verso).

428. A. LONGHI (?): *A cleric wearing a cap.* Venice,
Museo Correr (no. 579).

429. A. LONGHI (?): *Doge with his right arm raised.* Venice,
Museo Correr (no. 580).

430. A. LONGHI (?): *Portrait of Francesco Morosini*. Venice, Museo Correr (no. 581).

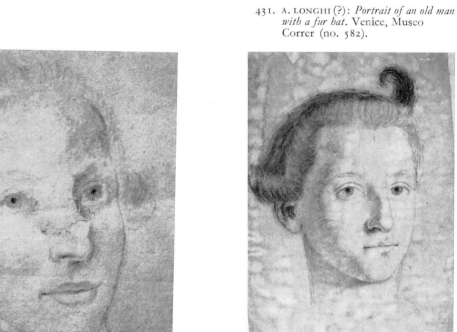

431. A. LONGHI (?): *Portrait of an old man with a fur hat*. Venice, Museo Correr (no. 582).

432. A. LONGHI (?): *Portrait of a balding old woman*. Venice, Museo Correr (no. 583 recto).

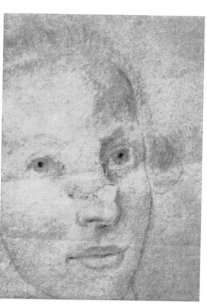

433. A. LONGHI (?): *Head of a young man*. Venice, Museo Correr (no. 583 verso).

434. A. LONGHI (?): *Head of a young woman*. Venice, Museo Correr (no. 1633).

435. A. LONGHI (?): *The wine shop at the sign of the Lion of St. Mark's*. Venice, Museo Correr (no. 584).

436. A. LONGHI (?): *Portrait of a gentleman*. Vienna, Albertina.

PAINTINGS OF UNCERTAIN ATTRIBUTION
AND PAINTINGS BY FOLLOWERS OF PIETRO LONGHI

*

LOST WORKS

437. C. FLIPART (?): *The Hairdresser*. Salzburg, Schloss Neuhaus, Topic Collection

438. P. LONGHI - C. FLIPART: *The Hairdresser* (print).

439. C. FLIPART (?): *The Concert*. Salzburg, Schloss Neuhaus, Topic Collection.

440. P. LONGHI - C. FLIPART: *The Concert* (print).

441. C. FLIPART (?): *Portrait of the Singer Scalzi*. Hartford (Conn.), Wadsworth Atheneum.

442. C. FLIPART (?): *Portrait of a Painter*. Paris, J. Cailleux Collection.

443. C. FLIPART (?): *Portrait of Rosa Pasquali*. Milan, Feltrinelli Doria Collection.

444. A. GRAMICCIA: *Family Gathering*. Udine, Museo Civico.

445. A. GRAMICCIA (?): *Family Gathering*. Venice, Ca' Rezzonico.

446. A. GRAMICCIA (?): *The Geography Lesson*. Venice, Ca' d'Oro.

447. A. GRAMICCIA (?): *Carlo Goldoni in his Study*. Formerly Milan, Crespi-Morbio Collection.

448. A. GRAMICCIA (?): *Portrait of a Gentleman on Horseback*. Venice, Ca' Rezzonico.

449. G. DE GOBBIS (?): *The Tooth-drawer*. Venice, Ca' Rezzonico.

450. G. DE GOBBIS (?): *The Singing Lesson*. Philadelphia, Museum of Art.

451. G. DE GOBBIS (?): *The Music Lesson*. Segromigno Monte,
Heirs to the Salom Collection.

452. G. DE GOBBIS (?): *The Coffee-House*. Segromigno Monte,
Heirs to the Salom Collection.

453. G. DE GOBBIS (?): *The Ridotto*. Segromigno Monte,
Heirs to the Salom Collection.

454. G. DE GOBBIS (?): *The Ridotto*. Baden-Salem, Collection of the Grand Dukes of Bavaria.

455. G. DE GOBBIS (?): *The Convent Parlour*. Baden-Salem, Collection of the Grand Dukes of Bavaria.

456. G. DE GOBBIS (?): *The Ridotto*. Formerly London, Sundin Collection.

457. G. DE GOBBIS (?): *The Convent Parlour*. Formerly London, Sundin Collection.

458. MASTER OF THE RIDOTTO: *The Ridotto*. Amsterdam, Rijksmuseum.

459. MASTER OF THE RIDOTTO:
*The Ridotto*. Venice,
Ca' Rezzonico.

460. MASTER OF THE RIDOTTO:
*The Convent Parlour*.
Venice, Ca' Rezzonico.

461. MASTER OF THE RIDOTTO: *The Embroidery Workroom*. Venice, Ca' Rezzonico.

462. MASTER OF THE RIDOTTO: *A Rustic Meal*. Venice, Ca' Rezzonico.

463. MASTER OF THE RIDOTTO: *The Ridotto*. Formerly Rome,
Palazzo Doria.

464. MASTER OF THE RIDOTTO: *The Convent Parlour*. Formerly Rome,
Palazzo Doria.

465. MASTER OF THE RIDOTTO: *The Masked Ball*. Formerly Rome,
Palazzo Doria.

466. MASTER OF THE REFLECTIONS: *The Spinet*. Milan, Treccani Collection.

467. MASTER OF THE REFLECTIONS: *The Game of Cards*.
Milan, Treccani Collection.

468. MASTER OF THE REFLECTIONS: *A Jewish Wedding*.
Milan, Private Collection.

469. MASTER OF THE REFLECTIONS: *The Declaration*. Whereabouts unknown.

470. P. LONGHI: *Old woman reading; gentleman*. Venice, Museo Correr (no. 572).

471. P. LONGHI: *Lady with a skein-winder*. Venice, Museo Correr (no. 465).

472. P. LONGHI - C. FLIPART: *The Declaration* (print).

473. MASTER OF THE REFLECTIONS: *The Lady's Awakening*. Segromigno Monte, Heirs to the Salom Collection.

474. P. LONGHI - C. FLIPART: *The Lady's Awakening* (print).

475. P. LONGHI: *Seated gentleman reading.* Venice, Museo Correr (no. 563).

476. P. LONGHI: *Lady rising.* Venice, Museo Correr (no. 561).

477. P. LONGHI: *Draping of a skirt.* Venice, Museo Correr (no. 562).

478. MASTER OF THE REFLECTIONS: *The Lady's Awakening*. Kansas City, William Rockhill Nelson Gallery of Art.

479. FOLLOWER OF PIETRO LONGHI: *Games at the Villa*. Bergamo, Accademia Carrara.

480. P. LONGHI (?): *The Rhinoceros*. Segromigno Monte, Heirs to the Salom Collection.

481. A. LONGHI: *The Pisani Family*. Venice, Heirs to the Bentivoglio d'Aragona Collection.

482. P. LONGHI (?): *St. Andrew and St. Peter*. Venice, Church of S. Pantalon.

483. A. LONGHI: *The Pisani Family*. Detail of plate 481.

484. A. LONGHI: *The Doge's Balotin*. Belluno, Museo Civico.

485. B. NAZZARI: *Portrait of a Nobleman*. Cambridge (Mass.), Fogg Art Museum.

486. P. LONGHI (?): *Portrait of a Senator*. Amiens,
Musée de Picardie.

486a. P. LONGHI (?): *Portrait of a Knight of Malta*.
Whereabouts unknown.

## LOST WORKS

487. P. LONGHI: *Coffee house keeper; glass ware*. Venice, Museo Correr (no. 436).

488. P. LONGHI - A. FALDONI: *The Lady's Stay in
the Country* (print).

489. A. LONGHI: *The Juggler* (print).

490. P. LONGHI - P. WAGNER: *The Coffee-house* (print).

491. P. LONGHI - F. BARTOLOZZI: *The Singing Lesson* (print).

492. P. LONGHI - C. DELL'ACQUA: *Antonio Diedo* (print).

493. P. LONGHI - GUTWEIN: *The Lady's Toilet* (print).

# SOURCES OF PHOTOGRAPHS

ALGIERS, Musée National des Beaux-Arts, 256.
AMIENS, Musée de Picardie, 486.
AMSTERDAM, Rijksmuseum, 458.
ANN ARBOR, University of Michigan, 418.
BERGAMO, Accademia Carrara, 172 285 300.
BERGAMO, Foto Lucchetti, 1, 270.
BERGAMO, Foto Wells, 479.
BERLIN, Kupferstichkabinett, 169, 215, 301, 302, 303, 304, 305, 306, 307.
BIELLA, Foto Rampazzi, 35.
BOSTON, Museum of Fine Arts, 251.
CAMBRIDGE, MASS., Fogg Art Museum, 250, 419, 485.
CHICAGO, Art Institute, 90, 137.
DUBLIN, National Gallery of Ireland, 48.
FERRARA, Foto Giulianelli, 20, 21, 22.
FLORENCE, Foto Alinari (Fiorentini), 13, 100, 164, 213.
FLORENCE, Museo Stibbert, 143.
FLORENCE, Soprintendenza alle Gallerie, 156.
GENOA, Foto Agosto, 231.
GENOA, Foto Cresta, 224.
HARTFORD, CONN., Wadsworth Atheneum, 441.
KANSAS CITY, MO. William Rockhill Nelson Gallery, 478.
LONDON, British Museum, 234.
LONDON, Christie, 162, 198, 198a.
LONDON, Photo A.C. Cooper, 19.
LONDON, Courtauld Institute of Art, 280.
LONDON, Photo John R. Freeman, 105, 308.
LONDON, Photo Grosvenor, 456, 457.
LONDON, National Gallery, 70, 80, 118, 135, 166.
LONDON, Sotheby, 106, 187, 190, 191, 192, 254.
LONDON, Whitechapel Art Gallery, 89.
LUCCA, Foto Cortopassi, 161, 163, 168, 211, 212, 253, 255, 256, 451, 452, 453, 473, 480.
MILAN, Foto Bassani, 157.
MILAN, Foto Perotti, 259, 292, 295, 296, 298, 420.
MILAN, Galleria d'Arte Moderna, 23, 86, 174.
MILAN, Galleria di Brera, 107, 117.
NEW YORK, Metropolitan Museum, 76, 78, 84, 103.
NEW YORK, Pierpont Morgan Library, 310, 311.
NORTHAMPTON, MASS. Smith College Museum of Art, 93.
OXFORD, Ashmolean Museum, 421.
PADUA, Museo Civico, 129.
PARIS, Cailleux Collection, 257.
PARIS, Talleyrand Collection, 314.

PARIS, Louvre, 44.
PHILADELPHIA, Museum of Art, 450.
PISA, Università degli Studi, 269.
PORT SUNLIGHT, Photo Card, 278.
PROVIDENCE, Rhode Island School of Design Museum of Art, 132.
ROME, Foto Danesi, 454, 455.
ROME, Foto Boccardi, 282.
SAINT LOUIS, MO. City Art Museum, 167.
SAN FRANCISCO, California Palace of the Legion of Honor, 54.
STANFORD, Stanford University, 193, 194.
TREVISO, Museo Civico, 260.
UDINE, Foto Brisighelli, 25, 26, 27, 31.
UDINE, Museo Civico, 230, 244, 444.
VENICE, Fondazione Giorgio Cini, 7, 10, 11, 12, 291.
VENICE, Foto Böhm, 3, 102, 104, 197, 284.
VENICE, Foto Ferruzzi, 214, 218, 265, 266, 267, 268, 482.
VENICE, Foto Rossi, 34, 37, 38, 41, 42, 94, 109, 112, 126, 165, 170, 180, 446, 448, 449, 484.
VENICE, Archivio Fotografico Museo Correr, 4, 8, 9, 14, 15, 16, 17, 24, 28, 29, 30, 36, 40, 43, 45, 46, 47, 50, 52, 55, 56, 58, 59, 60, 61, 63, 64, 65, 66, 69, 77, 79, 81, 82, 88, 92, 95, 96, 98, 99, 101, 108, 110, 111, 115, 116, 119, 121, 122, 123, 124, 125, 127, 128, 131, 134, 136, 139, 140, 142, 144, 145, 146, 155, 160, 173, 175, 176, 179, 181, 183, 184, 185, 186, 188, 189, 195, 202, 203, 204, 205, 206, 207, 208, 209, 210, 217, 219, 223, 227, 237, 240, 243, 245, 246, 247, 248, 249, 258, 261, 262, 263, 273, 277, 279, 287, 294, 299, 317 to 417, 422 to 435, 438, 440, 445, 459, 460, 461, 462, 470, 471, 472, 474, 475, 476, 477, 487, 488, 490, 492, 493.
VENICE, Pinacoteca Querini Stampalia, 32, 33, 120, 147, 148, 149, 150, 151, 152, 153, 154, 171, 221, 225, 233, 235, 236, 238, 239, 241, 242, 252, 293.
VENICE, Soprintendenza alle Gallerie, 2, 5, 6, 71, 72, 73, 74, 75, 226, 264, 283, 312, 313, 481, 483.
VERONA, Museo di Castelvecchio, 216.
VIENNA, Albertina, 436.
WASHINGTON, National Gallery, 67, 68.
WINDSOR, Royal Collections, 57, 62.
WORCESTER, Mass., Art Museum, 51.
PRIVATE COLLECTIONS, 39, 49, 83, 85, 87, 97, 113, 114, 130, 133, 138, 141, 158, 159, 177, 178, 182, 198, 199, 200, 201, 220, 222, 227, 229, 232, 271, 272, 274, 275, 281, 286, 288, 289, 290, 297, 309, 437, 439, 443, 447, 466, 467, 468.
From *Longhi* by A. Ravà, 1923, 53, 91, 196, 276, 463, 464, 465, 469.

*Paintings in the Royal Collection are reproduced by gracious permission of Her Majesty the Queen.*

# INDEX OF SUBJECTS

*This index refers to paintings only, which are classified as by Pietro Longhi (PL), paintings of uncertain attribution (Attr.) and lost works (L). The location of each is given and in the respective catalogues they are arranged according to their locations which are in alphabetical order. The figures in brackets refer to the plates.*

*Meeting of Dominoes* (XIX & 173) Venice, Ca' Rezzonico *(PL)*

*The Meeting of the Procuratore and his Wife* Moscow, Pushkin Museum *(Attr.)*

*The Meeting of the Procuratore and his Wife* (78) New York, Metropolitan Museum of Art *(PL)*

*The merry Couple* (17) Venice, Ca' Rezzonico *(PL)*

*The Michiel Family* (XXIV & 293) Venice, Pinacoteca Querini Stampalia *(PL)*

*The Milliner* (250) Cambridge, Mass., Fogg Art Museum *(PL)*

*The Milliner* (105) London, Brinsley Ford Collection *(PL)*

*The Milliner* Milan, A. Crespi Collection *(Attr.)*

*The Milliner* (103) New York, Metropolitan Museum of Art *(PL)*

*Milord's Salad* (83) Milan, A. Crespi Collection *(PL)*

*Milord's Visitor* (84) New York, Metropolitan Museum of Art *(PL)*

*A Miracle of St Lawrence* (158) Brescia, Suore Ancelle della Carità *(PL)*

*Monks, Canons and Friars of Venice* (221) Venice, Pinacoteca Querini Stampalia *(PL)*

*The Moor's Letter* (X & 119) Venice, Ca' Rezzonico *(PL)*

*The Morning Cup of Chocolate* (XXIII & 279) Venice, Ca' Rezzonico *(PL)*

*The Music Lesson* (54) San Francisco, Palace of the Legion of Honor *(PL)*

*The Music Lesson* (451) Segromigno Monte, Heirs to the Salom Collection *(Attr.)*

*The Needlework School* (96) Venice, Ca' Rezzonico *(PL)*

*The Nurse* (198) London, Private Collection *(PL)*

*The Nurse* (64) Venice, Ca' Rezzonico *(PL)*

*Oriental Child* Florence, Donzelli Collection *(Attr.)*

*Oriental Scene* (275) Formerly Venice, Brass Collection *(PL)*

*The Painter in his Studio* (48) Dublin, National Gallery of Ireland *(PL)*

*The Painter in his Studio* Formerly London, Cavendish Bentinck Collection *(Attr.)*

*The Painter in his Studio* Milan, Private collection *(Attr.)*

*The Painter in his Studio* (194) Stanford, Stanford University Museum *(PL)*

*The Painter in his Studio* (49) Formerly Stirling of Keir Collection *(PL)*

*The Painter in his Studio* (IV & 47) Venice, Ca' Rezzonico *(PL)*

*Painter and Model* Whereabouts unknown *(Attr.)*

*The Palmist* Formerly Brennenbroeck, Von Pannwitz Collection *(Attr.)*

*A Patrician Family* (123) Venice, Ca' Rezzonico *(PL)*

*Peasant Girl and a Man drinking* (22) Ferrara, Paulucci Collection *(PL)*

*Peasant Girl and Musician* (21) Ferrara, Paulucci Collection *(PL)*

*Peasants dancing* (20) Ferrara, Paulucci Collection *(PL*

*Peasants dancing* (20) Ferrara, Paulucci Collection *(PL)*

*Peasants dancing* (90) Chicago, The Art Institute, Worcester Collection *(PL)*

*Peasants dancing the Furlana* (93) Northampton, Mass., Museum of Art *(PL)*

*Peasants dancing the Furlana* Padua, Museo Civico *(Attr.)*

*Peasants dancing the Furlana* (92) Venice, Ca' Rezzonico *(PL)*

*Peasants dancing the Furlana* (268) Venice, Fornoni Bisacco Collection *(PL)*

*Peasants dancing the Furlana* (94) Venice, Pinacoteca Querini Stampalia *(PL)*

*Peasant dancing the Furlana* (91) Whereabouts unknown *(PL)*

*Peasants dancing the Furlana* (299d) Whereabouts unknown *(PL)*

*Peasants at an Inn* (244) Venice, Pinacoteca Querini Stampalia *(PL)*

*Peasants playing Cards* (264) Ferrara, Paulucci Collection *(PL)*

*The Pedlar* London, Earl of Harewood Collection *(Attr.)*

*The Perfume-Seller* Castagnola, Thyssen Collection *(Attr.)*

*The Perfume-Seller* (164) Venice, Ca' Rezzonico *(PL)*

*The Philosopher Pythagoras* (226) Venice, Gallerie dell'Accademia *(PL)*

*The Pisani Family* (481 483) Venice, Heirs and the Bentivoglio d'Aragona Collection *(Attr.)*

*A Poet reciting his Verses* (278) Port Sunlight, Lady Lever Art Gallery *(PL)*

*The Polenta* (18) Venice, Ca' Rezzonico *(PL)*

*The Polenta* (266) Venice, Fornoni Bisacco Collection *(PL)*

*The Polenta* (26) Zoppola, Castello *(PL)*

*Portrait of a Boy* Genova, Private collection *(Attr.)*

*Portrait of a Cardinal* Formerly Venice, Naya Collection *(Attr.)*

*Portrait of a Clerk* Modena, Pinacoteca Estense *(Attr.)*

*Portrait of the Doge Pietro Grimani* (VIII & 141) Bergamo, Private collection *(PL)*

*Portrait of the Doge's Steward* (231) Genoa, Trucchi Collection *(PL)*

*Portrait of Samuel Egerton* Venice, Ca' Rezzonico *(Attr.)*

*Portrait of Benedetto Ganassoni* (XXII & 261) Venice, Ca' Rezzonico *(PL)*

*Portrait of a Gentleman* (177) Bergamo, Private collection *(PL)*

*Portrait of a Gentleman* Boston Museum of Fine Arts *(Attr.)*

*Portrait of a Gentleman* New York, Drey Collection

*Portrait of a Gentleman* (260) Treviso, Museo Civico *(PL)*

*Portrait of a Gentleman* Venice, Brass Collection *(Attr.)*

*Portrait of a Gentleman* Formerly Venice, Brass Collection *(Attr.)*

*Portrait of a Gentleman* Venice, Gallerie dell'Accademia *(Attr.)*

*Portrait of a Gentleman* (228) Whereabouts unknown *(PL)*

*Portrait of a Gentleman* (299b) Whereabouts unknown *(PL)*

*Portrait of a Gentleman* Whereabouts unknown *(Attr.)*

*Portrait of a Gentleman on Horseback* (448) Venice, Ca' Rezzonico *(Attr.)*

*Portrait of a Gentleman in green* (259) Milan, A. Orsi Collection *(PL)*

*Portrait of the Great Captain* Whereabouts unknown *(Attr.)*

*Portrait of William Graham, second Duke of Montrose* (142) Venice, Ca' Rezzonico *(PL)*

*Portrait of Adriana Giustinian Barbarigo* (287) Venice, Ca' Rezzonico *(PL)*

*Portrait of Adriana Giustinian Barbarigo* (286) Whereabouts unknown *(PL)*

*Portrait of Carlo Goldoni* Budapest, Museum of Fine Arts *(Attr.)*

*Portrait of Carlo Goldoni* Venice, Ca' Rezzonico *(Attr.)*

*Portrait of Francesco Guardi* (XXI & 227) Venice, Ca' Rezzonico *(PL)*

*Portrait of Margarita Hanchin* Whereabouts unknown *(Attr.)*

*Portrait of a Knight of Malta* (486a) Whereabouts unknown *(Attr.)*

*Portrait of a Lady* Ferrara, Paulucci Collection *(Attr.)*

*Portrait of a Lady* Dresden, Gemäldegalerie *(Attr.)*

*Portrait of a Lady* (130) Milan, Private collection *(PL)*

*Portrait of a Lady* Milan, Private collection *(Attr.)*

*Portrait of a Lady* (178) Formerly New York, Newhouse Galleries *(PL)*

*Portrait of a Lady* Venice, Private collection *(Attr.)*

*Portrait of a Lady* Formerly Venice, Brass Collection *(Attr.)*

*Portrait of a Lady* (299a) Whereabouts unknown *(PL)*

*Portrait of Lucrezia Lupo Fantini* Milan, Private collection *(Attr.)*

*Portrait of a Man* Boston, Mass., Museum of Fine Arts *(Attr.)*

*Portrait of Magrath the Giant* (179) Venice, Ca' Rezzonico *(PL)*

*Portrait of Marchesa Concina* Frankfurt, Städelsches Kunstinstitut *(Attr.)*

*Portrait of M.V. Meneghel* Formerly Venice, Brass Collection *(Attr.)*

*Portrait of Conte Migazzi* Innsbruck, Ferdinandeum *(Attr.)*

*Portrait of Moser de Filsek* Milan, A. Crespi Collection *(Attr.)*
*Portrait of a Nobleman* (485) Cambridge, Mass., Fogg Art Museum *(Attr.)*
*Portrait of a Nobleman with a Whip* Formerly Venice, Private collection *(Attr.)*
*Portrait of Christopher Nugent* Dublin, National Gallery of Ireland *(Attr.)*
*Portrait of a Nun* Formerly Milan, Venier Collection *(Attr.)*
*Portrait of a Painter* (298) Milan, A. Orsi Collection *(PL)*
*Portrait of a Painter* (442) Paris, Cailleux Collection *(Attr.)*
*Portrait of a Painter* (294) Venice, Ca' Rezzonico *(PL)*
*Portrait of Rosa Pasquali* (443) Milan, Feltrinelli Doria Collection *(Attr.)*
*Portrait of Alessandro Petrettini* Padua, Museo Civico *(Attr.)*
*Portrait of Maria Petrettini* Padua, Museo Civico *(Attr.)*
*Portrait of a Lady of the Petrettini Family* Padua, Museo Civico *(Attr.)*
*Portrait of Francesca Maria Piccardi* Milan, Private collection *(Attr.)*
*Portrait of Senatore Pisani* New York, Chrysler Collection *(Attr.)*
*Portrait of a Polish Gentleman* (232) Venice, Brass Collection *(PL)*
*Portrait of Pope Clement XIII* (175) Venice, Ca' Rezzonico *(PL)*
*Portrait of Pope Clement XIII* Venice, Gallerie dell'Accademia *(Attr.)*
*Portrait of a Prelate* (296) Milan, A. Orsi Collection *(PL)*
*Portrait of a Priest* Rotterdam, Boymans Museum *(Attr.)*
*Portrait of a Procuratore* Zoppola, Castello *(Attr.)*
*Portrait of the Provveditore Andrea Querini* Venice, Pinacoteca Querini Stampalia *(Attr.)*
*Portrait of Caterina Contarini Querini* Venice, Pinacoteca Querini Stampalia *(Attr.)*
*Portrait of Stefano Querini* (257) Paris, Cailleux Collection *(PL)*
*Portrait of Marina Querini Benzon* (258) Formerly Venice, Charmet Padoan Collection *(PL)*
*Portrait of Matilde Querini Da Ponte* (256) Algiers, Musée National *(PL)*
*Portrait of Piero Rinaldi* (299) Venice, Ca' Rezzonico *(PL)*
*Portrait of Romualdo Sasso* Rovigo, Accademia dei Concordi *(Attr.)*
*Portrait of Eugene of Savoy* (145) Venice, Ca' Rezzonico *(PL)*
*Portrait of a Senator* (486) Amiens, Musée de Picardie *(Attr.)*
*Portrait of the Singer Scalzi* (441) Hartford, Conn., Wadsworth Atheneum *(Attr.)*
*Portrait of G.B. Toniolo* Venice, Toniolo Collection *(Attr.)*
*Portrait of Elisabetta Toniolo Nani* Venice, Toniolo Collection *(Attr.)*
*Portrait of a Violinist* Florence, Ventura Collection *(Attr.)*
*Portrait of a Violinist* (229) New York, R. Manning Collection *(PL)*
*Portrait of a Woman* Formerly Venice, Brass Collection *(Attr.)*
*Portrait of a young Girl* Milan, Private collection *(Attr.)*
*Portrait of a young Girl* Formerly Venice, Private collection *(Attr.)*
*Portrait of a young Man* Genoa, Private collection *(Attr.)*
*Portrait of a young Man* Boston, Museum of Fine Arts *(Attr.)*
*Portrait of a young Man with a Bird* Whereabouts unknown *(Attr.)*
*Portrait of a young Man with a Dog* Milan, A. Crespi Collection *(Attr.)*
*Portrait of a young Woman* Formerly Venice, O.V. Collection *(Attr.)*
*Portrait of a Writer* (295) Milan, A. Orsi Collection *(PL)*
*Preparing the Guns (Shooting in the Valley)* (XVI & 235) Venice, Pinacoteca Querini Stampalia *(PL)*
*The Procuratore pays a Call* (80) London, National Gallery *(PL)*
*The Procuratore Ludovico Manin* (230) Udine, Museo Civico *(PL)*
*A Procuratore receiving a Petition* Oxford, Ashmolean Museum *(Attr.)*
*The Quack* Frankfurt, Städelsches Kunstinstitut

*The Singing Test* (198a) Whereabouts unknown *(PL)*

*The Sleeper tickled* (214) Venice, Barone Rubin de Cervin Albrizzi Collection *(PL)*

*Sleeping Peasant Girl* (34) Venice, Pinacoteca Querini Stampalia *(PL)*

*The Spinet* (133) Milan, Senatore M. Crespi Collection *(PL)*

*The Spinet Recital* (192) London, Hallsborough Gallery *(PL)*

*The Tailor* (38) Venice, Gallerie dell'Accademia *(PL)*

*The Temptation* (100) Hartford, Conn., Wadsworth Atheneum *(PL)*

*The Temptations of St Anthony* (225) Venice, Pinacoteca Querini Stampalia *(PL)*

*Three Merry Fellows* (282) Rome, Morandotti Collection *(PL)*

*The Tickle* (53) Whereabouts unknown *(PL)*

*The Tooth-Drawer* (107) Milan, Galleria di Brera *(PL)*

*The Tooth-Drawer* (449) Venice, Ca' Rezzonico *(Attr.)*

*The Tooth-Drawer* (184) Venice, Heirs to the Ravà Collection *(PL)*

*The Tutor to the Grimani Family* (292) Milan, Orsi Collection *(PL)*

*Unloading Shooting Equipment (Shooting in the Valley)* (236) Venice, Pinacoteca Querini Stampalia *(PL)*

*The Usurers* (291) Formerly Venice, Barozzi Collection *(PL)*

*The Virgin and Child with Saints and Angels* (V & 71 to 75) Venice, Church of S. Pantalon *(PL)*

*The Visit to the Convent* (262) Venice, Ca' Rezzonico *(PL)*

*The Visit from a Domino* (203) Venice, Ca' Rezzonico *(PL)*

*The Visit from a Friar* (208) Venice, Ca' Rezzonico *(PL)*

*The Visit to Grandmama* (285) Bergamo, Accademia Carrara *(PL)*

*The Visit to Grandmama* (283) Venice, Curtis Collection *(PL)*

*The Visit to the Invalid* (263) Venice, Ca' Rezzonico *(PL)*

*The Visit from a Lady* (200) Milan, A. Crespi Collection *(PL)*

*The Visit to the Library* (51) Worcester, Mass., Art Museum *(PL)*

*The Washerwomen* Padua, Museo Civico *(Attr.)*

*The Washerwomen* (16) Venice, Ca' Rezzonico *(PL)*

*The Washerwomen* (25) Zoppola, Castello *(PL)*

*The Woman selling Doughnuts* (86) Milan, Galleria d'Arte Moderna *(PL)*

*The Woman selling Doughnuts* (88) Venice, Ca' Rezzonico *(PL)*

*A young Girl embroidering* (297) Bologna, Morandi Collection *(PL)*

*Young Girl with a Fan* Bergamo, Accademia Carrara *(Attr.)*

*Young Woman with a Mask* Venice, Private collection *(Attr.)*

**DATE DUE**

| Use | Only | In | The |
|-----|------|-----|-----|
| | Library | | |
| | | | |
| | | | |
| | | | |
| | | | |
| | | | |
| | | | |
| | | | |
| | | | |
| | | | |
| | | | |
| | | | |
| | | | |
| | | | |
| | | | |